CU00793395

THE PRELUDE

THE PRELUDE

1805

WILLIAM WORDSWORTH

Newly Edited from the Manuscripts and Fully Illustrated in Color

with Paintings and Drawings Contemporaneous with the Composition of the Poem

JAMES ENGELL & MICHAEL D. RAYMOND

with an Introduction, Maps, Notes, Glosses, and Chronology

OXFORD

UNIVERSITY PRESS

OXFORD
UNIVERSITY PRESS

Great Clarendon Street, Oxford, OX2 6DP, United Kingdom

Oxford University Press is a department of the University of Oxford. It furthers the University's
objective of excellence in research, scholarship, and education by publishing worldwide.
Oxford is a registered trade mark of Oxford University Press in the UK and in certain other countries.

Published in the United States by David R. Godine, *Publisher*, 15 Court Square, Ste. 320, Boston, MA 02108

Introduction, Editorial Matter, Textual and Critical Apparatus © 2016 James Engell
Chronology © 2016 Michael D. Raymond
The following illustrations: frontispiece, 1.2, 1.3, 1.4, 1.5, 1.10, 1.11, 1.12, 1.13, 2.4, 2.5, 3.2, 3.3,
3.5, 3.7, 7.1, 7.10, 8.12, 9.6, 9.11, 9.12, 11.7, 11.8, and 13.5 are © 2016 The Wordsworth Trust
Illustration 4.2 © 2016 Hawkshead Grammar School

The moral rights of the authors have been asserted.

All rights reserved. No part of this publication may be reproduced, stored in a retrieval system, or transmitted,
in any form or by any means, without the prior permission in writing of Oxford University Press, or as expressly
permitted by law, by licence or under terms agreed with the appropriate reprographics rights organization.
Enquiries concerning reproduction outside the scope of the above should be sent to the
Rights Department, Oxford University Press, at the address above.

You must not circulate this work in any other form and you must impose this same condition on any acquirer.

British Library Cataloguing in Publication Data
Data available
Library of Congress Control Number: 2016004335 | ISBN 978-0-19-879266-6
Links to third party websites are provided by Oxford in good faith and for information only. Oxford disclaims
any responsibility for the materials contained in any third party website referenced in this work.

FRONT ENDPAPER
Edward Lear (1812–1888). *Brothers Water from Patterdale*, 1836 (detail). Yale Center for British Art,
Gift of Donald C. Gallup, Yale BA 1934, PhD 1939. That "glittering lively lake," as Dorothy Wordsworth
described it in 1802, is named "From those two Brothers that were drowned therein" (*Prelude* 8.232).
It lies at the valley bottom of Kirkstone Pass, five miles northeast of Grasmere.

REAR ENDPAPER
John Robert Cozens (1752–1797). *Interlaken*, 1776 (detail). Yale Center for British Art, Paul Mellon
Collection. On September 14, 1790, Wordsworth and Robert Jones hiked through "the very heart of
the high Alps" and passed Interlaken, snug between the lakes of Thun and Brientz.

FRONTISPIECE
Henry Edridge (1769–1821). *William Wordsworth*, May 1806. The Wordsworth Trust. Edridge first met
Wordsworth at Dove Cottage in late summer 1804. The two met again in May 1806 in London at a
gathering that included William Godwin. Within the week, Wordsworth agreed to sit for this drawing.

FIRST EDITION PUBLISHED IN 2016 · FIRST IMPRESSION

TABLE OF CONTENTS

vii   Introduction
        The Prelude: Place, Self, Crisis, and Imagination

        Maps
xv   The Lake District
xvii Wordsworth's Walking Tour of the Alps, Summer 1790

        THE PRELUDE 1805

2   *Book First*
        INTRODUCTION—CHILDHOOD
        AND SCHOOL-TIME

26   *Book Second*
        SCHOOL-TIME CONTINUED

40   *Book Third*
        RESIDENCE AT CAMBRIDGE

60   *Book Fourth*
        SUMMER VACATION

76   *Book Fifth*
        BOOKS

94   *Book Sixth*
        CAMBRIDGE AND THE ALPS

116   *Book Seventh*
        RESIDENCE IN LONDON

138   *Book Eighth*
        RETROSPECT—LOVE OF NATURE
        LEADING TO LOVE OF MANKIND

164   *Book Ninth*
        RESIDENCE IN FRANCE

190   *Book Tenth*
        RESIDENCE IN FRANCE AND
        FRENCH REVOLUTION

222   *Book Eleventh*
        IMAGINATION, HOW IMPAIRED
        AND RESTORED

234   *Book Twelfth*
        SAME SUBJECT, CONTINUED

246   *Book Thirteenth*
        CONCLUSION

261   TO WILLIAM WORDSWORTH, S. T. Coleridge

265   A Note on the Text and Editorial Practice

267   Chronology

277   Selected Bibliography and Scholarly Editions of *The Prelude*

281   Acknowledgments

INTRODUCTION
The Prelude: Place, Self, Crisis, and Imagination

The Prelude is one of the greatest long poems in English or in any language. Tracing the growth of the individual creative imagination as it encounters nature, engages a wide range of human experience, and discovers connections between the two, *The Prelude* offers a mythology of the modern self. Fresh and compelling, it gives specific, personal expression to ideas, feelings, and turbulent historical events of Romanticism, a movement (roughly 1790–1840) that revolutionized culture and transformed society. When first published in 1850, a few months after Wordsworth's death at age eighty, *The Prelude* carried this subtitle: *or, Growth of a Poet's Mind: an Autobiographical Poem.* This description had some precedent. In 1807 Samuel Taylor Coleridge had praised his friend's poem "concerning the growth and history of his own mind." Wordsworth had just read aloud the entire composition to him, the version completed in 1805 and the one printed in this book. Wordsworth and his sister Dorothy knew *The Prelude* as the "poem to Coleridge." In the manuscript copy that Coleridge read, it is titled *Poem Title not yet fixed upon by William Wordsworth Addressed to S. T. Coleridge.* Wordsworth the narrator often addresses his immediate listener, Coleridge, as "dear Friend!" or "most belovèd Friend" (e.g., 1.144, 6.681).

The poem was daring and new. It was radical to produce what seemed like an epic poem without a traditional epic subject or hero. No one had written an autobiographical poem like it before. In 1805 the word *autobiography* had not even been used in English. Partly for this reason Wordsworth hesitated to publish the poem. He later referred to *The Prelude* as "The long poem on my own education." He meant this in a wide sense—a leading of the self out into the world, facing a crisis of values, and securing his own vocation as a poet. The poem finally conveys, in a phrase Seamus Heaney applied to Wordsworth, the "hard-

earned reward of resolved crisis." The poem received its title *The Prelude* only after he died. He had regarded it as "tributary" to a long philosophical poem, *The Recluse.* However, only one part of that poem, *The Excursion,* was completed. Between 1805 and 1839 he revised the manuscript of what would become known as *The Prelude,* and the poem was first published in 1850. Many readers prefer the 1805 version. Some editions print the 1805 and 1850 versions, and some include first efforts on the poem in 1798 and 1799 (see Scholarly Editions, pp. 278–79).

It would be hard to judge what the most widely read long poem in English is, Milton's *Paradise Lost* or Wordsworth's *Prelude,* for they are the two most plausible candidates. *Paradise Lost* has a gorgeous power, and Samuel Johnson said it was not the greatest epic *only* because it was not the first. (He was thinking of Homer.) There are other candidates, of course, Edmund Spenser's *Faerie Queene* and Geoffrey Chaucer's *Canterbury Tales,* though for most readers these texts require modernization of their English and a raft of notes. Accessible to every reader, *The Prelude* relates a story of personal growth that strikes a parallel with the history of many modern lives.

The Importance of Place

It is impossible to read or quote more than a handful of lines from *The Prelude* without an imagined vision of some specific place welling up vividly in the mind's eye. Places in the Lake District of northern England, where Wordsworth spent his early years and then lived almost the entire rest of his life, appear prominently. Others do as well—Cambridge, where he attended university, London, where he spent some time while young, Snowdonia, and numerous places he visited in Europe, for example, Paris at the time of the French Revolution, the Simplon Pass, the "soulless image" of the summit of Mont Blanc, the "Black drizzling crags" of the Gondo Ravine, and other landmarks that evoke natural grandeur or human turmoil. Some places in the Lake District that Wordsworth depicts remain as if time had stood still. This is due in part to his own preservation activities. His popular *Guide to the Lakes* (1822) pled for conservation. He proposed that the Lake District become "a sort of national property." His informing spirit moved two of the three founders of the National Trust, Canon Hardwicke Rawnsley and Octavia Hill. Not long after their efforts, Beatrix Potter further preserved the character of the Lake District. Her father Rupert Potter had been one of the first Life Members of the National Trust. The Lake District was designated and founded as a National Park in 1951.

Places in *The Prelude* include Grasmere, Brothers Water, Scafell Pike, Dove Crag, Grisedale Tarn, the "superior Mount" of Helvellyn, the "mouldering Pile, with fractured Arch" of Furness Abbey, and Claife Heights, location of an awareness early in Wordsworth's life—the spot where he first believed that he was a chosen poet, "a dedicated Spirit" to join the company of Chaucer, Shakespeare, and Milton. In Book Thirteenth, the climbing of Mount Snowdon in Wales, amidst "circumstance most awful and sublime," prompts one of the most moving meditations in English verse. Other scenes occur on the Continent, for example, the "melancholy Walls" of Goslar, Germany, or the magnificent Lake Como, "a treasure by the earth / Kept to itself."

When *The Prelude* traces the growth of the poet's creative imagination, it engages how that spirit anchors itself in, and arises from, a physical home in the world, from places remembered and cherished, from "spots" or "scenes" that form the stage for the emotional inner drama by which the self shapes its identity and realizes its inventive power. Such power and such places exist in and through one another—they cannot be separated. They reveal, too, that individual imagination and intellectual love "are each in each, and cannot stand / Dividually" (13.187–88).

During more than 160 years never out of print, *The Prelude* has enjoyed many editions. Of all long poems in English that deal with actual places and palpable scenes, Wordsworth's "poem to Coleridge" invites illustration, yet the full poem has never received illustration aside from a special, rare edition illustrated with abstract art. (For illustrated editions of Wordsworth's work, see Selected Bibliography, pp. 277–78). *Paradise Lost*, Coleridge's *Rime of the Ancient Mariner*, and Tennyson's *Idylls of the King* have each been famously illustrated, but their landscapes are imaginary or, with Tennyson's poem, set in a time so distant that no reliable location can be established—where is Camelot? Yet, reading *The Prelude* without a sense of particular places, especially those in the Lake District, is as impoverished as considering the novels of Thomas Hardy without conjuring his Wessex with identifiable scenes in Dorset, Devon, and

Somerset. Hardy himself declined an invitation to attend the coronation of George V because he had already arranged a holiday in the Lake District, as he noted, "spending it on Windermere."

When the young Wordsworth steals a small boat on Ullswater and guiltily feels pursued by the crags and mountains as he rows out into the lake; when he asks the River Derwent, "Was if for this . . . ?"—for his effort to become a poet—that in childhood he heard its waters blend their murmurs with his nurse's song; when he thinks of where he witnessed a drowned man, or remembers the spot, Claife Heights, where after a "night in dancing, gaiety and mirth," early the next morning, "More glorious than I ever had beheld," he realizes deep commitment to his art, where "The Sea was laughing at a distance; all / The solid Mountains were as bright as clouds," and "My heart was full; I made no vows, but vows / Were then made for me," vows to become a writer, "A dedicated Spirit"— these are all locations now invested with deep personal experience. When he recalls the scene associated with his father's death; when he crosses the Alps at the Simplon Pass yet realizes that crossing only in retrospect; when he recalls a young boy, soon afterward dead before the age of ten, who would mimic the hooting owls near the shores of Windermere, and whose grave he would visit in long silence; when Wordsworth as a boy himself shudders at the spot where a hanging, an execution, occurred, now desolate and lonely; when he recalls his "nook obscure!" at St. John's College, Cambridge, or a tree whose organic shape and branchings evoke for him the world of magic fiction; when he visits "the place in which / An honoured Teacher of my youth was laid" among "the churchyard graves / Of Cartmel's rural Town," and recalls that

> A week, or little less, before his death
> He had said to me, 'my head will soon lie low'
> (10.490–92, 500–501)

—in all these instances and many more the poem reveals how place and creative spirit become interconnected, how the growth of sympathy and love are nourished from roots in the physical world. In this sense, the idealism or transcendence of the poem, its visionary claim, is grounded on and co-exists in mutual support with its realism, its vision of a world revealed by the five senses. The only genuine idealism is at one and the same time a true and abiding realism.

Wordsworth relates his experience of each place, how he continues to feel its presence, how it moved into his heart and consciousness—how it may even have created some alienation—and he performs this alchemy through striking images, strong associations, and repeated memories. In *The Prelude* and other poems, he often uses "sketch" or "sketches," "spot" and "scene" to convey how vital the sense of place is. A poet, he says, not only writes but also "paints" and casts a "colouring of imagination" over what is painted. He began his career publishing *Descriptive Sketches* (1793). While he disliked crude visual efforts, "those mimic sights that ape / The absolute presence of reality," he esteemed accomplished artwork, the impact of "subtlest craft, / By means refined attaining purest ends" (7.248–49, 252–53). The poet develops an eye searching "from a stone, a tree, a withered leaf, / To the broad ocean and the azure heavens" (3.161–62). In *Moments of Vision*, Kenneth Clark has spoken eloquently of Wordsworth's "visual obsession" and ability to detach an object "from the habitual flux of impressions" so that it becomes "intensely clear and important" (see Selected Bibliography, p. 277). Such a gift is hard to acquire, for, as John Ruskin notes in *Modern Painters*, often "objects pass perpetually before the eyes without conveying any impression to the brain at all; and so pass actually unseen, not merely unnoticed, but in the full clear sense of the word, unseen."

Late in life Wordsworth would rail in verse against "Illustrated Books and Newspapers" (1846, published 1850) and address a sonnet "To a Painter" (1840, published 1842) on the inadequacy of visual art to satisfy Wordsworth's own memories. Yet, one of his finer poems, "Elegiac Stanzas" (1805, published 1807) was "suggested by a picture of Peele Castle" painted by his friend Sir George Beaumont, who also provided a painting, engraved by J. C. Bromley, for the frontispiece to *The White Doe of Rylstone* (1815). In 1815 the two-volume edition of *Poems* contained two engraved frontispieces, and some copies an additional four plates. His sonnet composed in August 1811, "Upon the Sight of a Beautiful Picture, Painted by Sir G. H. Beaumont, Bart.," begins "Praised be the Art whose subtle power could stay / Yon cloud." Wordsworth describes the visual capture of one instant as a "Soul-soothing Art!" that gives "To one brief moment caught from fleeting time / The appropriate calm of blest eternity."

Critics note that Wordsworth creates in his use of language an effect that approximates the technique in drawing or painting known as chiaroscuro, the alternation of light and dark. One recent critic also suggests that Wordsworth's visual imagination creates in words a position similar to that of someone looking at a photograph with intimate associations, a photographic subjectivity, so that images "can then be viewed in private isolation (as in the 'spots of time'), like a series of internalized photographs" (see Selected Bibliography, work by Nicola Trott and Scott Hess.) In its infancy in 1850, photography did not exist when Wordsworth composed *The Prelude*, yet his verse conveys a visual power that suggests the experience of an individual who views or composes evocative photographs.

The Prelude unfolds the growth of the poet's mind and its central power—the creative imagination—from infancy to maturity. Beginning with the bond between mother and child, moving through the parent-like relation of nature to the maturing self, and finally realizing the connection between individual and humanity, "love of nature leading to love of mankind," this growth arises through formal education only in part. True, one of the thirteen Books, Book Fifth, is called "Books," and others mention or allude to literature. While he is shaped by "the external universe, / By striking upon what is found within," yet this process comes with "the help / of Books, and what they picture and record" (8.768–69). Recounting his time at Cambridge, Wordsworth reflects that he "could shape the image of a Place" that

> should at once
> Have made me pay to science and to arts
> And written lore, acknowledged my liege Lord,
> A homage, frankly offered up, like that
> Which I had paid to Nature.
>
> (3.381, 383–87)

Yet, still, the growth of this poet's mind so often occurs through experiences in specific places found in the natural world. These places are the scene yet also the cause of revelations. They harbor insights and lessons not found in lectures or books. They are primal locations of conflict and of love. They are intense places of beauty and fear. The evolution of his creative spirit emerges from its environment, the places he inhabits, the scenes he visits, the locations he recalls. This is Wordsworth's version of Shakespeare's sense that imagination "gives to airy nothing /

A local habitation and a name." Wordsworth's soul is anchored in—his feelings tutored by—the physical world, most by nature (including its wild places), though by cities, too, above all by places where some event or realization either startles or creeps over him almost by stealth, understood only later through the power of memory—even years later—or, if startled, in the flash of seconds.

His famous phrase "spots of time," explicitly referring in Book Eleventh to episodes recounted there, has been expanded to refer to all such episodes and instances in the poem where the poet experiences something that awakens sympathy or recuperates loss. Each spot of time is a place and a time, a temporal *and* a spatial aspect. And these "spots" are vital. They structure the poem:

> There are in our existence spots of time,
> Which with distinct preeminence retain
> A renovating Virtue . . .
>
> (11.258–60)

In Book Eleventh, the first spot Wordsworth recounts is on a "rough and stony Moor" where "A Murderer had been hung in iron chains." Not far from the now mouldered gibbet-mast, he sees (he is not yet six years old)

> A naked Pool that lay beneath the hills,
> The Beacon on the summit, and more near
> A Girl who bore a Pitcher on her head
> And seemed with difficult steps to force her way
> Against the blowing wind.
>
> (11.304–08)

He experiences a "visionary dreariness," an existential moment of insight into the mystery of death and life, an uncomfortable quickening that later blends with "The spirit of pleasure, and youth's golden gleam" felt when, at age seventeen, he revisits the same spot with his sister Dorothy and future wife Mary Hutchinson.

Scholars (and whole books on the subject) debate the *exact* location of certain scenes in *The Prelude*, especially those in the Lake District. It is not the purpose of this book to settle those disputes—if they can be settled. Instead, using art generally contemporaneous with the poem's composition, the illustrations present what scholars agree are known

locales. Speculation over more precise locations appears in several books listed in the Selected Bibliography, p. 277.

The Mutual Transformation of Place and Self

Places in the poem are more than named locations. They constitute a living book, the Book of Nature newly understood, personally absorbed, and given significance for the life of the inner self. They are the very *scenes* of imagination, ones the poet associates with certain *acts* of imagination. In these places occur vows, anger, trauma, loss, joy, self-rebuke, and determined resolution. These places and what happens in them elicit, then discipline, his feelings. These places are agents. They cannot be separated from human powers of creativity but are partners, collaborators. They embody and blend receptivity, perception, and active creation, just as the individual mind

> Creates, creator and receiver both,
> Working but in alliance with the works
> Which it beholds.
>
> (2.273–75)

These places thus are more than catalysts for the internal transformation of mind and spirit, for a catalyst, at the end of a chemical reaction, is left unchanged. Once these places are experienced personally, they are never the same. Unlike the catalyst that precipitates but is not finally altered by the reaction, these places *are* transformed through our experience. We never look at—or remember—them in the same way again. We too are changed.

Wordsworth believed that the presence of nature could have a similar, profound effect on anyone, an effect that would strengthen and lift individual being. John Stuart Mill, in his *Autobiography*, testifies that reading Wordsworth had exactly that effect on him. When he was young, full of learning but dejected and a stranger to hope and joy, he read Wordsworth. It helped restore him to health and purpose in life.

Some places in the poem seem fully Nature's—mountains, gorges, waterfalls, lakes, vales, summits, a mountain pass. Others are dim, powerful presences that haunt the mind, the "huge and mighty Forms that do not live / Like living men." Yet other places are in nature but clearly touched by humankind: a public road through the countryside, culti-vated fields, a stone wall near the intersection of roads not far from Hawkeshead, a rural cottage, a frozen lake, Esthwaite Water or Winder-mere, where young Wordsworth would skate with companions, then leave them "To cut across the image of a star / That gleamed upon the ice"—or even a fashionable inn

> Upon the Eastern Shore of Windermere,
> Above the crescent of a pleasant Bay . . .
> Yet to this hour the spot to me is dear
> With all its foolish pomp.
>
> (2.145–46, 161–62)

Some places are almost totally dominated by human activity and drama—Cambridge, London, and Paris, where Wordsworth witnessed or saw the aftermath of some of the most violent and bloody events of the French Revolution.

The Poem, the Reader, and the World

While no reader will experience the same places and events that Wordsworth did, the growth and development of any creative spirit may find a pattern in his. We have private places of remembrance, places where childhood formed and attained distinct character, where perhaps we learned of a parent's or sibling's death, or recall making a promise to ourselves to pursue a dream or a career, where we witnessed or learned about an event of shocking historical importance, where we were overcome with guilt for some unworthy act, or where we rejoiced in friendship and unconditional love. In *The Prelude* we may come by extension to read the places in our own lives and the growth of our own spirits. Paradoxically, then, by being so particular, the poem becomes universal; it uses place to help discover acts of heart and mind as they reflect—and are formed by—situated experience.

The language of *The Prelude* enacts how the first poetic spirit of the mind grows until it realizes full exercise of imagination, a love of nature bonded with humanity. At every step the presence of what Wordsworth calls, in his lyric meditation "Tintern Abbey" (1798), "all the mighty world / Of eye and ear, both what they half-create, / And what per-ceive," accompanies him and becomes a partner in this development. An intuitive awareness of love joined with imagination is perceived, but half-created, too, at many places, including the summit of Mount Snowdon in Wales. Remembering an ascent he made as a young man, Wordsworth draws out the latent visionary power of that scene, which evokes for him "The perfect image of a mighty Mind, / Of one that feeds upon infinity." What Coleridge, using Wordsworth's own phrase, called his friend's ability to practice "the Vision and the Faculty divine," emerges from Wordsworth's transformation of what his eye and ear witnessed.

In late 1800, not long after he had composed early parts of *The Prelude* at Grasmere, and as if to highlight the symbiotic link between creative spirit and local nature (our word "genius" comes from an old usage that meant the god or goddess of a specific place), Coleridge rec-ognized this special relation between the poet and his chosen place: "Wordsworth . . . lives at Grasmere, a place worthy of him, & of which he is worthy—and neither to Man nor Place can higher praise be given."

Wordsworth is the first modern environmental poet. Other poems, including ancient ones, such as *De rerum natura* by Lucretius, had *described* nature, and famous, more recent ones such as James Thomson's *Seasons* (1726–44) did so in remarkable detail. Yet, aside from some passages in William Cowper's *The Task* (1785), a poem Wordsworth knew well, *The Prelude* is the first longer poem to fuse and reconcile individual human perception and feeling with external objects of experience and their representation in language. *The Prelude* shapes nature and the experi-encing self into a greater, transformed whole. As Coleridge remarked, the mystery and genius of the fine arts is to make the external internal and the internal external.

To repeat, specific places and scenes—and things in them, for example, the "whistling hawthorn" tree he associates with his father's death—foster the growth of imagination. Its growth occurs *in and through* such places and forms. Its activity fuses the objective world with the subjective self. It presents nature not as science describes and analy-ses it, but nature as experienced humanly, "nature humanized." This is Coleridge's phrase for what Shakespeare renders, a physical world not only observed but transformed by our experience, even as it transforms us. This reciprocal, transformative work of nature and self helps explain why Coleridge claimed that Wordsworth was capable of writing "the First Genuine Philosophic Poem." Samuel Johnson had remarked that the general effects of nature on the eye and ear are uniform, and poetry that simply describes nature has limits. However, he notes that nature "philosophically considered" is "inexhaustible" (*Rambler* 36).

The process of place and mind, nature and imagination, working upon one another in flux and reflux, can be stated more philosophically, yet in language simple enough. William James, founder of the modern science of psychology, noted in his essay "The Sentiment of Rationality" that "all great periods of revival, of expansion of the human mind"—and Romanticism is among the greatest of those periods—"display in common" one feature: "Each and all of them have said to the human being, 'the inmost nature of reality is congenial to the *powers* which you possess.'" James explained in *Psychology, Briefer Course*: "Mind and world in short have been evolved together, and in consequence are something of a mutual fit." This means, as he affirmed in his last important work, *The Varieties of Religious Experience*, that, "The practically real world for each one of us, the effective world of the individual, is the compound world, the physical facts and emotional values in indistinguishable combination." *The Prelude* presents this compound world, how it is built up by us and how sustained. As a young man in the 1870s, James had read Wordsworth and did so throughout his life.

The Prelude, then, is a poem to love not only for its own sake and for Wordsworth's experience of the places that shape his imagination, but also for its power to unlock one's own "spots of time." The poem becomes itself a friend. Coleridge had in a Notebook entry in January 1804, when he knew only a shorter, incomplete version of *The Prelude*, called it Wordsworth's "divine Self-biography." Wordsworth many times in his poem addresses Coleridge as "Friend!" So Coleridge, after hearing Wordsworth read the entire thirteen-book version aloud over successive evenings in early January 1807, soon addresses Wordsworth as "O Friend! my comforter and guide!" (see *To William Wordsworth*, below, page 261). It was a phrase Wordsworth never forgot but modified. When he later wrote a series of sonnets about the River Duddon, a series fulfilling Coleridge's idea for a work that would trace the progress of a stream from its source to the sea, in the last sonnet Wordsworth turns to the river that has been his companion and echoes Coleridge by addressing the entire travelled length of the Duddon not as a topographical feature but as a person, "my partner and my guide."

Authenticity, Crisis, and Original Imagination

Wordsworth knew the Lake District intimately from birth. He later chose to live there in order to dedicate himself to his craft. Since boyhood he had walked its paths, climbed its fells, and moved under "sun and shower" (12.5, 12.230) as they passed over pasture and hillside. It was his personal chiaroscuro, his native element, the landscape he had grown to love through intimacy with its splendid forms, tarns, fields, flowers, torrents, sands, and lakes. He enjoyed a familiarity with the Lake District no visitor could match. On the Continent, he had, mainly on foot and with the slow, keen, observant eye that only foot travel brings, noted details in a manner at once more minute *and* more imaginative than, say, the scenes of an earlier, well-known poem, *The Traveller* (1764) by Oliver Goldsmith. With his journey in Europe, Wordsworth presented a record better than many others in detail, and more imaginative in treatment. Instead of a conventional Grand Tour, which a young gentleman would take in Europe to complete his education by being exposed to (and occasionally obtaining) a wider sense of culture, *The Prelude* also relates Wordsworth's witness, both personally heartrending and intellectual, of the French Revolution in the early 1790s.

> I saw the revolutionary Power
> Toss like a Ship at anchor, rocked by storms.
>
> (9.48–49)

The poem in its later books recounts turmoil and crisis, personal and political. Wordsworth felt deep concern about the condition of his own country, its liberties, and its less fortunate citizens. He sympathized with idealistic aims of the French Revolution, yet later recoiled from its excesses and aggression. As a young man he tried to navigate the swift current of events that brought both promise and repression, events that at one point even made him wish no victory for his own nation. Books Ninth through Twelfth especially portray these engagements—nations in conflict internally and externally, shedding blood, and Wordsworth trying to find the right compass for his convictions.

When he found that the political revolution he had witnessed and the political theories he had encountered were deeply flawed, he determined to establish a poetic revolution in their place, one that would further the cause of justice, love, and sympathy.

The Prelude makes no mention of it, but he fathered a daughter during his stay in France, something not widely known until the early twentieth century. Revolutionary violence in the early 1790s, the hostility of England and France, and then the long Napoleonic Wars made it difficult for Wordsworth to visit his child and her mother. However, he did and offered support, in 1802. Yet, it was clear that he and Annette Vallon, whom he had passionately loved a decade earlier, would not marry. They saw each other again in the Louvre in 1820, and thereafter continued their cordial if separate existence. Annette remained unmarried. She called herself Madame Williams or Veuve Williams (William's Widow) and had her daughter christened Anne-Caroline Wordswodsth (sic).

One reason why *The Prelude* attains a fresh, convincing narrative is often not mentioned, perhaps because it rests on an aspect of experience so basic that it can be overlooked. Wordsworth presents the places as he encountered them growing up, when he explored and came to know them primarily from ages three or four to twenty-five or twenty-six. During that time such impressions are apt to be strong, often indelible.

> Youth maintains, I knew,
> In all conditions of society,
> Communion more direct and intimate
> With Nature and the inner strength she has,
> And hence, oft-times, no less with Reason too,
> Than Age or Manhood even.
>
> (10.604–09)

The places of youth haunt memory for a lifetime. They are in some sense unlike those we visit when character and emotions are fully formed; rather, they are what largely form our character and feelings in the first place. If we are receptive to their influence, these scenes of childhood and youth shape our being to an astonishing degree. Imbedded in the psyche, they are the landscape of dreams in later decades, no less true for city dwellers and children in a great metropolis than for Wordsworth's rural life.

> Our simple childhood sits upon a throne
> That hath more power than all the elements.
>
> (5.532–33)

And the very hopes of youth, as Wordsworth felt them for a time in France, can bring a joy never quite available again:

> Bliss was it in that dawn to be alive,
> But to be young was very heaven.
>
> (10.692–93)

In one instance Wordsworth completely misses recognizing a place crucial for his travel, even though he knows its name and looks forward to it eagerly. Then, having been there without realizing it, he reflects back on it. This is when he crosses the Alps at the Simplon Pass. At the instant of moving through the pass, he is unaware of the location. Only afterward does the realization come *"that we had crossed the Alps."* And when that recognition comes, it imbues the whole scene with a retrospective revelation. He seems to think of others who have crossed the Alps: the warriors Hannibal, Charlemagne, and, most recently, Napoleon. But for Wordsworth there are no "spoils or trophies." He feels the power not of armies but moves under the "banners militant" of imagination, the awful, tremendous power of creating what is not yet present, of seeing the actual world yet envisioning it anew, and of seeing even the invisible world:

> in such strength
> Of usurpation, in such visitings
> Of awful promise, when the light of sense
> Goes out in flashes that have shewn to us
> The invisible world, doth Greatness make abode.
>
> (6.532–36)

So, the places of imagination need not be near his home, though Grasmere becomes a special place, the place where he repairs, as he explains in Book First, to dedicate himself to "some work / Of glory" (1.85–86). His work expands the sense of home to something more than what is familiar to one individual. His song has the gift to make the spirit feel at home in nature wherever nature is encountered with open heart, and wherever sympathy is extended to humankind. The title of Book Eighth is "Retrospect—Love of Nature Leading to Love of Mankind."

While the importance of place is paramount to the poem, sound is a great part of its natural magic. Poetry is often enjoyed most when read aloud, as Wordsworth read his poem to Coleridge. This act discovers its music and rhythms; it amplifies resonances otherwise left faint; and, through an active process, it fixes images and engages memory. Strangely, it takes no longer time—often shorter—to feel pleasure from good verse read aloud rather than read silently: the textures of rich composition yield the resourcefulness of language at a moderate pace. Who would pass through an exquisite garden on a motorway and expect delight? To move through a poem silently is like reading program notes at a concert while largely ignoring the music. Wordsworth rejects in one of his Prefaces the idea that his verse should be accompanied by "the classical lyre or romantic harp," but he does urge "an animated or impassioned recitation, adapted to the subject." The reader, he says, should read naturally, and have "voluntary power to modulate, in subordination to the sense, the music of the poem;—in the same manner" as the reader's mind "is left at liberty, and even summoned, to act upon its thoughts and images."

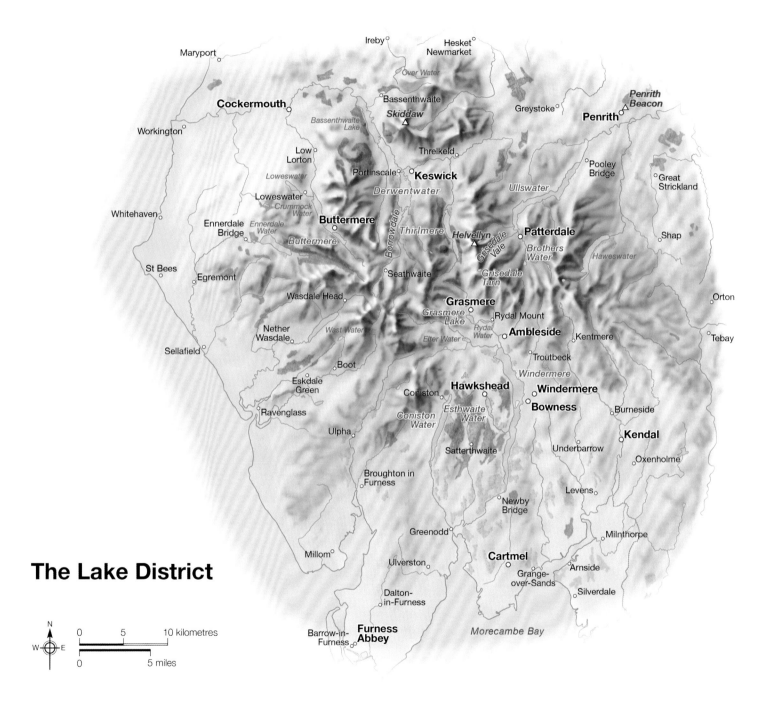

The Lake District

Maryport

Ireby

Hesket Newmarket

Over Water

Cockermouth

Bassenthwaite

Skiddaw

Greystoke

Penrith Beacon

Penrith

Workington

Bassenthwaite Lake

Threlkeld

Low Lorton

Loweswater

Portinscale

Keswick

Pooley Bridge

Whitehaven

Loweswater

Derwentwater

Ullswater

Great Strickland

Crummock Water

Ennerdale Bridge

Buttermere

Ennerdale Water

Borrowdale

Thirlmere

Helvellyn

Grisedale Vale

Patterdale

Shap

St Bees

Buttermere

Brothers Water

Egremont

Seathwaite

Grisedale Tarn

Haweswater

Wasdale Head

Grasmere

Orton

Sellafield

Nether Wasdale

Wast Water

Grasmere Lake

Rydal Mount

Rydal Water

Elter Water

Ambleside

Kentmere

Tebay

Boot

Troutbeck

Eskdale Green

Windermere

Ravenglass

Coniston

Hawkshead

Windermere

Esthwaite Water

Bowness

Burneside

Ulpha

Coniston Water

Kendal

Satterthwaite

Underbarrow

Oxenholme

Broughton in Furness

Levens

Millom

Newby Bridge

Milnthorpe

Greenodd

Cartmel

Arnside

Ulverston

Grange-over-Sands

Dalton-in-Furness

Silverdale

Barrow-in-Furness

Furness Abbey

Morecambe Bay

N
W—E
S

0   5   10 kilometres

0   5 miles

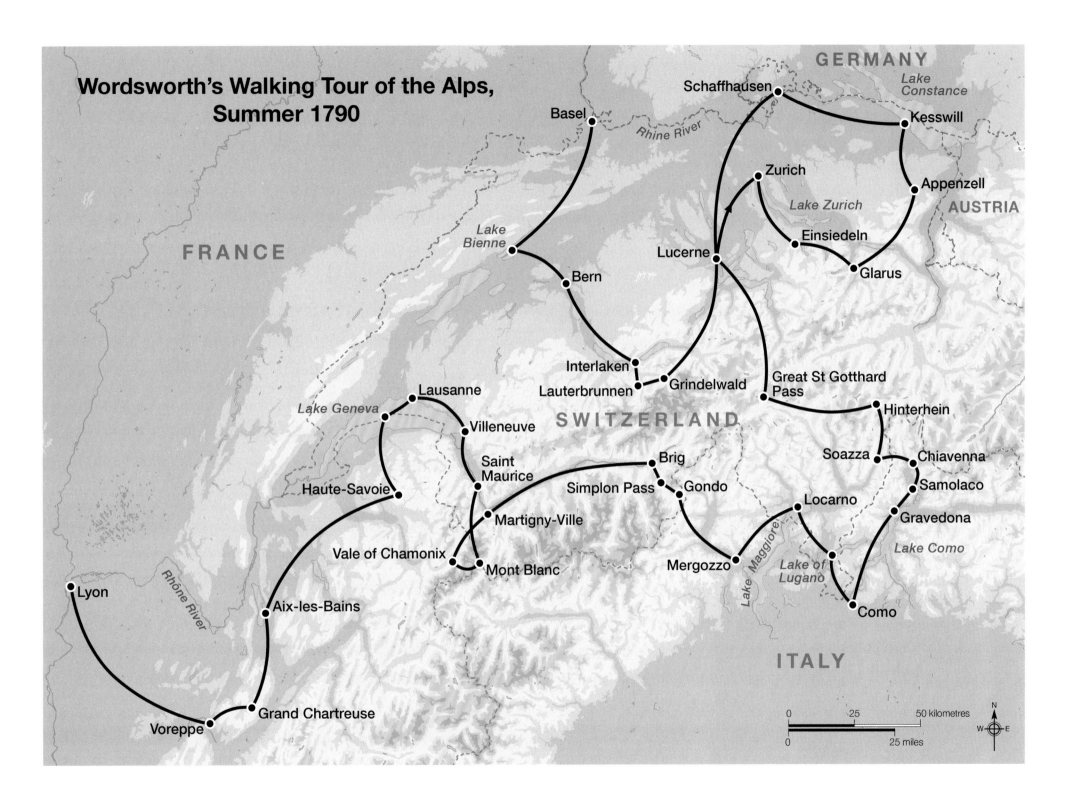

Wordsworth's Walking Tour of the Alps, Summer 1790

THE PRELUDE

Book First

INTRODUCTION—CHILDHOOD AND SCHOOL-TIME

Oh there is blessing in this gentle breeze

The poet invokes no divine or heavenly muse, but Nature itself.

That blows from the green fields and from the clouds
And from the sky: it beats against my cheek,
And seems half-conscious of the joy it gives.
O welcome Messenger! O welcome Friend!
A captive greets thee, coming from a house
Of bondage, from yon City's walls set free,
A prison where he hath been long immured.*
Now I am free, enfranchised and at large,
May fix my habitation where I will.   10
What dwelling shall receive me? In what Vale
Shall be my harbour? Underneath what grove
Shall I take up my home, and what sweet stream
Shall with its murmur lull me to my rest?
The earth is all before me: with a heart

Inspiration, his every breath, corresponds with the breeze to become a creative power.

Joyous, nor scared at its own liberty,
I look about, and should the guide I chuse
Be nothing better than a wandering cloud,
I cannot miss my way. I breathe again;
Trances of thought and mountings of the mind   20

LONG IMMURED: W could feel walled in ("immured") in cities. See also Exodus 13:3.

Come fast upon me: it is shaken off,
As by miraculous gift 'tis shaken off,
That burthen of my own unnatural self,
The heavy weight of many a weary day
Not mine, and such as were not made for me.
Long months of peace (if such bold word accord
With any promises of human life),
Long months of ease and undisturbed delight
Are mine in prospect; whither shall I turn
By road or pathway or through open field,   30
Or shall a twig or any floating thing
Upon the river, point me out my course?

Enough that I am free; for months to come
May dedicate myself to chosen tasks;
May quit the tiresome sea and dwell on shore,
If not a Settler on the soil, at least
To drink wild water, and to pluck green herbs,
And gather fruits fresh from their native bough.
Nay more, if I may trust myself, this hour
Hath brought a gift that consecrates my joy;   40
For I, methought, while the sweet breath of Heaven
Was blowing on my body, felt within
A corresponding mild creative breeze,
A vital breeze which travelled gently on
O'er things which it had made, and is become
A tempest, a redundant* energy

REDUNDANT: exuberant, overflowing

1.1 John Glover (1767–1849). *Thirlmere*, 1820–30. Tate Collection. Thirlmere is four miles north of Grasmere. Coleridge wrote in 1803, "O Thirlmere!—let me . . . celebrate the world in thy mirror."

Vexing its own creation. 'Tis a power
That does not come unrecognised, a storm,
Which breaking up a long-continued frost
Brings with it vernal promises, the hope   50
Of active days, of dignity and thought,
Of prowess in an honourable field,
Pure passions, virtue, knowledge, and delight,
The holy life of music and of verse.

■ *W always called this work not* The Prelude *but "the poem to Coleridge," his friend.*

■ Thus far, O Friend! did I, not used to make
A present joy the matter of my Song,
Pour out, that day, my soul in measured strains
Even in the very words which I have here
Recorded: to the open fields I told
A prophecy: poetic numbers came   60
Spontaneously, and clothed in priestly robe
My spirit, thus singled out, as it might seem,
For holy services: great hopes were mine;
My own voice cheared me, and, far more, the mind's
Internal echo of the imperfect sound;
To both I listened, drawing from them both
A chearful confidence in things to come.

1.2 James Northcote (1746–1831). *Samuel Taylor Coleridge*, 1804. The Wordsworth Trust. *The Prelude* is a sustained address to Wordsworth's great "Friend!"— S. T. Coleridge (1772–1834)—supplemented with a retrospective interior monologue.

Whereat being not unwilling now to give
A respite to this passion, I paced on
Gently, with careless steps, and came erelong   70
To a green shady place where down I sate

Beneath a tree, slackening my thoughts by choice
And settling into gentler happiness.

'Twas Autumn, and a calm and placid day,
With warmth as much as needed from a sun
Two hours declined towards the west, a day
With silver clouds, and sunshine on the grass,
And, in the sheltered grove where I was couched
A perfect stillness. On the ground I lay
Passing through many thoughts, yet mainly such   80
As to myself pertained. I made a choice

■ *He selects the Vale of Grasmere as home.*

■ Of one sweet Vale* whither my steps should turn
And saw, methought, the very house and fields
Present before my eyes: nor did I fail
To add, meanwhile, assurance of some work
Of glory, there forthwith to be begun,
Perhaps, too, there performed. Thus long I lay
Cheared by the genial pillow of the earth
Beneath my head, soothed by a sense of touch
From the warm ground, that balanced me, else lost   90
Entirely, seeing nought, nought hearing, save
When here and there, about the grove of Oaks
Where was my bed, an acorn from the trees
Fell audibly, and with a startling sound.

Thus occupied in mind, I lingered here
Contented, nor rose up until the sun
Had almost touched the horizon, bidding then
A farewell to the City left behind,
Even with the chance equipment of that hour

■ *Arduous work calls him, but he is uncertain, troubled.*

I journeyed towards the Vale that I had chosen.   100
It was a splendid evening; and my soul
Did once again make trial of the strength
Restored to her afresh; nor did she want
Eolian visitations; but the harp*
Was soon defrauded, and the banded host
Of harmony dispersed in straggling sounds
And, lastly, utter silence. 'Be it so,
It is an injury,' said I, 'to this day
To think of any thing but present joy.'
So like a Peasant I pursued my road   110
Beneath the evening sun, nor had one wish
Again to bend the sabbath of that time
To a servile yoke. What need of many words?
A pleasant loitering journey, through two days
Continued, brought me to my hermitage.*

I spare to speak, my Friend, of what ensued,
The admiration and the love, the life
In common things; the endless store of things
Rare, or at least so seeming, every day
Found all about me in one neighbourhood,   120
The self-congratulation,* the complete
Composure, and the happiness entire.
But speedily a longing in me rose
To brace myself to some determined aim,

■ Reading or thinking, either to lay up

ONE SWEET VALE: The Vale of Grasmere

HARP: Aeolian or stringed wind harp, from Aeolus, god of winds
MY HERMITAGE: W walked twenty miles from Ullswater to Grasmere, where he and his sister Dorothy would live in Dove Cottage.
SELF-CONGRATULATION: rejoicing (but not in pride)

1.3 James Bourne (1773–1854). *Grasmere Lake*, 1802. The Wordsworth Trust. Located in Wordsworth's "one sweet Vale" and near his "hermitage," Dove Cottage.

New stores, or rescue from decay the old
By timely interference, I had hopes
Still higher, that with a frame of outward life
I might endue, might fix in a visible home

Some portion of those phantoms of conceit
That had been floating loose about so long,
And to such Beings temperately deal forth
The many feelings that oppressed my heart.

But I have been discouraged; gleams of light
Flash often from the East, then disappear
And mock me with a sky that ripens not
Into a steady morning: if my mind,
Remembering the sweet promise of the past,
Would gladly grapple with some noble theme,
Vain is her wish; where'er she turns she finds   140
Impediments from day to day renewed.

And now it would content me to yield up
Those lofty hopes a while for present gifts
Of humbler industry. But, O dear Friend!
The Poet, gentle creature as he is,
Hath, like the Lover, his unruly times;
His fits when he is neither sick nor well,
Though no distress be near him but his own
Unmanageable thoughts. The mind itself
The meditative mind, best pleased, perhaps,   150
While she, as duteous as the Mother Dove,
Sits brooding, lives not always to that end,
But hath less quiet instincts, goadings on
That drive her as in trouble through the groves.
With me is now such passion, which I blame
No otherwise than as it lasts too long.

When, as becomes a man who would prepare
For such a glorious work, I through myself

Make rigorous inquisition, the report
Is often chearing; for I neither seem   160
To lack that first great gift! the vital soul,
Nor general truths which are themselves a sort
Of Elements and Agents, Under-Powers,
Subordinate helpers of the living mind.
Nor am I naked in external things,
Forms, images; nor numerous other aids
Of less regard, though won perhaps with toil,
And needful to build up a Poet's praise.
Time, place, and manners, these I seek, and these
I find in plenteous store; but nowhere such   170
As may be singled out with steady choice;
No little Band of yet remembered names
Whom I, in perfect confidence, might hope
To summon back from lonesome banishment
And make them inmates in the hearts of men
Now living, or to live in times to come.
Sometimes, mistaking vainly, as I fear,
Proud spring-tide swellings for a regular sea,
I settle on some British theme, some old
Romantic tale, by Milton left unsung;   180
More often resting at some gentle place
Within the groves of Chivalry, I pipe
Among the Shepherds, with reposing Knights
Sit by a Fountain-side, and hear their tales.
Sometimes, more sternly moved, I would relate

1.4 Amos Green (1735–1807). *Dove Cottage*, 1800. The Wordsworth Trust. Dove Cottage was home to William and Dorothy from December 1799 to May 1808. William's bride, Mary, joined them in 1802, followed by the births of three of their five children—John (1803), Dora (1804), and Thomas (1806).

Of Liberty, which fifteen hundred years
Survived, and, when the European came
With skill and power that could not be withstood,
Did like a pestilence maintain its hold,
And wasted down by glorious death that Race   200
Of natural Heroes: or I would record
How in tyrannic times some unknown man,
Unheard of in the Chronicles of Kings,
Suffered in silence for the love of truth;
How that one Frenchman,* through continued force
Of meditation on the inhuman deeds
Of the first Conquerors of the Indian Isles,
Went single in his ministry across
The Ocean, not to comfort the Oppressed,
But, like a thirsty wind, to roam about,   210
Withering the Oppressor: how Gustavus* found
Help at his need in Dalecarlia's Mines:
How Wallace fought for Scotland, left the name
Of Wallace to be found like a wild flower,
All over his dear Country, left the deeds
Of Wallace,* like a Family of Ghosts,
To people the steep rocks and river banks,
Her natural sanctuaries, with a local soul
Of independence and stern liberty.
Sometimes it suits me better to shape out   220
Some Tale from my own heart, more near akin
To my own passions and habitual thoughts,

W contemplates the histories, half fanciful, half factual, of ancient leaders.

How vanquished Mithridates northward passed,
And, hidden in the cloud of years, became
That Odin, Father of a Race by whom
Perished the Roman Empire: how the Friends
And Followers of Sertorius, out of Spain   190
Flying, found shelter in the Fortunate Isles;
And left their usages, their arts, and laws,
To disappear by a slow gradual death;
To dwindle and to perish one by one
Starved in those narrow bounds: but not the Soul

ONE FRENCHMAN: Dominique de Gourges in 1568 went to Florida to avenge a massacre of his country-men by Spaniards.
GUSTAVUS: Gustavus Vasa roused miners and liberated Sweden from Denmark in 1521–23.
WALLACE: William Wallace, Scottish hero executed by Edward I of England

Some variegated story, in the main
Lofty, with interchange of gentler things.

■ *But then sets on some philosophic song of daily life . . .*
■ But deadening admonitions will succeed
And the whole beauteous Fabric seems to lack
Foundation, and, withal, appears throughout
Shadowy and unsubstantial. Then, last wish,
My last and favourite aspiration! then
I yearn towards some philosophic Song   230
Of Truth that cherishes our daily life;
With meditations passionate from deep
Recesses in man's heart, immortal verse
Thoughtfully fitted to the Orphean lyre;*
But from this awful burthen I full soon

■ *. . . although he seems unready for what it demands . . .*
■ Take refuge, and beguile myself with trust
That mellower years will bring a riper mind
And clearer insight. Thus from day to day
I live, a mockery of the brotherhood

■ *. . . cannot start, rallies, then turns again discouraged.*
Of vice and virtue, with no skill to part   240
Vague longing that is bred by want of power
From paramount impulse not to be withstood,
A timorous capacity from prudence;
From circumspection, infinite delay.
Humility and modest awe themselves
Betray me, serving often for a cloak

■ *He asks the River Derwent, which flowed behind his childhood home, if his murmuring song acted as a second nurse to prepare him for the poet's task.*
To a more subtle selfishness, that now
Doth lock my functions up in blank reserve,*
Now dupes me by an over-anxious eye

ORPHEAN LYRE: from the myth of singer and philosopher Orpheus, important for W since his youth
BLANK RESERVE: mental paralysis, inaction

■ That with a false activity beats off   250
Simplicity and self-presented truth.
—Ah! better far than this, to stray about
Voluptuously through fields and rural walks,
And ask no record of the hours given up
To vacant musing, unreproved neglect
Of all things, and deliberate holiday;
Far better never to have heard the name
Of zeal and just ambition, than to live
Thus baffled by a mind that every hour
Turns recreant to her task, takes heart again,   260
Then feels immediately some hollow thought
Hang like an interdict upon her hopes.
This is my lot; for either still I find
Some imperfection in the chosen theme,
Or see of absolute accomplishment
Much wanting, so much wanting in myself,
That I recoil and droop, and seek repose
In listlessness from vain perplexity,
Unprofitably travelling towards the grave,
Like a false steward* who hath much received   270
■ And renders nothing back.—Was it for this
That one, the fairest of all Rivers, loved
To blend his murmurs with my Nurse's song
And from his alder shades and rocky falls,
And from his fords and shallows, sent a voice
That flowed along my dreams? For this didst Thou,

FALSE STEWARD: See Matthew 25:14–30.

1.5 Etched by John MacWhirter (1839–1911). Engraved by Georges-Henri Manesse (1854–1940). *Wordsworth's Birthplace, Cockermouth.* The Wordsworth Trust. Wordsworth was born in the finest home in Cockermouth on April 7, 1770—twenty miles northwest of Grasmere.

■ *He recalls his child's life in nature, how he would trap woodcocks, then feel guilt for taking birds caught by others . . .*

O Derwent! travelling over the green Plains
Near my sweet Birth-place,* didst thou, beauteous Stream,
Make ceaseless music through the night and day
Which with its steady cadence, tempering   280
Our human waywardness, composed my thoughts
To more than infant softness, giving me,
Among the fretful dwellings of mankind,

MY SWEET BIRTH-PLACE: Cockermouth. W takes the phrase from a poem by Coleridge.

A knowledge, a dim earnest, of the calm
That Nature breathes among the hills and groves.
When having left his Mountains, to the Towers*
Of Cockermouth that beauteous River came,
Behind my Father's House he passed, close by,
Along the margin of our Terrace Walk.
He was a Playmate whom we dearly loved.   290
Oh! many a time have I, a five years' Child,
A naked Boy, in one delightful Rill,
A little Mill-race severed from his stream,
Made one long bathing of a summer's day,
Basked in the sun, and plunged, and basked again
Alternate all a summer's day, or coursed
Over the sandy fields, leaping through groves
Of yellow grunsel,* or when crag and hill,
The woods, and distant Skiddaw's* lofty height,
Were bronzed with a deep radiance, stood alone   300
Beneath the sky, as if I had been born
On Indian Plains, and from my Mother's hut
Had run abroad in wantonness, to sport,
A naked Savage, in the thunder shower.

■ Fair seed-time had my soul, and I grew up
Fostered alike by beauty and by fear;
Much favoured in my birth-place, and no less
In that belovèd Vale* to which, erelong,
I was transplanted. Well I call to mind

TOWERS: high ruins of Cockermouth Castle
GRUNSEL: here, ragweed
SKIDDAW: 3,053 feet, one of the tallest peaks in the Lake District, visible from Cockermouth
BELOVÈD VALE: the Vale of Esthwaite, where W attended school in Hawkshead

1.6 J. M. W. Turner (1775–1851). *Cockermouth Castle*, 1810. Tate Collection. The Normans built Cockermouth Castle in 1134. Wordsworth's "sweet Birth-place" lies to the right on the southern bank of the River Derwent, "the fairest of all Rivers." As a child Wordsworth played inside the crumbling castle and swam in the Derwent.

('Twas at an early age, ere I had seen   310
Nine summers) when upon the mountain slope
The frost and breath of frosty wind had snapped
The last autumnal crocus, 'twas my joy
To wander half the night among the Cliffs
And the smooth Hollows, where the woodcocks ran
Along the open turf. In thought and wish
That time, my shoulder all with springes* hung,
I was a fell destroyer. On the heights
Scudding away from snare to snare, I plied
My anxious visitation, hurrying on,   320
Still hurrying, hurrying onward; moon and stars
Were shining o'er my head; I was alone,
And seemed to be a trouble to the peace
That was among them. Sometimes it befel
In these night-wanderings, that a strong desire
O'erpowered my better reason, and the bird
Which was the captive of another's toils

■ . . . hearing some strange power in pursuit of his own self.

■ The human mind is considered, and Nature as its teacher.

■ Became my prey; and when the deed was done
I heard among the solitary hills
Low breathings coming after me, and sounds   330
Of undistinguishable motion, steps
Almost as silent as the turf they trod.

Nor less in springtime when on southern banks
The shining sun had from her knot of leaves
Decoyed the primrose flower, and when the Vales

SPRINGES: snares

And woods were warm, was I a plunderer then
In the high places, on the lonesome peaks
Where'er, among the mountains and the winds,
The Mother Bird had built her lodge. Though mean
My object, and inglorious, yet the end   340
Was not ignoble. Oh! when I have hung
Above the raven's nest, by knots of grass
And half-inch fissures in the slippery rock
But ill sustained, and almost, as it seemed,
Suspended by the blast which blew amain,
Shouldering the naked crag; Oh! at that time,
While on the perilous ridge I hung alone,
With what strange utterance did the loud dry wind
Blow through my ears! the sky seemed not a sky
Of earth, and with what motion moved the clouds!   350

■ The mind of Man is framed even like the breath
And harmony of music. There is a dark
Invisible workmanship that reconciles
Discordant elements, and makes them move
In one society. Ah me! that all
The terrors, all the early miseries,
Regrets, vexations, lassitudes, that all
The thoughts and feelings which have been infused
Into my mind should ever have made up
The calm existence that is mine when I   360
Am worthy of myself. Praise to the end!

1.7 J. M. W. Turner (1775–1851). *View in the Lake District: Above Coniston*, 1797–98. Tate Collection. Yewdale Crag, above Coniston Water, lies two to three miles west of Hawkshead. When Wordsworth "hung / Above the raven's nest," he was likely speaking of Yewdale Crag. Ravens are enemies of lambs, and schoolboys were encouraged to raid the nests.

Thanks likewise for the means! But I believe
That Nature, oftentimes, when she would frame
A favored Being, from his earliest dawn
Of infancy doth open up the clouds,
As at the touch of lightning, seeking him
With gentlest visitation; not the less,
Though haply aiming at the self-same end,
Does it delight her sometimes to employ
Severer interventions, ministry   370
More palpable, and so she dealt with me.

One evening (surely I was led by her*)
I went alone into a Shepherd's Boat,
A Skiff that to a Willow tree was tied
Within a rocky Cave, its usual home.
'Twas by the shores of Patterdale,* a Vale
Wherein I was a Stranger, thither come
A School-boy Traveller, at the Holidays.
Forth rambled from the Village Inn alone
No sooner had I sight of this small Skiff,   380
Discovered thus by unexpected chance,
■ Than I unloosed her tether and embarked.
The moon was up, the Lake was shining clear
Among the hoary mountains; from the Shore
I pushed, and struck the oars and struck again
In cadence, and my little Boat moved on
Even like a Man who walks with stately step

■ *He steals a boat, rows in
youth's pride, and facing
rearward sees glittering
pools from the lusty dip-
ping of his oars.*

■ *As the boat moves from
land, a cliff looms higher
behind the lower land-
scape, as if pursuing
him across the waters.*

HER: Nature
SHORES OF PATTERDALE: on Ullswater

Though bent on speed. It was an act of stealth
And troubled pleasure; not without the voice
Of mountain-echoes did my Boat move on,   390
Leaving behind her still on either side
Small circles glittering idly in the moon,
Until they melted all into one track
Of sparkling light. A rocky Steep uprose
Above the Cavern of the Willow tree
And now, as suited one who proudly rowed
With his best skill, I fixed a steady view
Upon the top of that same craggy ridge,
The bound of the horizon, for behind
Was nothing but the stars and the grey sky.   400
She was an elfin Pinnace;* lustily
I dipped my oars into the silent Lake,
And, as I rose upon the stroke, my Boat
Went heaving through the water, like a Swan;
■ When from behind that craggy Steep, till then
The bound of the horizon, a huge Cliff,*
As if with voluntary power instinct,
Upreared its head. I struck, and struck again,
And, growing still in stature, the huge Cliff
Rose up between me and the stars, and still,   410
With measured motion, like a living thing,
Strode after me. With trembling hands I turned,
And through the silent water stole my way
Back to the Cavern of the Willow tree.

ELFIN PINNACE: small boat
HUGE CLIFF: Glenridding Dodd (less likely Black Crag), which would loom up behind Stybarrow Crag

1.8 Alfred William Hunt (1830–1896). *Stybarrow Crag, Ullswater*, 1847. National Museums, Liverpool. On the southern shore of Ullswater, the "craggy Steep," Stybarrow Crag, sits below the "huge Cliff" of Glenridding Dodd, which "Upreared its head" to young William.

There, in her mooring-place, I left my Bark,
And through the meadows homeward went with grave
And serious thoughts; and after I had seen

Rebuked, he returns to shore, changed for many days.

That spectacle, for many days my brain
Worked with a dim and undetermined sense
Of unknown modes of being; in my thoughts
There was a darkness, call it solitude,
Or blank desertion, no familiar shapes

420

1.9 Joseph Wright of Derby (1734–1797). *Derwent Water, with Skiddaw in the Distance*, 1795–96. Yale Center for British Art, Paul Mellon Collection. The double-summit Skiddaw is nine miles due east of Cockermouth. Many poets, including Dryden, Blake, and Wordsworth, thought the mountain a source of inspiration.

Of hourly objects, images of trees,
Of sea or sky, no colours of green fields;
But huge and mighty Forms that do not live
Like living men moved slowly through the mind
By day and were the trouble of my dreams.

Wisdom and Spirit of the universe!
Thou Soul that art the eternity of thought!
That giv'st to forms and images a breath   430
And everlasting motion! not in vain,
By day or star-light thus from my first dawn
Of Childhood didst Thou intertwine for me
The passions that build up our human Soul,
Not with the mean and vulgar works of Man,
But with high objects, with enduring things,
With life and nature, purifying thus
The elements of feeling and of thought,
And sanctifying, by such discipline,
Both pain and fear, until we recognise   440
A grandeur in the beatings of the heart.

Nor was this fellowship vouchsafed to me
With stinted kindness. In November days,
When vapours, rolling down the valleys, made
A lonely scene more lonesome; among woods
At noon, and 'mid the calm of summer nights,
When by the margin of the trembling Lake,

Beneath the gloomy hills I homeward went
In solitude, such intercourse was mine;
'Twas mine among the fields both day and night,   450
And by the waters all the summer long.

And in the frosty season, when the sun
Was set, and visible for many a mile
The cottage windows through the twilight blazed,
I heeded not the summons:—happy time
It was indeed for all of us; to me
It was a time of rapture: clear and loud
The village clock tolled six; I wheeled about,
Proud and exulting, like an untired horse,
That cares not for his home.—All shod with steel   460
We hissed along the polished ice in games
Confederate, imitative of the chace
And woodland pleasures, the resounding horn,
The Pack loud bellowing, and the hunted hare.
So through the darkness and the cold we flew,
And not a voice was idle; with the din,
Meanwhile, the precipices rang aloud,
The leafless trees, and every icy crag
Tinkled like iron, while the distant hills
Into the tumult sent an alien sound   470
Of melancholy, not unnoticed, while the stars,
Eastward, were sparkling clear, and in the west
The orange sky of evening died away.

Amid raucous school-mates skating, he feels the power of hills and stars, then seeks at times to be alone.

1.10 William Taylor Longmire (1841–1914). *January, Grasmere, Westmorland,* 1881. The Wordsworth Trust. As a schoolboy in Hawkshead, about five miles south of Grasmere, Wordsworth and his friends often "hissed along the polished ice" of Esthwaite Water.

Not seldom from the uproar I retired
Into a silent bay, or sportively
Glanced sideway, leaving the tumultuous throng,

To cut across the image of a star
That gleamed upon the ice: and oftentimes
When we had given our bodies to the wind,

And all the shadowy banks, on either side,   480
Came sweeping through the darkness, spinning still
The rapid line of motion; then at once
Have I, reclining back upon my heels,
Stopped short, yet still the solitary Cliffs
Wheeled by me, even as if the earth had rolled
With visible motion her diurnal* round;
Behind me did they stretch in solemn train
Feebler and feebler, and I stood and watched
Till all was tranquil as a dreamless sleep.

Ye Presences of Nature, in the sky   490
And on the earth! Ye Visions of the hills!
And Souls of lonely places! can I think
A vulgar hope was yours when Ye employed
Such ministry, when Ye through many a year
Haunting me thus among my boyish sports,
On caves and trees, upon the woods and hills,
Impressed upon all forms the characters*
Of danger or desire, and thus did make
The surface of the universal earth
With triumph, and delight, and hope, and fear,   500
Work like a sea?

■ *Varied young experi-
ences: domestic comforts,
study, games, cards, all
surrounded by the wider,
often wild world.*

                    Not uselessly employed,
I might pursue this theme through every change
Of exercise and play, to which the year

DIURNAL: daily
CHARACTERS: signs

Did summon us in its delightful round.
We were a noisy crew, the sun in heaven
Beheld not vales more beautiful than ours,
Nor saw a race in happiness and joy
More worthy of the ground where they were sown.
I would record with no reluctant voice
The woods of autumn and their hazel bowers   510
With milk-white clusters hung; the rod and line,
True symbol of the foolishness of hope,
Which with its strong enchantment led us on
By rocks and pools, shut out from every star
All the green summer, to forlorn cascades
Among the windings of the mountain brooks.
—Unfading recollections! at this hour
The heart is almost mine with which I felt,
From some hill-top, on sunny afternoons
The Kite high up among the fleecy clouds   520
Pull at its rein like an impatient Courser,
Or, from the meadows sent on gusty days,
Beheld her breast the wind, then suddenly
Dashed headlong—and rejected by the storm.

■ Ye lowly Cottages in which we dwelt,
A ministration of your own was yours,
A sanctity, a safeguard, and a love!
Can I forget you, being as you were
So beautiful among the pleasant fields

1.11 Joseph Wright of Derby (1734–1797). *Ullswater*, 1795. The Wordsworth Trust. Wordsworth thought Ullswater "perhaps, upon the whole, the happiest combination of beauty and grandeur, which any of the lakes affords." Here is "the level plain / Of waters coloured by the steady clouds."

In which ye stood? Or can I here forget 530
The plain and seemly countenance with which
Ye dealt out your plain comforts? Yet had ye
Delights and exultations of your own.
Eager and never weary we pursued
Our home amusements by the warm peat-fire
At evening; when with pencil and with slate,
In square divisions parcelled out, and all
With crosses* and with cyphers scribbled o'er,
We schemed and puzzled, head opposed to head,
In strife too humble to be named in Verse. 540
Or round the naked table, snow-white deal,*
Cherry or maple, sate in close array,
And to the combat, Lu or Whist,* led on
A thick-ribbed Army, not as in the world
Neglected and ungratefully thrown by
Even for the very service they had wrought,
But husbanded through many a long campaign.
Uncouth assemblage was it, where no few
Had changed their functions, some, plebeian cards,
Which Fate beyond the promise of their birth 550
Had glorified, and called to represent
The persons of departed Potentates.
Oh! with what echoes on the Board they fell!
Ironic Diamonds, Clubs, Hearts, Diamonds, Spades,
A congregation piteously akin.
Cheap matter did they give to boyish wit,

WITH CROSSES: tick-tack-toe (noughts and crosses)
DEAL: plain fir or pine
LU OR WHIST: Loo and Whist are card games.

1.12 Unknown artist. *House in which Wordsworth boarded while at Hawkshead school*, August 1850. The Wordsworth Trust. While attending Hawkshead Grammar School, Wordsworth was boarded here by his father with Ann Tyson from 1779 to 1783. He lodged in the upstairs room to the right. From 1783 to 1787 he boarded with Ann Tyson near Hawkshead in the hamlet of Colthouse.

Those sooty knaves, precipitated down
With scoffs and taunts, like Vulcan* out of Heaven,
The paramount Ace, a moon in her eclipse,
Queens, gleaming through their splendour's last decay, 560
And Monarchs, surly at the wrongs sustained
By royal visages. Meanwhile, abroad
The heavy rain was falling, or the frost
Raged bitterly, with keen and silent tooth,
And, interrupting oft the impassioned game,
From Esthwaite's neighbouring Lake the splitting ice,

VULCAN: Roman god of fire (hence volcano) and metalwork

While it sank down towards the water, sent,
Among the meadows and the hills, its long
And dismal yellings, like the noise of wolves
When they are howling round the Bothnic Main.*   570

Nor, sedulous as I have been to trace
How Nature by extrinsic passion first
Peopled my mind with beauteous forms or grand,
And made me love them, may I here forget
How other pleasures have been mine, and joys
Of subtler origin; how I have felt,
Not seldom, even in that tempestuous time,
Those hallowed and pure motions of the sense
Which seem, in their simplicity, to own
An intellectual charm,* that calm delight   580
Which, if I err not, surely must belong
To those first-born affinities that fit
Our new existence to existing things,
And, in our dawn of being, constitute
The bond of union betwixt life and joy.

■ *He is witness to forms,*
colors, ever moving mist,
cloud, sea, moon, and
earth, all presences of
natural beauty, eternal
because ever changing.

■ Yes, I remember, when the changeful earth,
And twice five seasons on my mind had stamped
The faces of the moving year, even then,
A Child, I held unconscious intercourse
With the eternal Beauty, drinking in   590
A pure organic pleasure from the lines

Bothnic Main: northernmost arm of the Baltic Sea
intellectual charm: here meaning spiritual charm

Of curling mist, or from the level plain
Of waters coloured by the steady clouds.

The Sands of Westmoreland, the Creeks and Bays
Of Cumbria's* rocky limits, they can tell
How when the Sea threw off his evening shade
And to the Shepherd's huts beneath the crags
Did send sweet notice of the rising moon,
How I have stood, to fancies such as these,
Engrafted in the tenderness of thought,   600
A stranger, linking with the spectacle
No conscious memory of a kindred sight,
And bringing with me no peculiar sense
Of quietness or peace, yet I have stood,
Even while mine eye has moved o'er three long leagues
Of shining water, gathering, as it seemed,
Through every hair-breadth of that field of light,
New pleasure, like a bee among the flowers.

Thus, often in those fits of vulgar* joy
Which, through all seasons, on a child's pursuits   610
Are prompt attendants, 'mid that giddy bliss
Which, like a tempest, works along the blood
And is forgotten; even then I felt
Gleams like the flashing of a shield; the earth
And common face of Nature spake to me
Rememberable things; sometimes, 'tis true,

Cumbria's: Cumberland's
vulgar: common, ordinary

1.13 Rev. Thomas Gisborne (1758–1846). *Ullswater from Gowbarrow Park*, 1796. The Wordsworth Trust. From the time he was a child, Wordsworth "held unconscious intercourse / With the eternal Beauty" of the natural world—including Ullswater and its own "lines / Of curling mist."

By chance collisions and quaint accidents
Like those ill-sorted unions,* work supposed
Of evil-minded fairies, yet not vain
Nor profitless, if haply they impressed   620
Collateral* objects and appearances,
Albeit lifeless then, and doomed to sleep
Until maturer seasons called them forth
To impregnate and to elevate the mind.
—And if the vulgar joy by its own weight
Wearied itself out of the memory,
The scenes which were a witness of that joy
Remained, in their substantial lineaments
Depicted on the brain, and to the eye
Were visible, a daily sight; and thus   630
By the impressive discipline of fear,
By pleasure and repeated happiness,
So frequently repeated, and by force
Of obscure feelings representative
Of joys that were forgotten, these same scenes,
So beauteous and majestic in themselves,
Though yet the day was distant, did at length
Become habitually dear, and all
Their hues and forms were by invisible links
Allied to the affections.

           I began   640
■ My story early, feeling as I fear,

ILL-SORTED UNIONS: poorly matched lovers
COLLATERAL: associated

The weakness of a human love, for days
Disowned by memory, ere the birth of spring
Planting my snowdrops among winter snows.
Nor will it seem to thee, my Friend!* so prompt
In sympathy, that I have lengthened out
With fond and feeble tongue a tedious tale.
Meanwhile, my hope has been that I might fetch
Invigorating thoughts from former years,
Might fix the wavering balance of my mind,   650
And haply meet reproaches, too, whose power
May spur me on, in manhood now mature,
To honourable toil. Yet should these hopes
Be vain, and thus should neither I be taught
To understand myself, nor Thou to know
With better knowledge how the heart was framed
Of him Thou lovest, need I dread from Thee
Harsh judgments, if I am so loth to quit
Those recollected hours that have the charm
Of visionary things, and lovely forms   660
And sweet sensations that throw back our life
And almost make our Infancy itself
A visible scene, on which the sun is shining.

One end hereby at least hath been attained,
My mind hath been revived, and if this mood
Desert me not, I will forthwith bring down,
Through later years, the story of my life.

MY FRIEND: Coleridge

■ *W in hope addresses his
friend Coleridge and,
resolved, looks forward
to continuing "the story
of my life."*

The road lies plain before me; 'tis a theme
Single and of determined bounds; and hence
I chuse it rather at this time, than work   670
Of ampler or more varied argument,

Where I might be discomfited or lost,
And certain hopes are with me that to Thee
This labour will be welcome, honoured Friend.

Book Second

SCHOOL-TIME CONTINUED

Thus far, O Friend!* have we, though leaving much
Unvisited, endeavoured to retrace
My life through its first years, and measured back
The way I travelled when I first began
To love the woods and fields; the passion yet
Was in its birth, sustained, as might befal,
By nourishment that came unsought; for still,
From week to week, from month to month, we lived

■ *He recalls his youth, full of activity . . .*

■ A round of tumult: duly were our games
Prolonged in summer till the day-light failed;   10
No chair remained before the doors, the bench
And threshold steps were empty; fast asleep

■ *. . . so distant in time, yet so present in memory that now he feels himself a being past and present, a double consciousness.*

The Labourer, and the Old Man who had sate,
A later lingerer, yet the revelry
Continued, and the loud uproar: at last,
When all the ground was dark, and the huge clouds
Were edged with twinkling stars, to bed we went
With weary joints, and with a beating mind.
Ah! is there one who ever has been young
And needs a monitory voice to tame   20

FRIEND: Coleridge

The pride of virtue, and of intellect?
And is there one, the wisest and the best
Of all mankind, who does not sometimes wish
For things which cannot be, who would not give,
If so he might, to duty and to truth
The eagerness of infantine desire?
A tranquillizing spirit presses now
On my corporeal frame: so wide appears
The vacancy between me and those days,
■ Which yet have such self-presence in my mind   30
That, sometimes, when I think of them, I seem
Two consciousnesses, conscious of myself
And of some other Being. A grey Stone*
Of native rock, left midway in the Square
Of our small market Village, was the home
And centre of these joys, and when, returned
After long absence, thither I repaired
I found that it was split, and gone to build
A smart Assembly-room* that perked and flared
With wash and rough-cast, elbowing the ground   40
Which had been ours. But let the fiddle scream
And be ye happy! yet, my Friends! I know
That more than one of you will think, with me,
Of those soft starry nights, and that old Dame*
From whom the Stone was named who there had sate
And watched her Table with its huxter's* wares
Assiduous, through the length of sixty years.

GREY STONE: Nanny's Stone in Hawkshead
ASSEMBLY-ROOM: Town Hall, 1790, whitewash and stucco
OLD DAME: Nanny Holme
HUXTER: seller (no pejorative sense)

2.1 J. M. W. Turner (1775–1851). *Windermere*, 1821. Abbot Hall Art Gallery. Reproduced by courtesy of Abbot Hall Art Gallery, Lakeland Arts Trust, Kendal, Cumbria, England. As a schoolboy Wordsworth enjoyed boat races between the islands of Windermere, including the Sister Isles called Lilies of the Valley (East and West), Belle Isle (the largest island), and Lady Holme, where he saw a hermit's "old stone Table, and a mouldered Cave."

We ran a boisterous race; the year span round
With giddy motion. But the time approached
That brought with it a regular desire   50
For calmer pleasures, when the beauteous forms
Of Nature were collaterally attached
To every scheme of holiday delight,
And every boyish sport, less grateful else,
And languidly pursued.

When summer came
It was the pastime of our afternoons
To beat along the plain of Windermere
With rival oars, and the selected bourne
Was now an Island, musical with birds
That sang for ever; now a Sister Isle,   60
Beneath the oak's umbrageous* covert, sown
With lillies of the valley, like a field;
And now a third small Island where remained
An old stone Table, and a mouldered Cave,
A Hermit's history. In such a race,
So ended, disappointment could be none,
Uneasiness, or pain, or jealousy;
We rested in the shade, all pleased alike,
Conquered and Conqueror. Thus the pride of strength,
And the vain-glory of superior skill   70
Were interfused with objects which subdued
And tempered them, and gradually produced

Youthful activity gives more pleasure when soon associated with forms of natural beauty.

The lads, learning victory and loss from sport, gain self-reliance. W finds, too, a strength in solitude.

Natural sustenance, exertion, support, and good regimen lead to joy.

UMBRAGEOUS: shady

A quiet independence of the heart.
And to my Friend, who knows me, I may add,
Unapprehensive of reproof, that hence
Ensued a diffidence and modesty,
And I was taught to feel, perhaps too much,
The self-sufficing power of solitude.

No delicate viands sapped our bodily strength;
More than we wished we knew the blessing then   80
Of vigorous hunger, for our daily meals
Were frugal, Sabine* fare! and then, exclude
A little weekly stipend, and we lived
Through three divisions of the quartered year
In pennyless poverty. But now, to School
Returned from the half-yearly holidays,
We came with purses more profusely filled,
Allowance which abundantly sufficed
To gratify the palate with repasts
More costly than the Dame* of whom I spake,   90
That ancient Woman, and her board* supplied.
Hence inroads into distant Vales, and long
Excursions far away among the hills,
Hence rustic dinners on the cool green ground,
Or in the woods, or near a river side,
Or by some shady fountain,* while soft airs
Among the leaves were stirring, and the sun,
Unfelt, shone sweetly round us in our joy.

SABINE: modest, as at Horace's farm
DAME: Ann Tyson
BOARD: table for eating
FOUNTAIN: spring

Nor is my aim neglected, if I tell

How twice in the long length of those half-years   100

We from our funds, perhaps, with bolder hand

Drew largely, anxious for one day, at least,

To feel the motion of the galloping Steed;

And with the good old Innkeeper, in truth,

On such occasion sometimes we employed

Sly subterfuge; for the intended bound

The schoolboys ride to Furness Abbey, ruined but enchanted, rest their horses up the hillsides, then race home to Hawkshead across the tidal sands.
Of the day's journey was too distant far

For any cautious man, a Structure famed

Beyond its neighbourhood, the antique Walls

Of that large Abbey, which within the Vale   110

Of Nightshade to St. Mary's honour built

Stands yet, a mouldering Pile, with fractured Arch,

Belfry, and Images, and living Trees,

A holy Scene! along the smooth green turf

Our Horses grazed: to more than inland peace

Left by the Sea wind passing overhead

(Though wind of roughest temper) trees and tow'rs

May in that Valley oftentimes be seen,

Both silent and both motionless alike;

Such is the shelter that is there, and such   120

The safeguard for repose and quietness.

Our steeds remounted, and the summons giv'n,

With whip and spur we by the Chauntry flew

In uncouth race, and left the cross-legg'd Knight,

And the Stone-Abbot, and that single Wren

Which one day sang so sweetly in the Nave

Of the old Church, that, though from recent showers

The earth was comfortless, and touched by faint

Internal breezes, sobbings of the place,

And respirations, from the roofless walls   130

The shuddering ivy dripped large drops, yet still,

So sweetly 'mid the gloom the invisible Bird

Sang to itself, that there I could have made

My dwelling-place, and lived for ever there

To hear such music. Through the walls we flew

And down the Valley, and a circuit made

In wantonness of heart, through rough and smooth

We scampered homeward. Oh! ye Rocks and Streams,

And that still Spirit of the evening air!

Even in this joyous time I sometimes felt   140

Your presence, when with slackened step we breathed

Along the sides of the steep hills, or when,

Lighted by gleams of moonlight from the sea,

We beat with thundering hoofs the level sand.*

Upon the Eastern Shore of Windermere,

Above the crescent of a pleasant Bay,

There stood an Inn, no homely-featured Shed,

Brother of the surrounding Cottages,

But 'twas a splendid place, the door beset

With Chaises, Grooms, and Liveries, and within   150

We . . . sand: repeated at 10.566

2.2 Frederick Henry Henshaw (1807–1891). *Furness Abbey*, 1840. Keble College, University of Oxford. Founded in 1123, the abbey was begun by the Savigny Order. Two decades later the Order merged with the Cistercians, who enlarged it. In 1537 Henry VIII's forces destroyed the abbey, eventually "a mouldering Pile, with fractured Arch."

Decanters, Glasses, and the blood-red Wine.
In ancient times, or ere the Hall was built
On the large Island,* had this Dwelling been
More worthy of a Poet's love, a Hut
Proud of its one bright fire, and sycamore shade.

■ *Clarke's* Survey of
the Lakes *(1787): The
"White Lyon" at Bowness
is "a very decent, clean
little inn. . . . Behind
the house is a small
bowling-green . . .
delightfully-enough
situated, but though
much elevated, does not
command a good
prospect of the Lake and
islands, as the view is
intercepted by some tall
trees." W adored the spot.*

■ *A boy, he loves the light
of sun and moon on
hills, cottages, and vale.
But for higher reasons
this love endures.*

■ But though the rhymes were gone which once inscribed
The threshold, and large golden characters
On the blue-frosted Sign-board had usurped
The place of the old Lion, in contempt
And mockery of the rustic Painter's hand,   160
Yet to this hour the spot to me is dear
With all its foolish pomp. The garden lay
Upon a slope surmounted by the plain
Of a small Bowling-green; beneath us stood
A grove, with gleams of water through the trees
And over the tree-tops; nor did we want*
Refreshment, strawberries and mellow cream.
And there, through half an afternoon, we played
On the smooth platform, and the shouts we sent
Made all the mountains ring. But ere the fall   170
Of night, when in our pinnace* we returned
Over the dusky Lake, and to the beach
Of some small Island steered our course with one,
The Minstrel* of our troop, and left him there,
And rowed off gently, while he blew his flute
Alone upon the rock; Oh! then the calm
And dead still water lay upon my mind

HALL . . . ISLAND: Curwen House on Belle Isle

WANT: lack

PINNACE: boat

MINSTREL: Robert Greenwood, who like W attended Cambridge

Even with a weight of pleasure, and the sky
Never before so beautiful, sank down
Into my heart, and held me like a dream.   180

Thus daily were my sympathies enlarged,
And thus the common range of visible things
Grew dear to me: already I began
To love the sun, a Boy I loved the sun,
■ Not as I since have loved him, as a pledge
And surety of our earthly life, a light
Which while we view, we feel we are alive;
But for this cause, that I had seen him lay
His beauty on the morning hills, had seen
The western mountain touch his setting orb,   190
In many a thoughtless hour, when, from excess
Of happiness, my blood appeared to flow
With its own pleasure, and I breathed with joy.
And from like feelings, humble though intense,
To patriotic and domestic love
Analogous, the moon to me was dear;
For I would dream away my purposes,
Standing to look upon her while she hung
Midway between the hills, as if she knew
No other region; but belonged to thee,   200
Yea, appertained by a peculiar right
To thee and thy grey huts,* my darling Vale!

GREY HUTS: cottages of local stone in the Vale of Esthwaite

Those incidental charms which first attached
My heart to rural objects, day by day
Grew weaker, and I hasten on to tell
How Nature, intervenient* till this time,
And secondary, now at length was sought
For her own sake. But who shall parcel out
His intellect by geometric rules,
Split, like a province,* into round and square?   210
Who knows the individual hour in which
His habits were first sown, even as a seed,
Who that shall point, as with a wand, and say,
'This portion of the river of my mind
Came from yon fountain?' Thou, my Friend! art one
More deeply read in thy own thoughts; to thee
Science appears but what in truth she is,
Not as our glory and our absolute boast,
But as a succedaneum,* and a prop
To our infirmity. Thou art no slave   220
Of that false secondary power,* by which,
In weakness, we create distinctions, then
Deem that our puny boundaries are things
Which we perceive, and not which we have made.
To Thee, unblinded by these outward shows,
The unity of all has been revealed
And Thou wilt doubt with me, less aptly skilled
Than many are to class the cabinet*
Of their sensations, and, in voluble phrase,

Run through the history and birth of each,   230
As of a single independent thing.
Hard task to analyse a soul, in which,
Not only general habits and desires,
But each most obvious and particular thought,
Not in a mystical and idle sense,
But in the words of reason deeply weighed,
Hath no beginning.

　　　　　Bless'd the infant Babe,
(For with my best conjectures I would trace
The progress of our Being) blest the Babe,
Nursed in his Mother's arms, the Babe who sleeps   240
Upon his Mother's breast, who, when his soul
Claims manifest kindred with an earthly soul,
Doth gather passion from his Mother's eye!
Such feelings pass into his torpid life
Like an awakening breeze, and hence his mind
Even in the first trial of its powers
Is prompt and watchful, eager to combine
In one appearance, all the elements
And parts of the same object, else detached
And loth to coalesce. Thus day by day,   250
Subjected to the discipline of love,
His organs and recipient faculties
Are quickened, are more vigorous, his mind spreads,
Tenacious of the forms which it receives.

■ *Knowledge, its parts but the parts of a greater whole, comes through imaginative as well as analytic faculties.*

■ *Elder collaborators, mothers humanize the first poetic acts of life: we perceive—we create— the world around us that is new. All are born creators; many later lose this power, yet some retain it always.*

INTERVENIENT: ancillary, merely accompanying
PROVINCE: area, esp. of knowledge
SUCCEDANEUM: support, compensation
FALSE . . . POWER: analytic understanding only, not "deeply weighed"
CABINET: display case, cabinet of curiosities

2.3 James Ward (1769–1859). *Mother and Infant*, 1798. Yale Center for British Art, Paul Mellon Collection. "The gravitation and the filial bond / Of nature": Wordsworth's mother died of consumption on March 8, 1778—a month before William's eighth birthday—"the heart / And hinge of all our learnings and our loves" was gone (5.257–58).

An inmate* of this *active* universe;
From nature largely he receives; nor so
Is satisfied, but largely gives again,
For feeling has to him imparted strength,
And powerful in all sentiments of grief,   270
Of exultation, fear, and joy, his mind,
Even as an agent of the one great mind,
Creates, creator and receiver both,
Working but in alliance with the works
Which it beholds.—Such verily is the first
Poetic spirit of our human life;
By uniform controul of after years
In most abated or suppressed, in some,
Through every change of growth or of decay
Pre-eminent till death.

           From early days,   280
Beginning not long after that first time
In which, a Babe, by intercourse of touch,
I held mute dialogues with my Mother's heart,
I have endeavoured to display the means
Whereby this infant sensibility,
Great birth-right of our Being, was in me
Augmented and sustained. Yet is a path
More difficult before me, and I fear
That in its broken windings we shall need
The Chamois'* sinews, and the Eagle's wing: 290

INMATE: member, dweller (no sense of prisoner)
CHAMOIS: Alpine hoofed mammal adept at climbing

The universe shuns stasis. It lives, eternally creating.

Growth of a visionary power, shaped first by his Mother, soon draws support from signs of ancient earth, moods of the mind, love, solitude, and a sense of endless possibility.

In one belovèd Presence, nay and more,
In that most apprehensive habitude
And those sensations which have been derived
From this belovèd Presence, there exists
A virtue which irradiates and exalts
All objects through all intercourse of sense.   260
No outcast he, bewildered and depressed:
Along his infant veins are interfused
The gravitation and the filial bond
Of nature, that connect him with the world.
Emphatically such a Being lives,

For now a trouble came into my mind
From unknown causes. I was left alone,
Seeking the visible world, nor knowing why.
The props of my affections were removed,
And yet the building stood, as if sustained
By its own spirit! All that I beheld
Was dear to me, and from this cause it came,
That now to Nature's finer influxes*
My mind lay open, to that more exact
And intimate communion which our hearts   300
Maintain with the minuter properties
Of objects which already are beloved,
And of those only. Many are the joys
Of youth; but Oh! what happiness to live
When every hour brings palpable access
Of knowledge, when all knowledge is delight,
And sorrow is not there. The seasons came,
And every season to my notice brought
A store of transitory qualities
Which, but for this most watchful power of love   310
Had been neglected, left a register
Of permanent relations, else unknown,
Hence life, and change, and beauty, solitude
More active, even, than 'best society',
Society made sweet as solitude
By silent inobtrusive sympathies,
And gentle agitations of the mind

■ *He recalls the hours of childhood that never vanish from the mind. Elusive yet permanent, their power—its origin obscure—both haunts and steadies.*

From manifold distinctions, difference
Perceived in things, where to the common eye
No difference is, and hence, from the same source   320
Sublimer joy; for I would walk alone
In storm and tempest, or in star-light nights
Beneath the quiet Heavens, and at that time
Have felt whate'er there is of power in sound
To breathe an elevated mood, by form
Or image unprofaned; and I would stand
Beneath some rock, listening to sounds that are
The ghostly language of the ancient earth,
Or make their dim abode in distant winds.
Thence did I drink the visionary power.   330
I deem not profitless these fleeting moods
Of shadowy exultation: not for this,
That they are kindred to our purer mind
And intellectual* life; but that the soul,
Remembering how she felt, but what she felt
Remembering not, retains an obscure sense
Of possible sublimity, to which,
With growing faculties she doth aspire,
With faculties still growing, feeling still
That whatsoever point they gain, they still   340
Have something to pursue.

                              And not alone,
■ In grandeur and in tumult, but no less

INFLUXES: influences, impressions

INTELLECTUAL: spiritual, not sensory

2.4 Richard Carruthers (1792–1876). *William Wordsworth*, 1818. The Wordsworth Trust. ". . . and I would stand / Beneath some rock, listening to sounds that are / The ghostly language of the ancient earth."

In tranquil scenes, that universal power
And fitness in the latent qualities

FRIEND: John Fleming, who also attended Cambridge

And essences of things, by which the mind
Is moved with feelings of delight, to me
Came strengthened with a superadded soul,
A virtue not its own. My morning walks
Were early; oft before the hours of School
I travelled round our little Lake, five miles   350
Of pleasant wandering, happy time! more dear
For this, that one was by my side, a Friend*
Then passionately loved: with heart how full
Will he peruse these lines, this page, perhaps
A blank to other men! for many years
Have since flowed in between us; and our minds,
Both silent to each other, at this time
We live as if those hours had never been.
Nor seldom did I lift our cottage latch
Far earlier, and before the vernal thrush   360
Was audible, among the hills I sate
Alone, upon some jutting eminence
At the first hour of morning, when the Vale
Lay quiet in an utter solitude.
How shall I trace the history, where seek
The origin of what I then have felt?
Oft in these moments such a holy calm
Did overspread my soul, that I forgot
That I had bodily eyes, and what I saw
Appeared like something in myself, a dream,   370
A prospect in my mind.

2.5 James Bourne (1773–1854). *Esthwaite Lake*, 1802. The Wordsworth Trust. Esthwaite Water lies less than a half mile southeast of Hawkshead. Wordsworth wandered happily "round our little Lake" countless times as a schoolboy.

      'Twere long to tell
What spring and autumn, what the winter snows,
And what the summer shade, what day and night,
The evening and the morning, what my dreams

And what my waking thoughts supplied, to nurse
That spirit of religious love in which
I walked with Nature. But let this at least
Be not forgotten, that I still retained

My first creative sensibility,
That by the regular action of the world   380
My soul was unsubdued. A plastic* power
Abode with me, a forming hand, at times

■ *Within him rises a force that colors all experi-ence—a will subservient yet superadded to all of Nature's acts.*

■ Rebellious, acting in a devious mood,
A local spirit of its own, at war
With general tendency, but for the most
Subservient strictly to the external things
With which it communed. An auxiliar light
Came from my mind which on the setting sun
Bestowed new splendor, the melodious birds,
The gentle breezes, fountains that ran on,   390
Murmuring so sweetly in themselves, obeyed
A like dominion; and the midnight storm
Grew darker in the presence of my eye.
Hence my obeisance, my devotion hence,
And hence my transport.

            Nor should this, perchance,
Pass unrecorded, that I still had loved
The exercise and produce of a toil

■ *In creative perceptions he now matures and sees "one life"—and feels that it is joy.*

Than analytic industry to me
More pleasing, and whose character, I deem,
Is more poetic, as resembling more   400
Creative agency. I mean to speak
Of that interminable building reared
By observation of affinities

PLASTIC: shaping, creative

In objects where no brotherhood exists
To common minds. My seventeenth year was come
And whether from this habit rooted now
So deeply in my mind, or from excess
Of the great social principle of life,
Coercing all things into sympathy,
To unorganic natures I transferred   410
My own enjoyments, or, the power of truth
Coming in revelation, I conversed
With things that really are, I at this time
Saw blessings spread around me like a sea.
Thus did my days pass on, and now at length
From Nature and her overflowing soul
I had received so much that all my thoughts
Were steeped in feeling; I was only then
Contented when with bliss ineffable
I felt the sentiment of Being spread   420
O'er all that moves, and all that seemeth still,
O'er all, that, lost beyond the reach of thought
And human knowledge, to the human eye
Invisible, yet liveth to the heart,
■ O'er all that leaps, and runs, and shouts, and sings,
Or beats the gladsome air, o'er all that glides
Beneath the wave, yea in the wave itself
And mighty depth of waters. Wonder not
If such my transports were; for in all things
I saw one life, and felt that it was joy.   430

One song they sang and it was audible,
Most audible then when the fleshly ear,
O'ercome by grosser prelude of that strain,
Forgot its functions, and slept undisturbed.

If this be error, and another faith
Find easier access to the pious mind,
Yet were I grossly destitute of all
Those human sentiments which make this earth
So dear, if I should fail, with grateful voice
To speak of you, Ye Mountains! and Ye Lakes,   440
And sounding Cataracts! Ye Mists and Winds
That dwell among the hills where I was born.
If in my youth, I have been pure in heart,
If, mingling with the world, I am content
With my own modest pleasures, and have lived,
With God and Nature communing, removed
From little enmities and low desires,

■ *Despite disappointments of his day and those who deny the visionary power, he retains a faith that through the gift of Nature it will endure.*

■ The gift is Yours: if in these times of fear,
This melancholy waste of hopes o'erthrown,
If, 'mid indifference and apathy   450
And wicked exultation, when good Men,
On every side, fall off we know not how,
To selfishness, disguised in gentle names
Of peace, and quiet, and domestic love,
Yet mingled, not unwillingly, with sneers
On visionary minds; if in this time

2.6 Thomas Creswick (1811–1869). *View from Mr. Southey's House, Keswick,* 1838. Yale Center for British Art, Paul Mellon Collection. "O Nature! Thou hast fed / My lofty speculations." Coleridge lived at Greta Hall in Keswick from 1800 to 1804. Fellow poet Robert Southey lived at Greta Hall after Coleridge until 1843.

Of dereliction and dismay, I yet
Despair not of our nature, but retain
A more than Roman confidence, a faith
That fails not, in all sorrow my support,   460
The blessing of my life, the gift is yours,
Ye Mountains! thine, O Nature! Thou hast fed
My lofty speculations; and in Thee,
For this uneasy heart of ours, I find
A never-failing principle of joy,
And purest passion.

                    Thou, my Friend! wert reared
In the great City,* 'mid far other scenes;
But we, by different roads at length, have gained
The self-same bourne. And for this cause to Thee
I speak, unapprehensive of contempt,   470

The insinuated scoff of coward tongues,
And all that silent language which so oft
In conversation betwixt man and man
Blots from the human countenance all trace
Of beauty and of love. For Thou hast sought
The truth in solitude, and Thou art one,
The most intense of Nature's worshippers,
In many things my Brother, chiefly here,
In this my deep devotion.

                    Fare Thee well!
Health, and the quiet of a healthful mind   480
Attend Thee! seeking oft the haunts of Men,
And yet more often living with Thyself,
And for Thyself, so haply shall thy days
Be many, and a blessing to mankind.

■ *Coleridge, of another temperament—gregarious yet alone, too—possesses allied though different gifts for human good, and W wishes his dear friend a quiet mind, long life, and health.*

GREAT CITY: Coleridge had lived and gone to school in London nine years.

Book Third

RESIDENCE AT CAMBRIDGE

It was a dreary morning when the Chaise*
Rolled over the flat Plains of Huntingdon
And through the open windows first I saw
The long-backed Chapel of King's College rear
His pinnacles above the dusky groves.

Soon afterwards we espied upon the road
A Student clothed in Gown and tasselled Cap;
He passed, nor was I master of my eyes
Till he was left a hundred yards behind.
■ The place as we approached seemed more and more   10
To have an eddy's force, and sucked us in
More eagerly at every step we took.
Onward we drove beneath the Castle, down
By Magdalene* Bridge we went and crossed the Cam,
And at the Hoop we landed, famous Inn!

My spirit was up, my thoughts were full of hope;
Some Friends I had, Acquaintances who there
Seemed Friends, poor simple School-boys, now hung round

■ *Never before outside the Lakes, W arrives at Cambridge with his cousin John Myers. His excitement is enormous . . .*

■ *. . . and for the moment he seems magically trans-formed.*

With honour and importance; in a world
Of welcome faces up and down I roved;   20
Questions, directions, counsel and advice
Flowed in upon me from all sides, fresh day
Of pride and pleasure! to myself I seemed
A man of business and expence, and went
From Shop to Shop about my own affairs,
To Tutors or to Tailors, as befel,
From Street to Street with loose and careless heart.

I was the Dreamer, they the Dream; I roamed
Delighted, through the motley spectacle;
Gowns grave or gaudy, Doctors, Students, Streets,   30
Lamps, Gateways, Flocks of Churches, Courts* and Towers.
Strange transformation for a mountain Youth,
A northern Villager! As if by word
Of magic, or some Fairy's power, at once
■ Behold me rich in monies, and attired
In splendid clothes, with hose of silk, and hair
Glittering like rimy* trees when frost is keen.
My lordly Dressing-gown I pass it by,
With other signs of manhood which supplied
The lack of beard.—The weeks went roundly on,   40
With invitations, suppers, wine and fruit,
Smooth housekeeping within, and all without
Liberal and suiting Gentleman's array!

CHAISE: light carriage or coach
MAGDALENE: as two syllables, môd´-lun

COURTS: college quadrangles or courtyards
RIMY: covered with rime or hoarfrost

3.1 Thomas Malton the Younger (1748–1804). *King's Parade, Cambridge, between 1798 and 1799.* Yale Center for British Art, Paul Mellon Collection. Wordsworth first saw "The long-backed Chapel of King's College" when he began studies at Cambridge on October 30, 1787.

3.2 Unknown artist. *St John's College, Cambridge.* The Wordsworth Trust. The College of St. John the Evangelist of the University of Cambridge was founded in 1511 with benefactions from Lady Margaret Beaufort, mother of Henry VII.

3.3 Unknown artist. Engraved by Georges-Henri Manesse (1854–1940). *Wordsworth's Room in St. John's College, Cambridge.* The Wordsworth Trust. Room 23: A noisy "nook obscure!" above the clattering college kitchens.

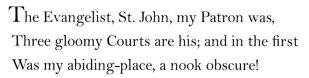
Settled in St. John's, he is not drawn to academic chores and competition . . .

The Evangelist, St. John, my Patron was,
Three gloomy Courts are his; and in the first
Was my abiding-place, a nook obscure!
■ Right underneath, the College Kitchens made
A humming sound, less tuneable than bees,
But hardly less industrious; with shrill notes
Of sharp command and scolding intermixed.   50
Near me was Trinity's loquacious Clock,

Who never let the Quarters, night or day,
Slip by him unproclaimed, and told the hours
Twice over with a male and female voice.
Her pealing organ was my neighbour, too;
And, from my Bed-room, I in moonlight nights
Could see, right opposite, a few yards off,
The Antechapel, where the Statue stood
Of Newton, with his Prism* and silent Face.

ANTECHAPEL . . . PRISM: His statue in Trinity's antechapel shows him holding a prism.

Of College labours, of the Lecturer's Room,   60
All studded round, as thick as chairs could stand,
With loyal Students, faithful to their books,
Half-and-half Idlers, hardy Recusants,*
And honest Dunces;—of important Days,
Examinations, when the Man was weighed
As in the balance!—of excessive hopes,
Tremblings withal, and commendable fears,
Small jealousies, and triumphs good or bad
I make short mention; things they were which then
I did not love, nor do I love them now.   70
Such glory was but little sought by me
And little won. But it is right to say
That even so early, from the first crude days
Of settling-time in this my new abode,

■ . . . yet wonders what
it all might mean, and
worries how it shapes
his future life.

■ Not seldom I had melancholy thoughts,
From personal and family regards,
Wishing to hope without a hope, some fears
About my future worldly maintenance,
And, more than all, a strangeness in my mind,
A feeling that I was not for that hour,   80
Nor for that place. But wherefore be cast down?
Why should I grieve? I was a chosen Son.

■ He turns to deeper
thoughts, things higher
than daily study . . .

For hither I had come with holy powers
And faculties, whether to work or feel:
To apprehend all passions and all moods
Which time, and place, and season do impress

RECUSANTS: here, those who disdain study

Upon the visible universe, and work
Like changes there by force of my own mind.
I was a Freeman: in the purest sense
Was free, and to majestic ends was strong.   90
I do not speak of knowledge, moral truth,
Or understanding; 'twas enough for me
To know that I was otherwise endowed.
When the first glitter of the show was past,
And the first dazzle of the taper light,
As if with a rebound my mind returned
Into its former self. Oft did I leave
My comrades, and the crowd, buildings and groves,
And walked along the fields, the level fields,
With Heaven's blue concave reared above my head.   100
And now it was, that from such change entire
And this first absence from those shapes sublime
Wherewith I had been conversant, my mind
Seemed busier in itself than heretofore;
At least, I more directly recognised
My powers and habits; let me dare to speak
A higher language, say that now I felt
The strength and consolation that were mine.
As if awakened, summoned, rouzed, constrained,
■ I looked for universal things, perused   110
The common countenance of earth and heaven,
And, turning the mind in upon itself,
Pored, watched, expected, listened; spread my thoughts,

And spread them with a wider creeping, felt
Incumbences more awful,* visitings
Of the Upholder of the tranquil Soul,
Which underneath all passion lives secure,
A steadfast life. But peace! it is enough
To notice that I was ascending now
To such community with highest truth.   120

A track pursuing not untrod before,
From deep analogies by thought supplied,
Or consciousnesses not to be subdued,
To every natural form, rock, fruit, or flower,
Even the loose stones that cover the high-way,
I gave a moral life, I saw them feel,
Or linked them to some feeling: the great mass
Lay bedded in a quickening soil, and all
That I beheld respired with inward meaning.
Thus much for the one Presence, and the Life   130
Of the great whole; suffice it here to add

*. . . and begins to see
and feel the world upon
another plane, in sight
and spirit.*

That, whatsoe'er of Terror or of Love,
Or Beauty, Nature's daily face put on
From transitory passion, unto this
I was as wakeful even as waters are
To the sky's motion; in a kindred sense
Of passion was obedient as a lute
That waits upon the touches of the wind.
So was it with me in my solitude;

Incumbences . . . awful: insistent broodings that create awe

3.4 William Turner of Oxford (1789–1862). *Donati's Comet*, 1858–59. Yale Center for British Art, Paul Mellon Collection. Wordsworth developed an eye searching "from a stone, a tree, a withered leaf, / To the broad ocean and the azure heavens."

So, often among multitudes of men.   140
Unknown, unthought of, yet I was most rich,
I had a world about me; 'twas my own,
I made it; for it only lived to me,
And to the God who looked into my mind.
Such sympathies would sometimes show themselves
By outward gestures and by visible looks.
Some called it madness: such, indeed, it was,
If child-like fruitfulness in passing joy,
If steady moods of thoughtfulness, matured

To inspiration, sort with such a name;   150
If prophecy be madness; if things viewed
By Poets in old time, and higher up*
By the first men, earth's first inhabitants,
May in these tutored days no more be seen
With undisordered sight: but leaving this
It was no madness: for I had an eye
Which in my strongest workings evermore
Was looking for the shades of difference
As they lie hid in all exterior forms
Near or remote, minute or vast, an eye   160
Which from a stone, a tree, a withered leaf,
To the broad ocean and the azure heavens
Spangled with kindred multitudes of stars,
Could find no surface where its power might sleep,
Which spake perpetual logic to my soul,
And by an unrelenting agency
Did bind my feelings, even as in a chain.

■ *This further growth of his creative power becomes a worthy theme . . .*

And here, O Friend!* have I retraced my life
Up to an eminence, and told a tale

■ *. . . but hard to speak, though all at times have felt its force.*

■ Of matters which, not falsely, I may call   170
The glory of my Youth. Of Genius, Power,
Creation, and Divinity itself
I have been speaking, for my theme has been
What passed within me. Not of outward things
Done visibly for other minds, words, signs,

Symbols, or actions; but of my own heart
Have I been speaking, and my youthful mind.
O Heavens! how awful is the might of Souls,
And what they do within themselves, while yet
The yoke of earth is new to them, the world   180
Nothing but a wild field where they were sown.
This is, in truth, heroic argument,
And genuine prowess; which I wished to touch
With hand however weak; but in the main
It lies far hidden from the reach of words.
Points have we all of us within our souls,
Where all stand single; this I feel, and make
Breathings for incommunicable powers.
Yet each man is a memory to himself:
■ And, therefore, now that I must quit this theme,   190
I am not heartless;* for there's not a man
That lives who hath not had his god-like hours,
And knows not what majestic sway we have,
As natural beings, in the strength of nature.

Enough: for now into a populous Plain
We must descend.—A Traveller I am
And all my Tale is of myself; even so,
So be it, if the pure in heart delight
To follow me; and Thou O honoured Friend!
Who in my thoughts art ever at my side,   200
Uphold, as heretofore, my fainting steps.

HEARTLESS: disheartened, faint of heart

HIGHER UP: even earlier
FRIEND: Coleridge

It hath been told already how my sight
Was dazzled by the novel show, and how
Erelong I did into myself return.
So did it seem, and so in truth it was.
Yet this was but short-lived: thereafter came
Observance less devout. I had made a change
In climate; and my nature's outward coat
Changed also, slowly and insensibly.

■ *He relates his lonelier meditations, yet shifts with idle, happy times among the student throng.*

■ To the deep quiet and majestic thoughts   210
Of loneliness succeeded empty noise
And superficial pastimes; now and then,
Forced labour; and, more frequently, forced hopes;
And worse than all, a treasonable growth
Of indecisive judgments that impaired
And shook the mind's simplicity. And yet
This was a gladsome time. Could I behold,
Who less insensible than sodden clay
On a sea River's bed at ebb of tide,
Could have beheld with undelighted heart   220
So many happy Youths, so wide and fair
A congregation, in its budding-time
Of health, and hope, and beauty; all at once
So many divers samples of the growth
Of life's sweet season, could have seen unmoved
That miscellaneous garland of wild flowers*
Upon the matron temples of a Place
So famous through the world?* To me, at least,

MISCELLANEOUS . . . FLOWERS: variety of students
MATRON . . . WORLD: the alma mater, Cambridge

It was a goodly prospect: for, through youth,
Though I had been trained up to stand unpropped,   230
And independent musings pleased me so
That spells seemed on me when I was alone,
Yet could I only cleave to solitude
In lonesome places; if a throng was near
That way I leaned by nature; for my heart
Was social, and loved idleness and joy.

Not seeking those who might participate*
My deeper pleasures (nay I had not once,
Though not unused to mutter lonesome songs,
Even with myself divided such delight,   240
Or looked that way for aught that might be cloathed
In human language) easily I passed
From the remembrances of better things,
And slipped into the week-day works of youth,
Unburthened, unalarmed, and unprofaned.
Caverns there were within my mind, which sun
Could never penetrate, yet did there not
Want store of leafy arbours where the light
Might enter in at will. Companionships,
Friendships, acquaintances, were welcome all;   250
We sauntered, played, we rioted, we talked
Unprofitable talk at morning hours,
Drifted about along the streets and walks,
Read lazily in lazy books, went forth

PARTICIPATE: share

To gallop through the country in blind zeal
Of senseless horsemanship; or on the breast
Of Cam sailed boisterously; and let the stars
Come out, perhaps, without one quiet thought.

Such was the tenor of the opening act
In this new life. Imagination slept,   260
And yet not utterly: I could not print
Ground, where the grass had yielded to the steps
Of generations of illustrious Men,
Unmoved: I could not always lightly pass
Through the same Gateways: sleep where they had slept,
Wake where they waked, range that enclosure old,
That garden of great intellects undisturbed.
Place also by the side of this dark sense
Of nobler feeling, that those spiritual Men,
Even the great Newton's own etherial Self   270
Seemed humbled in these precincts; thence to be
The more beloved; invested here with tasks
Of life's plain business, as a daily garb;
Dictators at the Plough,* a change that left
All genuine admiration unimpaired.

Beside the pleasant Mills of Trompington
I laughed with Chaucer,* in the hawthorn shade
Heard him, while birds were warbling, tell his tales
Of amorous passion. And that gentle Bard,

The university as the great legacy of the dead who have achieved so much there gives pause, even to the great them-selves.

3.5 Unknown artist. *Isaac Newton.* The Wordsworth Trust. Wordsworth read Newton's *Opticks* as early as age 14. A statue of Newton (1643–1727), a boyhood hero, stood in an antechapel, "a few yards off" from his college window—"the great Newton's own etherial Self."

DICTATORS . . . PLOUGH: alludes to the Roman Cincinnatus
CHAUCER: Two characters in his *Reeve's Tale* are Cambridge students from northern England.

3.6 William Blake (1757–1827). *Chaucer's Canterbury Pilgrims*, 1810 to 1820. Yale Center for British Art, Paul Mellon Collection. While at Cambridge, Wordsworth traveled two miles to the "pleasant Mills of Trompington" to read Chaucer, especially *The Reeve's Tale*, which satirizes the miller of Trumpington.

Invoking a Longinian ideal, W identifies with three mighty English poets long dead, though much alive to him. Spenser and Milton have Cambridge ties.

Chosen by the Muses for their Page of State,   280
Sweet Spenser, moving through his clouded heaven
With the moon's beauty, and the moon's soft pace,
■ I called him Brother, Englishman, and Friend.
Yea, our blind Poet, who, in his later days,
Stood almost single, uttering odious* truth,
Darkness before, and danger's voice behind;
Soul awful! if the earth hath ever lodged
An awful Soul, I seemed to see him here
Familiarly, and in his Scholar's dress

ODIOUS: giving offense, inconvenient

Bounding before me, yet a stripling Youth,   290
A Boy, no better, with his rosy cheeks
Angelical, keen eye, courageous look,
And conscious step of purity and pride.

Among the band of my Compeers was one,
My Class-fellow* at School, whose chance it was
To lodge in the Apartments which had been,
Time out of mind, honoured by Milton's name,
The very shell reputed of the abode

CLASS-FELLOW: Edward Birkett, who had attended school in Hawkshead

Embarrassed by easy zeal and drinking much to Milton's memory, beneath he harbors "private thoughts."

3.7 William Faithorne the Elder (1616–1691)? Engraved by Mellison. *John Milton.* The Wordsworth Trust. Milton (1608–1673) graduated from Cambridge in 1629. Wordsworth, during his first days there, "Poured out libations" with fellow students to toast "our blind Poet" in the room "Which he had tenanted . . . till"—as Wordsworth records—"my brain reeled" from too much wine.

Which he had tenanted. O temperate Bard!
One afternoon, the first time I set foot   300
In this thy innocent Nest and Oratory,

Seated with others in a festive ring
Of common-place convention, I to thee
Poured out libations, to thy memory drank,
Within my private thoughts, till my brain reeled;
Never so clouded by the fumes of wine
Before that hour, or since. Thence forth I ran
From that assembly, through a length of streets
Ran, Ostrich-like, to reach our Chapel Door
In not a desperate or opprobrious time,   310
Albeit long after the importunate Bell
Had stopped, with wearisome Cassandra* voice
No longer haunting the dark winter night.
Call back, O Friend!* a moment to thy mind,
The place itself and fashion of the rites.
Up-shouldering in a dislocated lump,
With shallow, ostentatious carelessness,
My Surplice, gloried in, and yet despised,
I clove in pride through the inferior throng
Of the plain Burghers, who in audience stood   320
On the last skirts of their permitted ground
Beneath the pealing Organ. Empty thoughts!
I am ashamed of them: and that great Bard
And thou, O Friend! who in thy ample mind
Hast stationed me for reverence and love,
Ye* will forgive the weakness of that hour
In some of its unworthy vanities,
Brother of many more.

CASSANDRA: Priam's daughter foretold Troy's fall but was not believed.
FRIEND: Coleridge
YE: Milton and Coleridge

In this mixed sort

The months passed on, remissly, not given up

To wilful alienation from the right,   330

Or walks of open scandal; but in vague

And loose indifference, easy likings, aims

Of a low pitch; duty and zeal dismissed,

Yet nature, or a happy course of things

Not doing in their stead the needful work.

The memory languidly revolved, the heart

Reposed in noontide rest; the inner pulse

Of contemplation almost failed to beat.

Rotted as by a charm, my life became

A floating island, an amphibious thing   340

Unsound, of spongy texture, yet withal,

Not wanting a fair face of water weeds

And pleasant flowers.—The thirst of living praise,

A reverence for the glorious Dead, the sight

■ Of those long Vistos,* Catacombs in which

Perennial minds lie visibly entombed,

Have often stirred the heart of Youth, and bred

A fervent love of rigorous discipline.

Alas! such high commotion touched not me;

No look was in these walls to put to shame   350

My easy spirits, and discountenance

Their light composure, far less to instil

A calm resolve of mind, firmly addressed

To puissant* efforts. Nor was this the blame

■ *He is moved by Cambridge, but not to excel at Cambridge.*

Vistos: vistas

puissant: strong, powerful

3.8 Thomas Creswick (1811–1869). *The Summer Bower, Derwent Water*, 1838. Yale Center for British Art, Paul Mellon Collection. Derwent Water has several islands plus one "floating island" of aquatic vegetation "of spongy texture." It occasionally rises with the help of methane gas escaping from the lake floor in late summer, the apparent origin of Wordsworth's image.

Of others but my own. I should, in truth,
As far as doth concern my single self
Misdeem most widely, lodging it elsewhere.
For I, bred up in Nature's lap, was even
As a spoiled Child; and rambling like the wind
As I had done in daily intercourse   360
With those delicious rivers, solemn heights,
And mountains, ranging like a fowl of the air,
I was ill tutored for captivity,
To quit my pleasure, and from month to month
Take up a station calmly on the perch
Of sedentary peace. Those lovely forms
Had also left less space within my mind,
Which, wrought upon instinctively, had found
A freshness in those objects of its love,
A winning power, beyond all other power.   370
Not that I slighted Books; that were to lack
All sense; but other passions had been mine
More fervent, making me less prompt, perhaps,
To in-door study than was wise or well

■ W can imagine a place that would inspire him as Nature does, though Cambridge at that time is not that place.

■ Or suited to my years: yet I could shape
The image of a Place which, soothed and lulled
As I had been, trained up in Paradise
Among sweet garlands and delightful sounds,
Accustomed in my loneliness to walk
With Nature magisterially, yet I,   380
Methinks, could shape the image of a Place

Which with its aspect should have bent me down
To instantaneous service, should at once
Have made me pay to science and to arts
And written lore, acknowledged my liege Lord,
A homage, frankly offered up, like that
Which I had paid to Nature. Toil and pains
In this recess which I have bodied forth
Should spread from heart to heart; and stately groves,
Majestic edifices, should not want   390
A corresponding dignity within.
The congregating temper which pervades
Our unripe years, not wasted, should be made
To minister to works of high attempt,
Which the enthusiast would perform with love;
Youth should be awed, possessed, as with a sense
Religious, of what holy joy there is
In knowledge, if it be sincerely sought
For its own sake, in glory and in praise,
If but by labour won, and to endure.   400
The passing Day should learn to put aside
Her trappings here, should strip them off, abashed
Before antiquity, and steadfast truth,
And strong book-mindedness; and over all
Should be a healthy, sound simplicity,
A seemly plainness, name it as you will,
Republican or pious.

<pre>
                          If these thoughts
           Be a gratuitous emblazonry
           That does but mock this recreant* age, at least
           Let Folly and False-seeming, we might say,   410
           Be free to affect whatever formal gait
           Of moral or scholastic discipline
           Shall raise them highest in their own esteem;
           Let them parade among the Schools at will,
           But spare the House of God. Was ever known
           The witless Shepherd who would drive his Flock
           With serious repetition to a pool
           Of which 'tis plain to sight they never taste?
           A weight must surely hang on days begun
</pre>

■ *Religious and academic*
practice seem overblown,
empty, and so his disil-
lusion grows.

<pre>
         ■ And ended with worst mockery: be wise,   420
           Ye Presidents and Deans, and to your Bells
           Give seasonable rest; for 'tis a sound
           Hollow as ever vexed the tranquil air;
           And your officious doings bring disgrace
           On the plain Steeples of our English Church
           Whose worship 'mid remotest village trees
           Suffers for this. Even Science too, at hand
           In daily sight of such irreverence,
           Is smitten thence with an unnatural taint,
           Loses her just authority, falls beneath   430
           Collateral suspicion, else unknown.
           This obvious truth did not escape me then,
           Unthinking as I was, and I confess
</pre>

RECREANT: unfaithful, cowardly

<pre>
           That, having in my native hills given loose
           To a School-boy's dreaming, I had raised a pile*
           Upon the basis of the coming time,
           Which now before me melted fast away,
           Which could not live, scarcely had life enough
           To mock the Builder. Oh! what joy it were
           To see a Sanctuary for our Country's Youth,   440
           With such a spirit in it as might be
           Protection for itself, a Virgin grove
           Primaeval in its purity and depth;
           Where, though the shades were filled with chearfulness,
           Nor indigent of songs, warbled from crowds
           In under-coverts, yet the countenance
           Of the whole place should bear a stamp of awe:
           A habitation sober and demure
           For ruminating creatures, a domain
           For quiet things to wander in, a haunt   450
           In which the Heron might delight to feed
           By the shy rivers, and the Pelican
           Upon the cypress spire in lonely thought
           Might sit and sun himself. Alas! alas!
           In vain for such solemnity we look;
           Our eyes are crossed by Butterflies, our ears
           Hear chattering Popinjays;* the inner heart
           Is trivial, and the impresses without
           Are of a gaudy region.
</pre>

PILE: here, a castle in the air
BUTTERFLIES . . . POPINJAYS: mere distractions . . . parrots, vain people

3.9 William Turner of Oxford (1789–1862). *Shepherd Boy on a Hillside*, 1840. Yale Center for British Art, Paul Mellon Collection. Wordsworth was raised near shepherds. Several appear in *The Prelude*, including the Cumbrian shepherd and his son searching for lost sheep, and the shepherd guide in Book Thirteenth. However "witless" some might be, Wordsworth thinks them wiser than "Presidents and Deans" who mislead their flocks. Another contrast with shepherds appears (3.579–82).

This he contrasts with studies in a virtuous, frugal past, a university of *plain living* and *highest thought.*

Those venerable Doctors saw of old   460
When all who dwelt within these famous Walls
Led in abstemiousness a studious life,
When, in forlorn and naked chambers cooped
And crowded, o'er the ponderous Books they sate,
Like caterpillars eating out their way,
In silence, or with keen devouring noise
Not to be tracked or fathered.* Princes then
At matins* froze, and couched at curfew-time,
Trained up, through piety and zeal, to prize
Spare diet, patient labour, and plain weeds.*   470
O Seat of Arts! renowned throughout the world,
Far different service in those homely days
The Nurslings of the Muses underwent
From their first childhood; in that glorious time,
When Learning, like a Stranger come from far,
Sounding through Christian Lands her Trumpet, rouzed
The Peasant and the King; when Boys and Youths,
The growth of ragged villages and huts,
Forsook their homes, and, errant in the quest
Of Patron, famous School or friendly Nook,   480
Where, pensioned, they in shelter might sit down,
From Town to Town and through wide-scattered Realms
Journeyed with their huge Folios* in their hands;
And often, starting from some covert place,
Saluted the chance comer in the road,

Yet he knows the world imperfect and ideals easy to prefer; the time must be worked as it is.

TRACKED OR FATHERED: pinned to a source, academically traced
MATINS: early morning prayers
WEEDS: clothes
FOLIOS: large books, about 12 × 15 inches

Crying, 'an obolus,* a penny give
To a poor Scholar': when illustrious Men,
Lovers of truth, by penury constrained,
Bucer, Erasmus, or Melancthon* read
Before the doors or windows of their Cells   490
By moonshine, through mere lack of taper light.

But peace to vain regrets! We see but darkly
Even when we look behind us; and best things
Are not so pure by nature that they needs
Must keep to all, as fondly all believe,
Their highest promise. If the Mariner,
When at reluctant distance he hath passed
Some fair enticing Island, did but know
What fate might have been his, could he have brought
His Bark to land upon the wished-for spot,   500
Good cause full often would he have to bless
The belt of churlish Surf that scared him thence,
Or haste of the inexorable wind.
For me, I grieve not; happy is the Man
Who only misses what I missed, who falls
No lower than I fell.

        I did not love,
As hath been noticed heretofore, the guise
Of our scholastic studies; could have wished
The river* to have had an ampler range,
And freer pace; but this I tax* not; far,   510

OBOLUS: associated with begging, a halfpenny
BUCER ... MELANCTHON: Reformation scholars
RIVER: the river of the mind (2.214) and its studies
TAX: blame

Far more I grieved to see among the Band
Of those who in the field of contest stood
As combatants, passions that did to me
Seem low and mean; from ignorance of mine,

■ *He turns from academic strife and its ungenerous side to pass time with souls less striving . . .* ■ In part, and want of just forbearance, yet
My wiser mind grieves now for what I saw.
Willingly did I part from these, and turn
Out of their track, to travel with the shoal*
Of more unthinking Natures, easy Minds
And pillowy, and not wanting love that makes   520
The day pass lightly on, when foresight sleeps,
And wisdom, and the pledges interchanged
With our own inner being are forgot.

To Books, our daily fare prescribed, I turned
With sickly appetite, and when I went,
At other times, in quest of my own food,
I chaced not steadily the manly deer,
But laid me down to any casual feast
Of wild wood-honey; or, with truant eyes
Unruly, peeped about for vagrant fruit.   530

■ *. . . though nowhere finds a way to voice his inner self.* ■ And as for what pertains to human life,
The deeper passions working round me here,
Whether of envy, jealousy, pride, shame,
Ambition, emulation, fear, or hope,
Or those of dissolute pleasure, were by me
Unshared; and only now and then observed,

SHOAL: crowd

3.10 Robert Dighton (1752–1814). *A Lesson Westward, or, a Morning Visit to Betsy Cole*, 1782. Yale Center for British Art, Paul Mellon Collection. Wordsworth, for the first time in his life, "now and then observed" Cambridge prostitutes—never indulging himself, remaining "Unshared" in the "dissolute pleasure" of the town.

So little was their hold upon my being,
As outward things that might administer
To knowledge or instruction. Hushed, meanwhile,
Was the under soul, locked up in such a calm   540
That not a leaf of the great nature stirred.

Yet was this deep vacation* not given up
To utter waste. Hitherto I had stood
In my own mind remote from human life,
At least from what we commonly so name,
Even as a shepherd on a promontory,
Who, lacking occupation, looks far forth
Into the endless sea, and rather makes

■ *Still, for "mortal business" such schooling is better preparation than many.*

■ Than finds what he beholds. And sure it is
That this first transit from the smooth delights,   550
And wild outlandish walks of simple youth,
To something that resembled an approach
Towards mortal business, to a privileged world

■ *Academic officers and teachers are observed and compared with Nature's school.*

Within a world, a midway residence
With all its intervenient imagery,
Did better suit my visionary mind,
Far better, than to have been bolted* forth,
Thrust out abruptly into Fortune's way,
Among the conflicts of substantial life;
By a more just gradation did lead on   560
To higher things, more naturally matured,

VACATION: though at school, time with no serious work
BOLTED: forced or flushed out

For permanent possession, better fruits
Whether of truth or virtue to ensue.

In playful zest of fancy did we note,
(How could we less?) the manners and the ways
Of those who in the livery were arrayed
Of good or evil fame; of those with whom
By frame of academic discipline
Perforce we were connected, men whose sway
And whose authority of Office served   570
To set our minds on edge, and did no more.
Nor wanted we rich pastime of this kind,
Found every where; but chiefly in the ring
Of the grave Elders, Men unscoured, grotesque

■ In character; tricked out like agèd trees
Which, through the lapse of their infirmity,
Give ready place to any random seed
That chuses to be reared upon their trunks.

Here, on my view, confronting as it were
Those Shepherd Swains whom I had lately left,   580
Did flash a different image of old age,
How different! yet both withal alike:
A Book of rudiments for the unpractised sight,
Objects embossed! and which with sedulous care
Nature holds up before the eye of Youth

In her great School; with further view, perhaps,
To enter early on her tender scheme
Of teaching comprehension with delight,
And mingling playful with pathetic thoughts.

The surfaces of artificial life   590
And manners finely spun, the delicate race
Of colours, lurking, gleaming up and down
Through that state arras,* woven with silk and gold,
This wily interchange of snaky hues,
Willingly and unwillingly revealed
I had not learned to watch, and at this time
Perhaps, had such been in my daily sight
I might have been indifferent thereto
As Hermits are to tales of distant things.

His entertainments are not refined nor from privilege, but simple, common . . .

■ Hence for those rarities elaborate   600
Having no relish yet, I was content
With the more homely produce, rudely piled
In this our coarser warehouse. At this day
I smile in many a mountain solitude
At passages and fragments that remain

. . . yet they, too, reflect the actual world, and virtues that have lost their way.

Of that inferior exhibition, played
By wooden images, a theatre
For Wake or Fair. And oftentimes do flit
Remembrances before me of old Men,
Old Humourists* who have been long in their graves,   610

And having almost in my mind put off
Their human names, have into Phantoms passed,
Of texture midway betwixt life and books.

I play the Loiterer: 'tis enough to note
That here, in dwarf proportions, were expressed
The limbs of the great world, its goings on
Collaterally pourtrayed, as in mock fight,
A Tournament of blows, some hardly* dealt,
Though short of mortal Combat; and whate'er
Might in this pageant be supposed to hit   620
A simple Rustic's notice, this way less,
More that way, was not wasted upon me.
—And yet this spectacle may well demand
A more substantial name, no mimic show,
Itself a living part of a live whole,
A creek of the vast sea. For all Degrees
And Shapes of spurious fame and short-lived praise
Here sate in state, and fed with daily alms
Retainers won away from solid good;

■ And here was Labour, his own Bond-slave, Hope   630
That never set the pains against the prize,
Idleness, halting with his weary clog,
And poor misguided Shame, and witless Fear,
And simple Pleasure foraging for Death,
Honour misplaced, and Dignity astray;

STATE ARRAS: tapestry reflecting elite power
HUMOURISTS: eccentrics, character actors

HARDLY: with force, strongly

3.11 Richard Banks Harraden (1778–1862). *Procession of Boats on the River Cam below Clare College, Cambridge,* early 19th century. Yale Center for British Art, Paul Mellon Collection. Wordsworth grew uneasy with the "goings on" at Cambridge—"poor misguided Shame, and witless Fear, / And simple Pleasure foraging for Death, / Honour misplaced." He came to feel he "was not . . . for that place."

Feuds, Factions, Flatteries, Enmity, and Guile;
Murmuring Submission, and bald* Government;
The Idol weak as the Idolater,
And Decency and Custom starving Truth;
And blind Authority, beating with his Staff   640
The Child that might have led him; Emptiness
Followed, as of good omen; and meek Worth
Left to itself unheard-of, and unknown.

Of these and other kindred notices
I cannot say what portion is in truth
The naked recollection of that time
And what may rather have been called to life
By after meditation. But delight,
That, in an easy temper lulled asleep,
Is still with innocence its own reward,   650
This surely was not wanting. Carelessly
I gazed, roving as through a Cabinet*
Or wide Museum (thronged with fishes, gems,
Birds, crocodiles, shells), where little can be seen

Well understood, or naturally endeared,
Yet still does every step bring something forth
That quickens, pleases, stings; and here and there
A casual rarity is singled out,
And has its brief perusal, then gives way
To others, all supplanted in their turn.   660

Meanwhile, amid this gaudy Congress, framed
Of things, by nature, most unneighbourly,
The head turns round, and cannot right itself;
And, though an aching and a barren sense
Of gay confusion still be uppermost,
With few wise longings and but little love,
Yet something to the memory sticks at last,
Whence profit may be drawn in times to come.

Thus, in submissive idleness, my Friend,
The labouring time of Autumn, Winter, Spring,   670
Nine months, rolled pleasingly away; the tenth
Returned me to my native hills again.

■ *From all the welter of his first nine months away, something yet of value still remains.*

BALD: crude, overbearing
CABINET: cabinet of wonders or curiosities (2.228)

4.1 Julius Caesar Ibbetson (1759–1817). *Lake Windermere*, between 1801 and 1805. Yale Center for British Art, Paul Mellon Collection. Returning from Cambridge in 1788 and climbing the "Heights of Kendal" soon to see, "as from a rampart's edge . . . the bed of Windermere," Wordsworth continues by ferry "towards home," to the Vale of Esthwaite and Ann Tyson's cottage at Colthouse.

Book Fourth

SUMMER VACATION

A pleasant sight it was when, having clomb*
The Heights of Kendal, and that dreary Moor
Was crossed,* at length, as from a rampart's edge,
I overlooked the bed of Windermere.
I bounded down the hill, shouting amain
A lusty summons to the farther shore
For the old Ferryman, and when he came
I did not step into the well-known Boat
Without a cordial welcome. Thence right forth
I took my way, now drawing towards home,   10
To that sweet Valley* where I had been reared;
'Twas but a short hour's walk ere, veering round,
I saw the snow-white Church upon its hill
Sit like a thronèd Lady, sending out
A gracious look all over its domain.
Glad greetings had I, and some tears perhaps
From my old Dame,* so motherly and good,
While she perused me with a Parent's pride.
The thoughts of gratitude shall fall like dew
Upon thy grave, good Creature! While my heart   20

Can beat I never will forget thy name.
Heaven's blessing be upon thee where thou liest,
After thy innocent and busy stir
In narrow cares, thy little daily growth
Of calm enjoyments, after eighty years,
And more than eighty, of untroubled life,*
Childless, yet by the strangers to thy blood
Honoured with little less than filial love.
Great joy was mine to see thee once again,
Thee and thy dwelling; and a throng of things   30
About its narrow precincts all beloved,
And many of them seeming yet my own.
Why should I speak of what a thousand hearts
Have felt, and every man alive can guess?
The rooms, the court, the garden were not left
Long unsaluted, and the spreading Pine
And broad stone Table underneath its boughs,
Our summer seat in many a festive hour;
And that unruly Child of mountain birth,
The froward Brook,* which soon as he was boxed   40
Within our Garden, found himself at once,
As if by trick insidious and unkind,
Stripped of his voice, and left to dimple down
Without an effort and without a will,
A channel pavèd by the hand of man.
I looked at him, and smiled, and smiled again,
And in the press of twenty thousand thoughts,

Back from Cambridge, W crosses Windermere on the ferry and returns to the Vale of Esthwaite and Ann Tyson's cottage. He cherishes her.

CLOMB: climbed
CROSSED: as one walks from Kendal to Windermere
SWEET VALLEY: Vale of Esthwaite
OLD DAME: Ann Tyson, since 1784 at Colthouse near Hawkshead

LIFE: She died in 1796, age 83.
FROWARD BROOK: Spring Wood Ghyll, ungoverned till channeled

4.2 Unknown artist. *Hawkshead Towards the Grammar School*, 1700. Hawkshead Grammar School. Wordsworth's "thronèd Lady," St. Michael and All Angels Church, is the first building one sees approaching the village. The exterior "snow-white" wash was removed in 1875. To the left is Hawkshead Grammar School, where Wordsworth studied until leaving for Cambridge.

'Ha,' quoth I, 'pretty Prisoner, are you there!'
And now, reviewing soberly that hour,
I marvel that a fancy did not flash   50
Upon me, and a strong desire, straitway,
At sight of such an emblem that showed forth
So aptly my late course of even days*
And all their smooth enthralment, to pen down
A satire on myself. My agèd Dame
Was with me at my side; She guided me;
I willing, nay—nay—wishing to be led.
—The face of every neighbour whom I met
Was as a volume to me. Some I hailed
Far off, upon the road, or at their work,   60
Unceremonious greetings, interchanged
With half the length of a long field between.
Among my School-fellows I scattered round
A salutation that was more constrained,
Though earnest, doubtless with a little pride,
But with more shame, for my habiliments,*
The transformation, and the gay attire.

Delighted did I take my place again
At our domestic Table; and, dear Friend!*
Relating simply, as my wish hath been,   70
A Poet's history, can I leave untold
The joy with which I laid me down at night

In my accustomed Bed, more welcome now,
Perhaps, than if it had been more desired,
Or been more often thought of with regret?
That Bed whence I had heard the roaring wind
And clamorous rain, that Bed where I, so oft,
Had lain awake, on breezy nights, to watch
The moon in splendour couched among the leaves
Of a tall Ash, that near our Cottage stood,   80
Had watched her with fixed eyes, while to and fro,
In the dark summit of the moving Tree
She rocked with every impulse of the wind.

Among the faces which it pleased me well
To see again, was one, by ancient right
Our Inmate,* a rough Terrier of the hills,
By birth and call of Nature pre-ordained
To hunt the badger, and unearth the fox,
Among the impervious crags; but having been
From youth our own adopted, he had passed   90
Into a gentler service. And when first
The boyish spirit flagged, and day by day
Along my veins I kindled with the stir,
The fermentation, and the vernal heat
Of Poesy, affecting private shades
Like a sick lover, then this Dog was used
To watch me, an attendant and a friend

Secure again in his old bed, he recalls witnessing what went on just outside, storms, or the moon borrowing motion from wind-swept branches of the nearby ash.

He meets again his faithful dog that kept him company on earlier walks . . .

EVEN DAYS: W's first year at Cambridge, 1787–88
HABILIMENTS: clothes
FRIEND: Coleridge

INMATE: housemate

Obsequious* to my steps, early and late,
Though often of such dilatory walk
Tired, and uneasy at the halts I made.   100
A hundred times when, in these wanderings
I have been busy with the toil of verse,
Great pains and little progress, and at once
Some fair enchanting Image in my mind
Rose up, full formed like Venus from the sea,
Have I sprung forth towards him, and let loose
My hand upon his back with stormy joy,
Caressing him again, and yet again.
And when in the public roads at eventide
I sauntered, like a river murmuring   110
And talking to itself, at such a season
It was his custom to jog on before;
But duly, whensoever he had met
A passenger* approaching, would he turn
To give me timely notice, and straitway,
Punctual to such admonishment, I hushed
My voice, composed my gait, and shaped myself
To give and take a greeting that might save
My name from piteous rumours, such as wait
On men suspected to be crazed in brain.   120

Those walks, well worthy to be prized and loved,
Regretted! that word too, was on my tongue,
But they were richly laden with all good,

OBSEQUIOUS: following, obedient
PASSENGER: pedestrian, passerby

And cannot be remembered but with thanks
And gratitude, and perfect joy of heart.
Those walks did now like a returning spring
Come back on me again. When first I made
Once more the circuit of our little Lake*
If ever happiness hath lodged with Man,
That day consummate happiness was mine,   130
Wide-spreading, steady, calm, contemplative.
The sun was set or setting when I left
Our cottage door, and evening soon brought on
A sober hour, not winning or serene,
For cold and raw the air was, and untuned:
But as a face we love is sweetest then
When sorrow damps it, or, whatever look
It chance to wear is sweetest if the heart
Have fulness in itself, even so with me
It fared that evening. Gently did my soul   140
Put off her veil, and, self-transmuted, stood
Naked as in the presence of her God.
As on I walked, a comfort seemed to touch
A heart that had not been disconsolate,
Strength came where weakness was not known to be,
At least not felt, and restoration came,
Like an intruder, knocking at the door
Of unacknowledged weariness. I took
The balance in my hand and weighed myself.
I saw but little, and thereat was pleased;   150

LAKE: Esthwaite Water

... when he composed
verse (as he so often did)
out loud. With the terrier
warning of someone
coming near, W hushes
his own voice.

This present walk,
though "cold and raw,"
invokes all previous ones
and conjures how deep
the human powers that
create can be.

Little did I remember, and even this
Still pleased me more; but I had hopes and peace
And swellings of the spirit, was wrapped* and soothed,
Conversed with promises; had glimmering views
How Life pervades the undecaying mind,
How the immortal Soul with God-like power
Informs, creates, and thaws the deepest sleep
That time can lay upon her; how on earth,
Man, if he do but live within the light
Of high endeavour, daily spreads abroad   160
His being with a strength that cannot fail.

■ Nor was there want of milder thoughts, of love
Of innocence, and holiday repose;
And more than pastoral quiet, in the heart
Of amplest projects; and a peaceful end
At last, or glorious, by endurance won.
Thus musing, in a wood I sate me down,
Alone, continuing there to muse: meanwhile,
The mountain heights were slowly overspread
With darkness, and before a rippling breeze   170
The long Lake lengthened out its hoary* line
And in the sheltered coppice* where I sate,
Around me, from among the hazel leaves,
Now here, now there, stirred by the straggling wind
Came intermittingly a breath-like sound,
A respiration short and quick, which oft,
Yea, might I say, again and yet again,

Mistaking for the panting of my Dog,
The off and on Companion of my walk,
I turned my head, to look if he were there.   180

■ A freshness also found I at this time
In human Life, the life, I mean, of those
Whose occupations really I loved.
The prospect often touched me with surprize,
Crowded and full, and changed, as seemed to me,
Even as a garden in the heat of Spring,
After an eight days' absence. For (to omit
The things which were the same, and yet appeared
So different) amid this solitude,
The little Vale where was my chief abode,   190
'Twas not indifferent to a youthful mind
To note, perhaps, some sheltered Seat in which
An old Man had been used to sun himself,
Now empty; pale-faced Babes whom I had left
In arms, known children of the neighbourhood,
Now rosy prattlers, tottering up and down;
And growing Girls, whose beauty, filched away
With all its pleasant promises, was gone
To deck some slighted Play-mate's homely cheek.

Yes, I had something of another eye,   200
And often, looking round, was moved to smiles,
Such as a delicate work of humour breeds.

WRAPPED: immersed, caught up in
HOARY: whitish, here as wind whips water
COPPICE: small wood

■ *Thus layered with the past, the walk prompts him to think of high efforts, to sit and muse, until in mutual mimicry the panting of his dog and what seem breathings of the wind catch attention.*

■ *The common round of work and all who practice it impress upon his thoughts a truthfulness to human life.*

4.3 Thomas Gainsborough (1727–1788). *Sunset: Carthorses Drinking at a Stream*, c. 1760. Tate Collection. Wordsworth attended to "those plain-living People, in a sense / Of love and knowledge."

I read, without design,* the opinions, thoughts
Of those plain-living People, in a sense
Of love and knowledge; with another eye
I saw the quiet Woodman in the Woods,
The Shepherd on the Hills. With new delight,
This chiefly, did I view my grey-haired Dame,*
Saw her go forth to Church, or other work
Of state, equipped in monumental* trim,   210
Short Velvet Cloak (her Bonnet of the like)
A Mantle such as Spanish Cavaliers
Wore in old time. Her smooth domestic life,
Affectionate without uneasiness
Her talk, her business* pleased me, and no less
Her clear, though shallow stream of piety,
That ran on Sabbath days a fresher course.
With thoughts unfelt till now, I saw her read
Her Bible on the Sunday afternoons;
And loved the Book, when she had dropped asleep,   220
And made of it a pillow for her head.

Nor less do I remember to have felt
Distinctly manifested at this time
A dawning, even as of another sense,
A human-heartedness about my love
For objects, hitherto the gladsome air
Of my own private being, and no more;
Which I had loved, even as a blessed Spirit,

DESIGN: specific or conscious motive
DAME: Ann Tyson
MONUMENTAL: impressive
BUSINESS: activities

Lives that no biography records he sees in a new way, most the life and faith of Ann Tyson, now 75.

4.4 Thomas Barker of Bath (1769–1847). *The Woodman and his Dog in a Storm*, c. 1787. Tate Collection. "I saw the quiet Woodman in the Woods, / The Shepherd on the Hills."

Or Angel, if he were to dwell on earth,
Might love in individual happiness.   230
But now there opened on me other thoughts,
Of change, congratulation, and regret,
A new-born feeling. It spread far and wide;
The trees, the mountains shared it, and the brooks;
The stars of Heaven, now seen in their old haunts,
White Sirius, glittering o'er the southern crags,
Orion with his belt, and those fair Seven,*
Acquaintances of every little Child,
And Jupiter, my own belovèd Star.
Whatever shadings of mortality   240
Had fallen upon these objects heretofore
Were different in kind; not tender: strong,
Deep, gloomy were they, and severe, the scatterings
Of Childhood; and moreover had given way,
In later Youth, to beauty, and to love
Enthusiastic, to delight and joy.

■ *Reflections on the surface and peering into water's depths . . .*

■ *. . . are akin to present time and past; a superficial glance can well distract from deeper views.*

■ As one who hangs down-bending from the side
Of a slow-moving Boat, upon the breast
Of a still water, solacing himself
With such discoveries as his eye can make,   250
Beneath him, in the bottom of the deeps,
Sees many beauteous sights, weeds, fishes, flowers,
Grots, pebbles, roots of trees, and fancies more;

Yet often is perplexed, and cannot part
The shadow from the substance, rocks and sky,
Mountains and clouds, from that which is indeed
The region, and the things which there abide
In their true dwelling; now is crossed by gleam
Of his own image, by a sunbeam now
And motions that are sent he knows not whence,   260
Impediments that make his task more sweet.
—Such pleasant office have we long pursued
Incumbent* o'er the surface of past time
With like success; nor have we often looked
On more alluring shows (to me, at least)
More soft or less ambiguously descried*
Than those which now we have been passing by,
■ And where we still are lingering. Yet, in spite
Of all these new employments of the mind,
There was an inner falling-off. I loved,   270
Loved deeply, all that I had loved before,
More deeply even than ever; but a swarm
Of heady thoughts, jostling each other, gauds,*
And feast, and dance, and public revelry,
And sports, and games (less pleasing in themselves
Than as they were a badge, glossy and fresh,
Of manliness and freedom): these did now
Seduce me from the firm habitual quest
Of feeding* pleasures, from that eager zeal,

FAIR SEVEN: the Pleiades, daughters of Atlas changed into stars

INCUMBENT: resting
DESCRIED: noticed, observed
GAUDS: showy acts or things
FEEDING: meaningful, formative

Those yearnings which had every day been mine,   280
A wild, unworldly-minded Youth, given up
To Nature and to Books, or, at the most,
From time to time by inclination shipped,*
One among many, in societies
That were, or seemed, as simple as myself.
But now was come a change; it would demand
Some skill, and longer time than may be spared,
To paint even to myself these vanities,
And how they wrought. But sure it is that now
Contagious air did oft environ me,   290
Unknown among these haunts in former days.

■ *W attends a party of seeming great excitement . . .*

The very garments that I wore appeared
To prey upon my strength, and stopped the course
And quiet stream of self-forgetfulness.
Something there was about me that perplexed
The authentic sight of reason, pressed too closely
On that religious dignity of mind,
That is the very faculty of truth;
Which wanting, either from the very first,
A function never lighted up, or else   300
Extinguished, Man, a creature great and good,
Seems but a pageant play-thing with wild claws,
And this great frame of breathing elements
A senseless Idol.

                    That vague heartless* chace
Of trivial pleasures was a poor exchange
For Books and Nature at that early age.
'Tis true some casual knowledge might be gained
Of character or life; but at that time
Of manners put to school I took small note
And all my deeper passions lay elsewhere.   310
Far better had it been to exalt the mind
By solitary study, to uphold
Intense desire by thought and quietness.
And yet in chastisement of these regrets
The memory of one particular hour
■ Doth here rise up against me. In a throng,
A festal company of Maids and Youths,
Old Men and Matrons staid, promiscuous rout,*
A medley of all tempers, I had passed
The night in dancing, gaiety and mirth,   320
With din of instruments and shuffling feet,
And glancing forms and tapers glittering,
And unaimed prattle flying up and down,
Spirits upon the stretch, and here and there
Slight shocks of young love-liking interspersed,
That mounted up like joy into the head
And tingled through the veins. Ere we retired
The Cock had crowed, the sky was bright with day.
Two miles I had to walk along the fields

SHIPPED: included

HEARTLESS: empty, discouraging

PROMISCUOUS ROUT: diverse, boisterous company

4.5 English School. *The Old Ferry Hotel, Windermere*, 19th century. Hill Top, Sawrey, Cumbria, UK / National Trust Photographic Library / Bridgeman Images. Windermere's summer regatta consisted of yacht and rowing races and numerous social gatherings, including parties at the delightful Ferry Inn (demolished in 1879). William came to feel that, after one summer night of revelry, when in the early morning he was returning, soon in a different mood, to Ann Tyson's cottage, "vows / Were then made for me" to become a "dedicated Spirit"—perhaps the primary turning point in his young life.

Before I reached my home. Magnificent   330
The Morning was, in memorable pomp,

■ More glorious than I ever had beheld.
The Sea was laughing at a distance; all
The solid Mountains were as bright as clouds,
Grain-tinctured,* drenched in empyrean* light;
And in the meadows and the lower grounds
Was all the sweetness of a common dawn,
Dews, vapours, and the melody of birds,
And Labourers going forth into the fields.
—Ah! need I say, dear Friend, that to the brim   340
My heart was full; I made no vows, but vows
Were then made for me, bond unknown to me
Was given, that I should be, else sinning greatly,
A dedicated Spirit. On I walked
In blessedness which even yet remains.

Strange rendezvous my mind was at that time,
A party-coloured* show of grave and gay,
Solid and light, short-sighted and profound,
Of inconsiderate habits and sedate,
Consorting in one mansion unreproved.   350
I knew the worth of that which I possessed,
Though slighted and misused. Besides, in truth,
That Summer, swarming as it did with thoughts
Transient and loose, yet wanted not a store
Of primitive* hours, when by these hindrances

GRAIN-TINCTURED: dyed with color
EMPYREAN: highest heaven
PARTY-COLOURED: varied, alternating in shade or hue
PRIMITIVE: original, archetypal, touched by early experience

Unthwarted, I experienced in myself
Conformity as just as that of old
To the end and written spirit of God's works,
Whether held forth in Nature or in Man.

From many wanderings that have left behind   360
Remembrances not lifeless, I will here
Single out one, then pass to other themes.

■ A favourite pleasure hath it been with me
From time of earliest youth, to walk alone
Along the public Way, when, for the night
Deserted, in its silence it assumes
A character of deeper quietness
Than pathless solitudes. At such an hour
Once, ere those summer months were passed away,
I slowly mounted up a steep ascent   370
Where the road's watery surface to the ridge
Of that sharp rising glittered in the moon,
And seemed before my eyes another stream
Creeping with silent lapse* to join the brook
That murmured in the Valley. On I went
Tranquil, receiving in my own despite
Amusement, as I slowly passed along,
From such near objects as from time to time
Perforce intruded on the listless sense
Quiescent, and disposed to sympathy   380

LAPSE: flow, current

■ *. . . but it is the glorious natural morning afterward that moves his spirit and leaves him changed.*

■ *.At night, on one of his habitual walks that gives him rest and sweet tranquility . . .*

With an exhausted mind, worn out by toil,
And all unworthy of the deeper joy
Which waits on distant prospect, cliff or sea,
The dark blue vault, and universe of stars.
Thus did I steal along that silent road,
My body from the stillness drinking in
A restoration like the calm of sleep,
But sweeter far. Above, before, behind,
Around me, all was peace and solitude,
I looked not round, nor did the solitude   390
Speak to my eye; but it was heard and felt.
O happy state! what beauteous pictures now
Rose in harmonious imagery—they rose
As from some distant region of my soul
And came along like dreams; yet such as left
Obscurely mingled with their passing forms
A consciousness of animal delight,
A self-possession felt in every pause
And every gentle movement of my frame.

While thus I wandered, step by step led on,   400
It chanced a sudden turning of the road
Presented to my view an uncouth shape
So near, that slipping back into the shade
Of a thick hawthorn, I could mark him well,
Myself unseen. He was of stature tall,
A foot above Man's common measure tall,

4.6 Pupil of Francis Towne (1740–1816). *The Road to the Lake*, undated. Yale Center for British Art, Paul Mellon Collection. Wordsworth often walked "Along the public Way," relishing as a "favourite pleasure" its solitude at night.

Stiff in his form and upright, lank and lean,
A man more meagre, as it seemed to me,
Was never seen abroad by night or day.

■ *. . . he espies some form that shakes all sense and habit, a ghostly seeming stranger.*

■ His arms were long, and bare his hands, his mouth   410
Showed ghastly* in the moonlight; from behind
A mile-stone propped him, and his figure seemed
Half-sitting, and half-standing. I could mark
That he was clad in military garb,
Though faded, yet entire. He was alone,
Had no attendant, neither Dog, nor Staff,
Nor knapsack; in his very dress appeared
A desolation, a simplicity
That seemed akin to solitude. Long time
Did I peruse him with a mingled sense   420
Of fear and sorrow. From his lips, meanwhile,
There issued murmuring sounds, as if of pain
Or of uneasy thought, yet still his form
Kept the same steadiness, and at his feet
His shadow lay and moved not. In a Glen
Hard by, a Village stood, whose roofs and doors
Were visible among the scattered trees,
Scarce distant from the spot an arrow's flight;
I wished to see him move, but he remained
Fixed to his place, and still from time to time   430
Sent forth a murmuring voice of dead complaint,
Groans scarcely audible. Without self-blame
I had not thus prolonged my watch, and now

GHASTLY: ghostly

4.7 Hercules Brabazon Brabazon (1821–1906), After Sir Joshua Reynolds, 1723–1792. *Study after Joshua Reynolds's Portrait of Cornet Nehemiah Winter, 11th Dragoons,* undated. Yale Center for British Art, Bequest of Joseph F. McCrindle. Wordsworth encountered "an uncouth shape . . . of stature tall . . . his mouth / Showed ghastly in the moonlight."

■ W reveals himself to the
discharged soldier, hears
his brief history, and
offers a local home to try
for hospitality.

■ Subduing my heart's specious cowardise
I left the shady nook where I had stood
And hailed him. Slowly from his resting-place
He rose, and with a lean and wasted arm
In measured gesture lifted to his head
Returned my salutation, then resumed
His station as before, and when erelong   440
I asked his history, he in reply
Was neither slow nor eager, but unmoved,
And with a quiet uncomplaining voice,
A stately air of mild indifference,
He told in simple words a Soldier's tale,

■ The veteran, in con-
trolled and simple words,
answers the queries of
his young companion
guide. A cottager will
take the man that night.

That in the Tropic Islands* he had served,
Whence he had landed, scarcely ten days past,
That on his landing he had been dismissed,
And now was travelling to his native home.
At this, I turned and looked towards the Village   450
But all were gone to rest, the fires all out,
And every silent window to the Moon
Shone with a yellow glitter. 'No one there,'
Said I, 'is waking; we must measure back
The way which we have come: behind yon wood
A Labourer dwells, and, take it on my word
He will not murmur should we break his rest,
And with a ready heart will give you food
And lodging for the night.' At this he stooped
And from the ground took up an oaken Staff   460

TROPIC ISLANDS: West Indies, within the Tropic of Cancer

By me yet unobserved, a Traveller's Staff
Which I suppose from his slack hand had dropped,
And lain till now neglected in the grass.

Towards the Cottage without more delay
We shaped our course; as it appeared to me
He travelled without pain, and I beheld
With ill-suppressed astonishment his tall
And ghastly figure moving at my side;
Nor while we journeyed thus could I forbear
To question him of what he had endured   470
From hardship, battle, or the pestilence.
■ He all the while was in demeanour calm,
Concise in answer: solemn and sublime
He might have seemed, but that in all he said
There was a strange half-absence, and a tone
Of weakness and indifference, as of one
Remembering the importance of his theme
But feeling it no longer. We advanced
Slowly, and, ere we to the wood were come,
Discourse had ceased. Together on we passed,   480
In silence, through the shades, gloomy and dark;
Then turning up along an open field
We gained the Cottage. At the door I knocked,
Calling aloud, 'my Friend, here is a Man
By sickness overcome; beneath your roof
This night let him find rest, and give him food,

*W finds his plea, that
the stranger henceforth
ask for help, answered
with dignity and deep
forbearance by a soul
whose ghost-like form
has reasons to seem so.*

If food he need, for he is faint and tired.'

■ Assured that now my Comrade would repose
In comfort, I entreated that henceforth
He would not linger in the public ways   490
But ask for timely furtherance and help
Such as his state required.—At this reproof,
With the same ghastly mildness in his look,
He said, 'my trust is in the God of Heaven
And in the eye of him that passes me.'

The Cottage door was speedily unlocked,
And now the Soldier touched his hat again
With his lean hand, and in a voice that seemed
To speak with a reviving interest,
Till then unfelt, he thanked me; I returned   500
The blessing of the poor unhappy Man,
And so we parted. Back I cast a look,
And lingered near the door a little space,
Then sought with quiet heart my distant home.

Book Fifth
BOOKS

■ *From Nature as a guide he turns now to human works . . .*

■ *. . . though grieves to feel that in the arc of time all trace of their recorded worth must disappear, poetry and science, fragile in their preservation.*

Even in the steadiest mood of reason, when
All sorrow for thy transitory pains
Goes out, it grieves me for thy state, O Man,
Thou paramount Creature! and thy race, while Ye
Shall sojourn on this planet; not for woes
Which thou endur'st; that weight, albeit huge,
I charm away; but for those palms* atchieved
Through length of time, by study and hard thought,
The honours of thy high endowments, there
■ My sadness finds its fuel. Hitherto,   10
In progress through this Verse, my mind hath looked
Upon the speaking face of earth and heaven
As her prime Teacher, intercourse with Man
Established by the sovereign Intellect,
Who through that bodily Image hath diffused
A soul divine which we* participate,
A deathless spirit. Thou also, Man, hast wrought,
For commerce of thy nature with itself,
Things worthy of unconquerable life;

And yet we feel, we cannot chuse but feel   20
That these must perish. Tremblings of the heart
It gives, to think that the immortal being
No more shall need such garments;* and yet Man,
As long as he shall be the Child of Earth,
Might almost 'weep to have'* what he may lose,
Nor be himself extinguished; but survive
Abject, depressed, forlorn, disconsolate.
A thought is with me sometimes, and I say,
Should earth by inward throes be wrenched throughout
Or fire be sent from far to wither all   30
Her pleasant habitations, and dry up
Old Ocean in his bed left singed and bare,
Yet would the living Presence still subsist
Victorious; and composure would ensue,
And kindlings like the morning presage sure,
Though slow, perhaps, of a returning day.
But all the meditations of mankind,
Yea, all the adamantine holds* of truth,
By reason built, or passion, which itself
Is highest reason in a soul sublime;   40
■ The consecrated works of Bard and Sage,
Sensuous* or intellectual, wrought by Men,
Twin labourers and heirs of the same hopes,
Where would they be? Oh! why hath not the mind
Some element to stamp her image on

PALMS: gains, awards, marks of progress
WHICH WE: in which we

GARMENTS: here, mortal achievements
'WEEP TO HAVE': from Shakespeare, sonnet 64
HOLDS: repositories, fortresses
SENSUOUS: of the senses (no carnal or sensual meaning)

5.1 Samuel Colman (1780–1845). *The Rock of Salvation*, 1837. Yale Center for British Art, Paul Mellon Collection. "A soul divine which we participate, / A deathless spirit."
The poet speaks of "Nature's self, which is the breath of God" (5.222).

A friend reading
Don Quixote by the
sea dreams of a
Bedouin, who holds a
Book of science and
a Shell, which is a Book
of verse and hope.

In nature somewhat nearer to her own?
Why, gifted with such powers to send abroad
Her spirit, must it lodge in shrines so frail?

One day, when in the hearing of a Friend*
I had given utterance to thoughts like these,   50
He answered with a smile, that in plain truth
'Twas going far to seek disquietude;
But on the front of his reproof, confessed
That he, at sundry seasons, had himself
Yielded to kindred hauntings.—And forthwith
Added, that once upon a summer's noon,
While he was sitting in a rocky cave
By the Sea-side, perusing, as it chanced,
The famous History of the Errant Knight*
Recorded by Cervantes, these same thoughts   60
Came to him; and to height unusual rose
While listlessly he sate, and having closed
The Book, had turned his eyes towards the Sea.
On Poetry and geometric Truth,*
The knowledge that endures, upon these two,
And their high privilege of lasting life,
Exempt from all internal injury,
He mused; upon these chiefly: and at length,
His senses yielding to the sultry air,
Sleep seized him, and he passed into a dream.   70

Yet, the sounding Shell
tells of a deluge advanc-
ing soon to drown all
human life.

He saw before him an Arabian Waste,
A Desart; and he fancied that himself
Was sitting there in the wide wilderness,
Alone upon the sands. Distress of mind
Was growing in him when, behold! at once
To his great joy a Man was at his side
Upon a Dromedary mounted high.
He seemed an Arab of the Bedouin Tribes,
A Lance he bore, and underneath one arm
A Stone, and in the opposite hand a Shell   80
Of a surpassing brightness. Much rejoiced
The dreaming Man that he should have a Guide
To lead him through the Desart; and he thought,
While questioning himself what this strange freight
Which the New-comer carried through the Waste
Could mean, the Arab told him that the Stone,
To give it in the language of the Dream,
Was Euclid's Elements;* 'and this,' said he,
'This other,' pointing to the Shell, 'this Book
Is something of more worth.' And at the word,   90
The Stranger, said my Friend continuing,
Stretched forth the Shell towards me, with command
That I should hold it to my ear: I did so,
And heard that instant in an unknown Tongue,
Which yet I understood, articulate sounds,
A loud prophetic blast of harmony,

FRIEND: possibly Coleridge
HISTORY . . . KNIGHT: *Don Quixote*, which W read when young
GEOMETRIC TRUTH: suggesting, too, all objective knowledge

ELEMENTS: geometry text still used in W's day

5.2 John Frederick Lewis (1804–1876). *A Bedouin Encampment; or, Bedouin Arabs*, 1841. Yale Center for British Art, Paul Mellon Collection. "He seemed an Arab of the Bedouin Tribes."

An Ode, in passion uttered, which foretold
Destruction to the Children of the Earth,
By Deluge now at hand. No sooner ceased
The Song, but with calm look the Arab said   100
That all was true; that it was even so

■ As had been spoken; and that he himself
Was going then to bury those two Books:
The one that held acquaintance with the stars,
And wedded man to man by purest bond
Of nature, undisturbed by space or time;
Th'other that was a God, yea many Gods,
Had voices more than all the winds, and was
A joy, a consolation, and a hope.
My friend continued, 'strange as it may seem,   110
I wondered not, although I plainly saw
The one to be a Stone, th'other a Shell,
Nor doubted once but that they both were Books,
Having a perfect faith in all that passed.
A wish was now engendered in my fear
To cleave unto* this Man, and I begged leave
To share his errand with him. On he passed
Not heeding me; I followed, and took note
That he looked often backward with wild look,
Grasping his twofold treasure to his side.   120

■ —Upon a Dromedary, Lance in rest
He rode, I keeping pace with him, and now
I fancied that he was the very Knight

*Thus the Arab strives
to bury the two great
Books he holds, to save
them from destruction.*

*The Arab now seems
Quixote, too, and rides
to flee the rising flood,
leaving the dreamer
terrified, awake again
with Quixote by his
side, the sea in front.*

*W identifies with the
Arab-Quixote, obsession
growing from the power
of poets to enchant.*

CLEAVE UNTO: stay with, follow closely

Whose Tale Cervantes tells, yet not the Knight,
But was an Arab of the Desart too;
Of these was neither, and was both at once.
His countenance, meanwhile, grew more disturbed,
And looking backwards when he looked, I saw
A glittering light, and asked him whence it came.
"It is," said he, "the waters of the deep   130
Gathering upon us"; quickening then his pace
He left me; I called after him aloud,
He heeded not; but with his twofold charge
Beneath his arm, before me full in view
I saw him riding o'er the Desart Sands,
With the fleet* waters of the drowning world
In chace of him, whereat I waked in terror
And saw the Sea before me; and the Book
In which I had been reading at my side.'

Full often taking from the world of sleep   140
This Arab Phantom which my Friend beheld,
This Semi-Quixote, I to him have given
A substance, fancied him a living Man,
A gentle Dweller in the Desart, crazed
By love and feeling, and internal thought
Protracted among endless solitudes;
Have shaped him, in the oppression of his brain,
Wandering upon this quest, and thus equipped.

■ And I have scarcely pitied him, have felt

FLEET: The word first meant water fast flowing, swift.

5.3 John Martin (1789–1854). *The Deluge*, 1834. Yale Center for British Art, Paul Mellon Collection. The "fleet waters of the drowning world."

A reverence for a Being thus employed;   150
And thought that in the blind and awful lair
Of such a madness, reason did lie couched.
Enow* there are on earth to take in charge
Their Wives, their Children, and their virgin Loves,
Or whatsoever else the heart holds dear;
Enow to think of these; yea, will I say,
In sober contemplation of the approach
Of such great overthrow made manifest
By certain evidence, that I, methinks,
Could share that Maniac's anxiousness, could go   160
Upon like errand. Oftentimes, at least,
Me hath such deep entrancement half-possessed,
When I have held a Volume in my hand,
Poor earthly casket of immortal Verse!
Shakespeare, or Milton, Labourers divine!

Mighty indeed, supreme must be the power
Of living Nature which could thus so long
Detain me from the best of other thoughts.
Even in the lisping time of Infancy,
And later down, in prattling Childhood, even   170
While I was travelling back among those days,
How could I ever play an ingrate's part?
Once more should I have made those bowers resound,
And intermingled strains of thankfulness
With their own thoughtless melodies; at least,

■ *Heart and mind learn
from the written word,
from verse of every
kind, whose authors, a
force second to Nature's
self alone, give delight
to high and low alike.*

Enow: enough

It might have well beseemed me to repeat
Some simply-fashioned tale; to tell again,
In slender* accents of sweet Verse, some tale
That did bewitch me then, and soothes me now.
O Friend! O Poet! Brother of my soul,*   180
Think not that I could ever pass along
Untouched by these remembrances; no, no,
But I was hurried forward by a stream,
And could not stop. Yet wherefore should I speak,
Why call upon a few weak words to say
What is already written in the hearts
Of all that breathe! what in the path of all
Drops daily from the tongue of every Child,
Wherever Man is found. The trickling tear
Upon the cheek of listening Infancy   190
Tells it, and the insuperable look
That drinks as if it never could be full.

That portion of my Story I shall leave
There registered; whatever else there be
Of power or pleasure sown or fostered thus,
Peculiar to myself, let that remain
Where it lies hidden in its endless home
■ Among the depths of time. And yet it seems
That here, in memory of all Books which lay
Their sure foundations in the heart of Man;   200
Whether by native prose or numerous verse:

SLENDER: here, soft
FRIEND . . . SOUL: Coleridge

W asks what he and Coleridge would have become if words for them had been narrowed at the start, their paths set by rote rather than let to wander in lands of invention.

That in the name of all inspired Souls,
From Homer, the great Thunderer; from the voice
Which roars along the bed of Jewish Song;
And that more varied and elaborate,
Those trumpet-tones of harmony that shake
Our Shores in England; from those loftiest notes
Down to the low and wren-like warblings, made
For Cottagers and Spinners at the wheel,
And weary Travellers when they rest themselves   210
By the highways and hedges; ballad tunes,
Food for the hungry ears of little Ones,
And of old Men who have survived their joy.
It seemeth, in behalf of these, the works
And of the Men who framed them, whether known,
Or sleeping nameless in their scattered graves,
That I should here assert their rights, attest
Their honours; and should, once for all, pronounce
Their benediction; speak of them as Powers
For ever to be hallowed; only less,   220
For what we may become, and what we need,
Than Nature's self, which is the breath of God.

Rarely, and with reluctance, would I stoop
To transitory themes; yet I rejoice
And by these thoughts admonished, must speak out
Thanksgivings from my heart, that I was reared
Safe from an evil* which these days have laid

Upon the Children of the Land, a pest
That might have dried me up, body and soul.
This Verse is dedicate to Nature's self,   230
And things that teach as Nature teaches, then
Oh! where had been the Man, the Poet where?
Where had we been, we two, belovèd Friend,
If we, in lieu of wandering as we did,
Through heights and hollows, and bye-spots of tales
Rich with indigenous produce, open ground
Of Fancy, happy pastures ranged at will!
Had been attended, followed, watched, and noosed,
Each in his several* melancholy walk
Stringed like a poor man's Heifer, at its feed   240
Led through the lanes in forlorn servitude;
Or rather, like a stallèd Ox shut out
From touch of growing grass, that may not taste
A flower till it have yielded up its sweets,
A prelibation to the mower's scythe.

Behold the Parent Hen amid her Brood,
Though fledged* and feathered, and well pleased to part
And straggle from her presence, still a Brood,
And she herself from the maternal bond
Still undischarged; yet doth she little more   250
Than move with them in tenderness and love,
A centre of the circle which they make;
And now and then, alike from need of theirs

AN EVIL: here, certain new kinds of education

SEVERAL: respective, own
FLEDGED: cared for until able to fly

And call of her own natural appetites,

She scratches, ransacks up the earth for food

Which they partake at pleasure. Early died

My honoured Mother,* she who was the heart

And hinge of all our learnings and our loves:

She left us destitute, and as we might

Trooping together. Little suits it me

To break upon the sabbath of her rest

With any thought that looks at others' blame,

Nor would I praise her but in perfect love.

■ *Knowing others helped raise him, he yet feels deep debts for his mother's care and love.*

■ Hence am I checked. But I will boldly say,

In gratitude, and for the sake of truth,

Unheard by her, that she, not falsely taught,

Fetching her goodness rather from times past

Than shaping novelties from those to come,

Had no presumption, no such jealousy;

Nor did by habit of her thoughts mistrust

Our Nature; but had virtual* faith that He

Who fills the Mother's breasts with innocent milk,

Doth also for our nobler part provide,

Under his great correction and controul,

■ *The prodigy of knowledge and propriety appears with no compeer. Yet, there seems no love of Nature. It is . . .*

As innocent instincts, and as innocent food.

This was her creed, and therefore she was pure

From feverish dread of error or mishap

And evil, overweeningly so called;

Was not puffed up by false unnatural hopes;

Nor selfish with unnecessary cares;

260

270

280

Nor with impatience from the season asked

More than its timely produce, rather loved

The hours for what they are than from regards

Glanced on their promises in restless pride.

Such was She; not from faculties more strong

Than others have, but from the times, perhaps,

And spot in which she lived, and through a grace

Of modest meekness, simple-mindedness,*

A heart that found benignity and hope,

Being itself benign.

My drift hath scarcely,   290

I fear, been obvious; for I have recoiled

From showing as it is the monster birth

Engendered by these too industrious times.

Let few words paint it: 'tis a Child, no Child,

But a dwarf Man in knowledge, virtue, skill;

In what he is not, and in what he is,

The noontide shadow of a Man complete,

A worshipper of worldly seemliness,

Not quarrelsome, for that were far beneath

■ His dignity; with gifts he bubbles o'er   300

As generous as a fountain; selfishness

May not come near him, gluttony or pride;

The wandering Beggars propagate his name,

Dumb creatures find him tender as a Nun.

Yet deem him not for this a naked dish

MOTHER: She died a month before W turned eight.

VIRTUAL: strong, certain

SIMPLE-MINDEDNESS: sincere, straightforward (no sense of feeble)

Of goodness merely, he is garnished out.*

Arch are his notices, and nice* his sense

Of the ridiculous; deceit and guile,

Meanness and falsehood he detects, can treat

With apt and graceful laughter; nor is blind   310

To the broad follies of the licensed world;

Though shrewd, yet innocent himself withal

And can read* lectures upon innocence.

He is fenced round, nay armed, for aught we know

In panoply* complete; and fear itself,

Natural or supernatural alike,

Unless it leap upon him in a dream,

Touches him not. Briefly, the moral part

Is perfect,* and in learning and in books

He is a prodigy. His discourse moves slow,   320

Massy and ponderous as a prison door,

Tremendously embossed with terms of art;

Rank growth of propositions overruns

The Stripling's brain; the path in which he treads

Is choked with grammars; cushion of Divine

Was never such a type of thought profound

As is the pillow where he rests his head.

The Ensigns of the Empire which he holds,

The globe and sceptre of his royalties

Are telescopes, and crucibles, and maps.   330

Ships he can guide across the pathless Sea,

And tell you all their cunning: he can read

■ *. . . an empty life rather than one of childish tales, which yet prepare the child for later leaps and strife.*

The inside of the earth, and spell* the stars.

He knows the policies of foreign Lands,

Can string you names of districts, cities, towns,

The whole world over, tight as beads of dew

Upon a gossamer thread; he sifts, he weighs,

Takes nothing upon trust. His Teachers stare,

The Country People pray for God's good grace,

And tremble at his deep experiments.*   340

All things are put to question; he must live

Knowing that he grows wiser every day

Or else not live at all; and seeing, too,

Each little drop of wisdom as it falls

Into the dimpling cistern of his heart.

Meanwhile, old Grandame* Earth is grieved to find

The playthings which her love designed for him

Unthought of: in their woodland beds the flowers

Weep, and the river sides are all forlorn.

■ Now this is hollow, 'tis a life of lies*   350

From the beginning, and in lies must end.

Forth bring him to the air of Common sense,

And fresh and showy as it is, the Corps

Slips from us into powder. Vanity,

That is his soul, there lives he, and there moves;

It is the soul of every thing he seeks;

That gone, nothing is left which he can love.

Nay, if a thought of purer birth should rise

GARNISHED OUT: promoted or self-promoted

NICE: fine, consciously practiced

READ: deliver, recite

PANOPLY: arms and armor, defense mechanisms

PERFECT: worked up (ironic)

SPELL: interpret, forecast by the stars

DEEP EXPERIMENTS: forbidden or arcane knowledge

GRANDAME: grandmother

LIES: pretenses, things inadequate for human needs

To carry him towards a better clime,
Some busy helper still is on the watch   360
To drive him back and pound him like a Stray
Within the pinfold of his own conceit;*
Which is his home, his natural dwelling-place.
Oh! give us once again the Wishing-cap
Of Fortunatus, and the invisible Coat
Of Jack the Giant-killer, Robin Hood,
And Sabra in the forest with Saint George!*
The Child whose love is here, at least doth reap
One precious gain, that he forgets himself.

■ *Sharp utility would bind the young down and pose only problems already known. Creative thought will thrive with less restraint.*

■ These mighty workmen of our later age   370
Who with a broad highway have overbridged
The froward* chaos of futurity,
Tamed to their bidding; they who have the skill
To manage books and things, and make them work
Gently on infant minds, as does the sun
Upon a flower; the Tutors of our Youth,
The Guides, the Wardens of our faculties,
And Stewards of our labour, watchful men

■ *There was a boy . . .*

And skillful in the usury of time,
Sages, who in their prescience would controul   380
All accidents, and to the very road

■ *. . . who seemed as one with the owls he mimicked, and with all waters, rocks, and woods—here, now, always . . .*

Which they have fashioned would confine us down
Like engines,* when will they be taught
That in the unreasoning progress of the world

To . . . CONCEIT: The image is of a stray animal impounded.
WISHING-CAP . . . GEORGE: fairytale, folktale, and legendary figures, many with magic powers
FROWARD: ungovernable, energetic
ENGINES: mechanical beings, mechanisms

A wiser Spirit is at work for us,
A better eye than theirs, more prodigal
Of blessings, and more studious of our good
Even in what seem our most unfruitful hours.

■ There was a Boy, ye knew him well, ye Cliffs
And Islands of Winander!* many a time   390
At Evening, when the Stars had just begun
To move along the edges of the hills,
Rising or setting, would he stand alone,
Beneath the trees, or by the glimmering Lake,
And there, with fingers interwoven, both hands
Pressed closely, palm to palm, and to his mouth
Uplifted, he, as through an instrument,
Blew mimic hootings to the silent Owls
That they might answer him.—And they would shout
Across the watery Vale, and shout again,   400
Responsive to his call, with quivering peals,
And long halloos, and screams, and echoes loud
Redoubled and redoubled, concourse wild
■ Of mirth and jocund din! And when it chanced
That pauses of deep silence mocked his skill,
Then sometimes, in that silence, while he hung
Listening, a gentle shock of mild surprize
Has carried far into his heart the voice
Of mountain torrents, or the visible scene
Would enter unawares into his mind   410

WINANDER: older form of Windermere (Winandermere)

5.4 Henry Oliver Walker (1843–1929). *The Boy of Winander*, 1898–1907. Thomas Jefferson Building, Library of Congress, Prints & Photographs Division, photograph by Carol M. Highsmith. "There was a Boy, ye knew him well, ye Cliffs / And Islands of Winander!" The original version of the passage was written in the first person.

5.5 Francis Towne (1740–1816). *Windermere at Sunset,* 1786. Yale Center for British Art, Paul Mellon Collection. "At Evening, when the Stars had just begun / To move along the edges of the hills, / Rising or setting, would he stand alone."

With all its solemn imagery, its rocks,
Its woods, and that uncertain Heaven received
Into the bosom of the steady Lake.

This Boy* was taken from his Mates, and died
In childhood, ere he was full ten years old.
—Fair are the woods, and beauteous is the Spot,

THIS BOY: W's schoolmate John Tyson, who died August 25, 1782.

■ *. . . but he rests silently in the churchyard.*

■ The Vale* where he was born: the Church-yard hangs
   Upon a Slope above the Village School
   And there along that bank, when I have passed
   At evening, I believe that oftentimes   420
   A full half-hour together I have stood
   Mute—looking at the grave in which he lies.

   Even now, methinks, I have before my sight
   That self-same Village Church, I see her sit,
   The thronèd Lady spoken of erewhile,
   On her green hill; forgetful of this Boy
   Who slumbers at her feet; forgetful, too,
   Of all her silent neighbourhood of graves,
   And listening only to the gladsome sounds
   That, from the rural School ascending, play   430

■ *A just degree of freedom blessed the youths W knew, companions loving books and nature both.*

■ Beneath her and about her. May she long
   Behold a race of Young ones like to those
   With whom I herded! (easily, indeed,
   We might have fed upon a fatter soil
   Of Arts and Letters, but be that forgiven)
   A race of real Children, not too wise,
   Too learned, or too good: but wanton,* fresh,
   And bandied up and down by love and hate,
   Fierce, moody, patient, venturous, modest, shy;
   Mad at their sports like withered leaves in winds;   440
   Though doing wrong, and suffering, and full oft
   Bending beneath our life's mysterious weight

VALE: Vale of Esthwaite

WANTON: lively, willful, hard to discipline

5.6 Edmund Bristow (1787–1876). *The Rat Trap*, early to mid-19th century. Yale Center for British Art, Paul Mellon Collection. "A race of real Children, not too wise, / Too learned, or too good: but wanton, fresh."

Of pain and fear; yet still in happiness
Not yielding to the happiest upon earth.

Simplicity in habit, truth in speech,
Be these the daily strengtheners of their minds!
May books and nature be their early joy!
And knowledge, rightly honoured with that name,
Knowledge not purchased with the loss of power!

Well do I call to mind the very week*   450
When I was first entrusted to the care
Of that sweet Valley,* when its paths, its shores,
And brooks, were like a dream of novelty
To my half-infant thoughts; that very week
While I was roving up and down alone,
Seeking I knew not what, I chanced to cross
One of those open fields, which, shaped like ears,
Make green peninsulas on Esthwaite's Lake.
Twilight was coming on; yet through the gloom,
I saw distinctly on the opposite Shore   460
A heap of garments, left, as I supposed,
By one who there was bathing: long I watched,
But no one owned* them: meanwhile the calm Lake
Grew dark, with all the shadows on its breast,
And now and then a fish upleaping snapped
The breathless stillness. The succeeding day,
(Those unclaimed garments telling a plain Tale)
Went there a Company, and in their Boat
Sounded with grappling irons and long poles.
■ At length, the dead Man,* 'mid that beauteous scene   470

■ *W's encounter with
death in fictions that he
read now reconciles him,
somehow, when not yet
nine, to the shocking
sight of the drowned
man.*

■ *He recalls reading*
The Thousand and
One Nights, *a small
selection . . .*

Of trees, and hills, and water, bolt upright
Rose with his ghastly face: a spectre-shape
Of terror even! and yet no vulgar fear,
Young as I was, a Child not nine years old,
Possessed me; for my inner eye had seen
Such sights before, among the shining streams
Of Fairy land, the Forests of Romance.
Thence came a Spirit hallowing what I saw
With decoration* and ideal grace,
A dignity, a smoothness, like the works   480
Of Grecian Art, and purest Poesy.

■ I had a precious treasure at that time,
A little, yellow canvas-covered Book,
A slender abstract of the Arabian Tales;
And when I learned, as now I first did learn
From my Companions in this new abode,
That this dear prize of mine was but a block
Hewn from a mighty quarry; in a word,
That there were four large Volumes, laden all
With kindred matter, 'twas in truth to me   490
A promise scarcely earthly. Instantly
I made a league, a covenant with a Friend
Of my own age, that we should lay aside
The monies we possessed, and hoard up more,
Till our joint savings had amassed enough
To make this Book our own. Through several months

VERY WEEK: in May 1779
SWEET VALLEY: Vale of Esthwaite
OWNED: claimed
DEAD MAN: James Jackson, schoolmaster in Sawrey, drowned June 18, 1779.

DECORATION: what is fitting, decorum

Religiously* did we preserve that vow,
And spite of all temptation, hoarded up
And hoarded up; but firmness failed at length,
Nor were we ever masters of our wish.   500

■ . . . and the books he
treasured at his father's
house, too, ones that stole
his time from fishing in
the Derwent.

■ A bond of writing and
of tales nurtures child-
hood long into later life,
and storytellers are as
friends, granting their
empires without bound
of space or time.

■ And afterwards, when to my Father's House
Returning at the holidays, I found
That golden store of books which I had left
Open to my enjoyment, once again
What heart was mine! Full often through the course
Of those glad respites in the summer-time,
When armed with rod and line we went abroad
For a whole day together, I have lain
Down by thy side, O Derwent! murmuring Stream,
On the hot stones and in the glaring sun,   510
And there have read, devouring as I read,
Defrauding the day's glory, desperate,
Till, with a sudden bound of smart reproach,
Such as an Idler deals with in his shame,
I to the sport betook myself again.

A gracious Spirit o'er this earth presides,
And o'er the heart of Man: invisibly
It comes, directing those to works of love
Who care not, know not, think not what they do;
The Tales that charm away the wakeful night   520
In Araby, Romances, Legends, penned,

For solace, by the light of monkish Lamps;
Fictions for Ladies, of their Love, devised
By youthful Squires; adventures endless, spun
By the dismantled* Warrior in old age,
Out of the bowels of those very thoughts
In which his youth did first extravagate;
These spread like day, and something in the shape
Of these will live till Man shall be no more.
Dumb* yearnings, hidden appetites are ours,   530
■ And they must have their food: our childhood sits,
Our simple childhood sits upon a throne
That hath more power than all the elements.
I guess not what this tells of Being past,
Nor what it augurs of the life to come;
But so it is, and in that dubious hour,
That twilight when we first begin to see
This dawning earth, to recognise, expect;
And in the long probation that ensues,
The time of trial, ere we learn to live   540
In reconcilement with our stinted powers,
To endure this state of meagre vassalage;
Unwilling to forego, confess, submit,
Uneasy and unsettled; yoke-fellows
To custom, mettlesome, and not yet tamed
And humbled down, Oh then we feel, we feel,
We know when we have Friends.—Ye dreamers, then,
Forgers of lawless Tales!* we bless you then,

RELIGIOUSLY: keeping a strict rule

DISMANTLED: not armed or dressed for battle
DUMB: mute, voiceless
FORGERS . . . TALES: makers of fantastic stories

Impostors, drivellers, dotards, as the ape*
Philosophy will call you: then we feel   550
With what, and how great might ye are in league,
Who make our wish our power, our thought a deed,
An empire, a possession; Ye whom Time
And Seasons serve, all Faculties; to whom
Earth crouches, th'elements are potter's clay,
Space like a Heaven filled up with Northern lights,
Here, nowhere, there, and everywhere at once.

■ *Yet from that childhood
we mature in less fan-
tastic things, and find
delight in very words
themselves.*

It might demand a more impassioned strain
To tell of later pleasures linked to these,
■ A tract of the same isthmus which we cross   560
In progress from our native continent
To earth and human life. I mean to speak
Of that delightful time of growing Youth

■ *He recalls, at this time
of youth, sharing with
a friend a conscious love
of meaning, music,
sense and feeling, all
unlocked by poetry.*

When cravings for the marvellous relent,
And we begin to love what we have seen;
And sober truth, experience, sympathy
Take stronger hold of us; and words themselves
Move us with conscious pleasure.

            I am sad
At thought of raptures, now for ever flown,
Even unto tears, I sometimes could be sad   570
To think of, to read over, many a page,
Poems, withal of name,* which at that time

APE: narrowly rational, lacking imagination

WITHAL OF NAME: even famous or well-known ones

Did never fail to entrance me, and are now
Dead in my eyes as is a theatre
■ Fresh emptied of Spectators. Thirteen years
Or haply less I might have seen, when first
My ears began to open to the charm
Of words in tuneful order, found them sweet
For their own sakes, a passion and a power,
And phrases pleased me, chosen for delight,   580
For pomp or love. Oft in the public roads,
Yet unfrequented, while the morning light
Was yellowing the hill-tops, with that dear Friend,*
The same whom I have mentioned heretofore,
I went abroad, and for the better part
Of two delightful hours we strolled along
By the still borders of the misty Lake,
Repeating favourite Verses with one voice,
Or conning* more; as happy as the birds
That round us chaunted. Well might we be glad,   590
Lifted above the ground by airy fancies
More bright than madness or the dreams of wine,
And though full oft the objects of our love
Were false, and in their splendour overwrought,
Yet, surely, at such time no vulgar power
Was working in us, nothing less, in truth,
Than that most noble attribute of Man,
Though yet untutored and inordinate,*
That wish for something loftier, more adorned

FRIEND: John Fleming (2.352)

CONNING: getting by heart, memorizing

INORDINATE: without direction or order

Than is the common aspect, daily garb   600
Of human life. What wonder then if sounds
Of exultation echoed through the groves!
For images, and sentiments, and words,
And every thing with which we had to do
In that delicious world of poesy,
Kept holiday, a never-ending show,
With music, incense, festival and flowers!

He receives from Nature much, but from surpassing poets a second Nature, too, and these two blend as words and wind. Language in verse reveals and alters more than ear and eye alone can sense.

Here must I pause: this only will I add
From heart-experience, and in humblest sense
Of modesty, that he, who, in his youth   610
A wanderer among the woods and fields,
With living Nature hath been intimate,
Not only in that raw unpractised time
Is stirred to ecstasy, as others are,
By glittering Verse; but he doth furthermore,
In measure only dealt out to himself,
Receive enduring touches of deep joy
From the great Nature that exists in works

Having told only what his earliest years owed to books, W now projects the history of his growth more than first conceived, for otherwise it would have ended here.

Of mighty Poets. Visionary Power
Attends upon the motions of the winds   620
Embodied in the mystery of words.
There darkness makes abode, and all the host
Of shadowy things do work their changes there,
As in a mansion like their proper home:
Even forms and substances are circumfused
By that transparent veil with light divine,
And through the turnings intricate of Verse
Present themselves as objects recognised,
In flashes, and with a glory scarce their own.

Thus far a scanty record is deduced   630
Of what I owed to Books in early life;
Their later influence yet remains untold.
But as this work was taking in my thoughts
Proportions that seemed larger than had first
Been meditated, I was indisposed
To any further progress at a time
When these acknowledgements were left unpaid.

Book Sixth
CAMBRIDGE AND THE ALPS

The leaves were yellow when to Furness Fells,
The haunt of Shepherds, and to cottage life
I bade adieu; and one among the Flock
Who by that season are convened, like birds
Trooping together at the Fowler's lure,
Went back to Granta's* cloisters; not so fond
Or eager, though as gay and undepressed
In spirit, as when I thence had taken flight
A few short months before. I turned my face
Without repining from the mountain pomp*   10
Of Autumn, and its beauty entered in
With calmer Lakes, and louder Streams: and You,
Frank-hearted Maids of rocky Cumberland,
You and your not unwelcome days of mirth
I quitted, and your nights of revelry,
And in my own unlovely Cell* sate down
In lightsome mood; such privilege has Youth,
That cannot take long leave of pleasant thoughts.

■ *W returns
to Cambridge . . .*

GRANTA: Cambridge; a name for the River Cam
POMP: here, magnificent display from colors
CELL: W's room in St. John's (3:46)

6.1 J. M. W. Turner (1775–1851). *Morning amongst the Coniston Fells, Cumberland,*
c. 1798. Tate Collection. "Furness Fells" refers to the upland region of southwest
Cumbria, which forms a peninsula between the Irish Sea and Morecambe Bay.

We need not linger o'er the ensuing time,

■ . . . and falls into an
undistinguished routine.

But let me add at once that now the bonds   20

Of indolent and vague society

Relaxing in their hold, I lived henceforth

More to myself, read more, reflected more,

Felt more, and settled daily into habits

More promising. Two winters* may be passed

Without a separate notice; many books

Were read in process of this time, devoured,

Tasted or skimmed, or studiously perused,

But with no settled plan. I was detached

Internally from academic cares,   30

From every hope of prowess and reward,

And wished to be a lodger in that house

Of Letters, and no more: and should have been

Even such, but for some personal concerns

That hung about me in my own despite

Perpetually, no heavy weight, but still

A baffling and a hindrance, a controul

Which made the thought of planning for myself

■ Yet, he develops a sense
of calling to the poet's
craft . . .

A course of independent study seem

An act of disobedience towards them   40

Who loved me, proud rebellion and unkind.

This bastard virtue, rather let it have

A name it more deserves, this cowardice

Gave treacherous sanction to that overlove

Of freedom planted in me from the very first

TWO WINTERS: 1788–89 and 1789–90

And indolence,* by force of which I turned

■ From regulations even of my own,

As from restraints and bonds. And who can tell,

Who knows what thus may have been gained both then

And at a later season, or preserved;   50

What love of nature, what original strength

Of contemplation, what intuitive truths

The deepest and the best, and what research

Unbiassed, unbewildered, and unawed?

The Poet's soul was with me at that time,

Sweet meditations, the still overflow

Of happiness and truth. A thousand hopes

Were mine, a thousand tender dreams, of which

No few have since been realized, and some

Do yet remain, hopes for my future life.   60

Four years and thirty, told this very week,*

Have I been now a sojourner on earth,

And yet the morning gladness is not gone

Which then was in my mind. Those were the days

■ Which also first encouraged me to trust

With firmness, hitherto but lightly touched

With such a daring thought, that I might leave

Some monument behind me which pure hearts

Should reverence. The instinctive humbleness,

Upheld even by the very name and thought   70

Of printed books and authorship, began

INDOLENCE: i.e., indolence also received "treacherous sanction"

VERY WEEK: on April 7, 1804

To melt away, and further, the dread awe
Of mighty names was softened down, and seemed
Approachable, admitting fellowship
Of modest sympathy. Such aspect now,
Though not familiarly, my mind put on;
I loved, and I enjoyed, that was my chief
And ruling business, happy in the strength
And loveliness of imagery and thought.
All winter long, whenever free to take   80
My choice, did I at night frequent our Groves
And tributary walks,* the last, and oft
The only one who had been lingering there
Through hours of silence, till the Porter's Bell,
A punctual follower on the stroke of nine,
Rang with its blunt unceremonious voice,
Inexorable summons. Lofty Elms,
Inviting shades of opportune recess,
Did give composure to a neighbourhood

■ . . . of which one "fairy work of earth" becomes an emblem.

■ Unpeaceful in itself. A single Tree   90
There was, no doubt yet standing there, an Ash
With sinuous trunk, boughs exquisitely wreathed;
Up from the ground and almost to the top
The trunk and master branches every where
Were green with ivy, and the lightsome twigs

■ Stock "poetic" phrases and those from older languages, he now sees, suffice no longer.

And outer spray profusely tipped with seeds
That hung in yellow tassels and festoons,
Moving or still, a favourite trimmed out

GROVES . . . WALKS: near or belonging to the colleges

By Winter for himself, as if in pride,
And with outlandish grace. Oft have I stood   100
Foot-bound, uplooking at this lovely Tree
Beneath a frosty moon. The hemisphere
Of magic fiction, verse of mine perhaps
May never tread; but scarcely Spenser's self
Could have more tranquil visions in his youth,
More bright appearances could scarcely see
Of human Forms and superhuman Powers,
Than I beheld, standing on winter nights
Alone, beneath this fairy* work of earth.
'Twould be a waste of labour to detail   110
The rambling studies of a truant Youth,
Which further may be easily divined,
What, and what kind they were. My inner knowledge
(This barely will I note) was oft in depth
And delicacy like another mind
Sequestered from my outward taste in books,
And yet the books which then I loved the most
Are dearest to me now: for being versed
In living Nature, I had there a guide
Which opened frequently my eyes, else shut,   120
A standard which was usefully applied,
Even when unconsciously, to other things
■ Which less I understood. In general terms,
I was a better judge of thoughts than words,
Misled as to these latter, not alone

FAIRY: amazing, imaginative

By common inexperience of youth

But by the trade in classic niceties,

Delusion to young Scholars incident

And old ones also, by that overprized

And dangerous craft of picking phrases out   130

From languages that want* the living voice

To make of them a nature to the heart,

To tell us what is passion, what is truth,

What reason, what simplicity and sense.

Yet must I not entirely overlook

The pleasure gathered from the elements

Of geometric science. I had stepped

In these inquiries but a little way,

No farther than the threshold: with regret

Sincere I mention this; but there I found   140

Enough to exalt, to chear me and compose.

With Indian* awe and wonder, ignorance

Which even was cherished, did I meditate

Upon the alliance of those simple, pure

Proportions and relations with the frame

And laws of Nature, how they would become

Herein a leader to the human mind,

And made endeavours frequent to detect

The process by dark guesses of my own.

Yet from this source more frequently I drew   150

A pleasure calm and deeper, a still sense

WANT: lack

INDIAN: refers to Native Americans

6.2 Samuel Prout (1783–1852). *The Wreck of the Dutton, An East Indiaman*, 1815. Yale Center for British Art, Gift of Rutgers Barclay, Yale BA 1957. "And as I have read of one by shipwreck thrown / With fellow Sufferers whom the waves had spared / Upon a region uninhabited" are lines influenced by *An Authentic Narrative of Some Remarkable and Interesting Particulars in the Life of ********* (1764) by John Newton (1725–1807).

Of permanent and universal sway

And paramount endowment in the mind,

An image not unworthy of the one

Surpassing Life, which out of space and time,

Nor touched by welterings of passion, is

And hath the name of God. Transcendent peace

And silence did await upon these thoughts

That were a frequent comfort to my youth.

And as I have read* of one by shipwreck thrown   160

READ: in John Newton's *Authentic Narrative* (1764)

With fellow Sufferers whom the waves had spared
Upon a region uninhabited,
An island of the Deep, who having brought
To land a single Volume and no more,

■ *In geometry he finds
intellectual magic to
calm a mind immersed
in images—and itself.*

■ *He indulges a pensive,
moody side.*

■ A Treatise of Geometry, was used,
Although of food and clothing destitute
And beyond common wretchedness depressed,
To part from company and take this book
(Then first a self-taught pupil in those truths)
To spots remote and corners of the Isle   170
By the sea-side, and draw his diagrams
With a long stick upon the sand, and thus
Did oft beguile his sorrow, and almost
Forget his feeling; even so, if things
Producing like effect, from outward cause
So different, may rightly be compared,
So was it with me then, and so will be
With Poets ever. Mighty is the charm
Of those abstractions to a mind beset
With images, and haunted by itself;   180
And specially delightful unto me
Was that clear Synthesis built up aloft
So gracefully, even then when it appeared
No more than as a plaything or a toy
Embodied to the sense, not what it is
In verity, an independent world
Created out of pure Intelligence.

Such dispositions then were mine, almost
Through grace of Heaven and inborn tenderness.
And not to leave the picture of that time   190
Imperfect, with these habits I must rank
■ A melancholy from humours of the blood*
In part, and partly taken up,* that loved
A pensive sky, sad days, and piping winds,
The twilight more than dawn, Autumn than Spring;
A treasured and luxurious gloom, of choice
And inclination mainly, and the mere
Redundancy of youth's contentedness.
Add unto this a multitude of hours
Pilfered away by what the Bard who sang   200
Of the Enchanter Indolence* hath called
'Good-natured lounging,' and behold a map
Of my Collegiate life, far less intense
Than Duty called for, or without regard
To Duty, might have sprung up of itself
By change of accident, or even, to speak
Without unkindness, in another place.

In summer among distant nooks I roved
Dovedale, or Yorkshire Dales, or through bye-tracts
Of my own native region, and was blest   210
Between these sundry wanderings with a joy
Above all joys that seemed another morn
Risen on mid noon, the presence, Friend,* I mean

MELANCHOLY . . . BLOOD: black bile, one of four traditional humors
PARTLY TAKEN UP: partly cultivated
BARD . . . INDOLENCE: James Thomson's *The Castle of Indolence* (1748)
FRIEND: Coleridge

6.3 Joseph Wright of Derby (1734–1797). *Matlock Tor by Moonlight*, 1777 and 1780. Yale Center for British Art, Paul Mellon Collection. "A pensive sky, sad days, and piping winds, / The twilight more than dawn": Wordsworth experienced melancholy—at times "A treasured and luxurious gloom, of choice / And inclination mainly" supplemented with a fondness for the English graveyard poets and for Thomas Gray.

6.4 J. M. W. Turner (1775–1851). *Ingleborough from Chapel-Le-Dale*, 1810–15. Yale Center for British Art, Paul Mellon Collection. "I roved / Dovedale, or Yorkshire Dales." Ingleborough is the second highest mountain in the Yorkshire Dales (2,372 feet), about 22 miles southeast of Windermere.

He recalls how he and
Dorothy, reunited after
years, had walked near
Penrith . . .

Of that sole Sister, she who hath been long

Thy Treasure also, thy true Friend and mine,

Now, after separation desolate

Restored to me, such absence that she seemed

A gift* then first bestowed. The gentle Banks

Of Emont,* hitherto unnamed in Song,   220

And that monastic Castle,* on a Flat

Low-standing by the margin of the Stream,

A Mansion not unvisited of old

By Sidney, where, in sight of our Helvellyn,

Some snatches he might pen, for aught we know,

Of his Arcadia, by fraternal love

Inspired;* that River and that mouldering Dome

Have seen us sit in many a summer hour,

My sister and myself, when having climbed

In danger through some window's open space,

We looked abroad, or on the Turret's head   230

Lay listening to the wild flowers and the grass

As they gave out their whispers to the wind.

. . . with
Mary Hutchinson.

Another Maid* there was, who also breathed

A gladness o'er that season, then to me

By her exulting outside look of youth

And placid under countenance first endeared,

That other Spirit, Coleridge, who is now

So near to us, that meek confiding heart,

So reverenced by us both. O'er paths and fields

In all that neighbourhood, through narrow lanes   240

SISTER . . . GIFT: Dorothy, whose name means "gift of God"

EMONT: the River Eamont

CASTLE: Brougham Castle, though not monastic

SIDNEY . . . INSPIRED: Sir Philip Sidney dedicated it to his sister, the Countess of Pembroke.

MAID: Mary Hutchinson, who married W in 1802

6.5 J. M. W. Turner (1775–1851). *Brougham Castle, near the Junction of the Rivers Eamont
and Lowther*, 1824. Tate Collection. In the late 1780s, along with "Another Maid," Mary
Hutchinson, Wordsworth and his "sole Sister," Dorothy, visited the ruins of 13th-
century Brougham Castle, a short walk from their grandparents' home in Penrith.

Of eglantine, and through the shady woods,

And o'er the Border Beacon,* and the Waste*

Of naked Pools and common Crags that lay

Exposed on the bare Fell, was scattered love,

A spirit of pleasure and youth's golden gleam.

O Friend! we had not seen thee at that time;*

And yet a power is on me and a strong

Confusion, and I seem to plant Thee there.

Far art Thou wandered now in search of health,*

BORDER BEACON: Penrith Beacon, a stone tower on Beacon Hill

WASTE: uncultivated land

THAT TIME: Coleridge did not know W in 1787.

FAR . . . HEALTH: Coleridge in April 1804 sailed to Malta.

And milder breezes, melancholy lot!

But Thou art with us, with us in the past,

The present, with us in the times to come:

There is no grief, no sorrow, no despair,

No languor, no dejection, no dismay,

No absence scarcely can there be for those

Who love as we do. Speed Thee well!* divide

Thy pleasure with us, thy returning strength,

Receive it daily as a joy of ours;

Share with us thy fresh spirits, whether gift

Of gales Etesian,* or of loving thoughts.

I, too, have been a Wanderer: but, alas!

How different is the fate of different men

Though Twins almost in genius and in mind!

Unknown unto each other, yea, and breathing

As if in different elements, we were framed

To bend at last to the same discipline,

Predestined, if two Beings ever were,

To seek the same delights, and have one health,

One happiness. Throughout this narrative,

Else sooner ended, I have known full well

For whom I thus record the birth and growth

Of gentleness, simplicity, and truth,

And joyous loves that hallow innocent days

Of peace and self-command. Of Rivers, Fields,

And Groves, I speak to Thee, my Friend, to Thee,

Who, yet a liveried* School-Boy, in the depths

Of the huge City,* on the leaded Roof

Of that wide Edifice, thy Home and School,

Wast used to lie and gaze upon the clouds

Moving in Heaven; or haply tired of this,

To shut thine eyes and by internal light

See trees and meadows, and thy native Stream*

Far distant, thus beheld from year to year

Of thy long exile.* Nor could I forget

In this late portion of my argument

That scarcely had I finally resigned

My rights among those academic Bowers*

When Thou wert thither guided. From the heart

Of London, and from Cloisters there Thou cam'st,

And didst sit down in temperance and peace,

A rigorous Student. What a stormy course

Then followed: oh! it is a pang that calls

For utterance, to think how small a change

Of circumstances might to Thee have spared

A world of pain, ripened ten thousand hopes

For ever withered. Through this retrospect

Of my own College life I still have had

Thy after sojourn in the self-same place

Present before my eyes: I have played with times

(I speak of private business of the thought)

And accidents as children do with cards,

Or as a man who when his house is built,

250

260

270

280

290

300

Composing Book Sixth, W wishes good fortune to Coleridge, then heading for Malta.

From age eight to nineteen Coleridge lost his father, only sister, and four older brothers. Brilliant at school but often lonely and disordered, he left Cambridge without a degree.

SPEED THEE WELL: Coleridge sailed on *Speedwell.*
ETESIAN: northwesterly summer winds in the Mediterranean

LIVERIED: Boys at Christ's Hospital wore a blue-coat uniform.
CITY: London
NATIVE STREAM: the River Otter in Devon
EXILE: In nine years Coleridge rarely returned to Devon.
ACADEMIC BOWERS: Cambridge University

A frame locked up in wood and stone, doth still,
In impotence of mind, by his fire-side
Rebuild it to his liking. I have thought
Of Thee, thy learning, gorgeous eloquence,
And all the strength and plumage of thy Youth,
Thy subtle speculations, toils abstruse
Among the Schoolmen,* and platonic forms
Of wild ideal pageantry, shaped out   310
From things well matched, or ill, and words for things,
The self-created sustenance of a mind
Debarred from Nature's living images,
Compelled to be a life unto itself,
And unrelentingly possessed by thirst
Of greatness, love, and beauty. Not alone,
Ah! surely not in singleness of heart
Should I have seen the light of evening fade
Upon the silent Cam, if we had met,

■ *W wishes he could have been a support to his friend earlier.*

■ Even at that early time: I needs must hope,   320
Must feel, must trust, that my maturer age,
And temperature less willing to be moved,
My calmer habits and more steady voice
Would with an influence benign have soothed
Or chased away the airy wretchedness
That battened on thy youth. But thou hast trod,
In watchful meditation thou hast trod
A march of glory, which doth put to shame
These vain regrets: health suffers in thee; else

■ *W and Jones, Cambridge almost done, head for a walking tour on the Continent.*

SCHOOLMEN: Scholastics; medieval scholars

Such grief for Thee would be the weakest thought   330
That ever harboured in the breast of Man.

A passing word erewhile did lightly touch
On wanderings of my own; and now to these
My Poem leads me with an easier mind.
The employments of three winters when I wore
A Student's Gown have been already told,
Or shadowed forth, as far as there is need.
When the third summer* brought its liberty
A Fellow Student and myself, he, too,
■ A Mountaineer,* together sallied forth   340
And, Staff in hand, on foot pursued our way
Towards the distant Alps. An open slight
Of College cares and study was the scheme,
Nor entertained without concern for those
To whom my worldly interests were dear:
But Nature then was sovereign in my heart,
And mighty forms* seizing a youthful Fancy
Had given a charter to irregular hopes.
In any age, without an impulse sent
From work of Nations and their goings-on,   350
I should have been possessed by like desire:
But 'twas a time when Europe was rejoiced,
France standing on the top of golden hours,
And human nature seeming born again.
Bound, as I said, to the Alps, it was our lot

THIRD SUMMER: 1790
MOUNTAINEER: Robert Jones, from rugged north Wales
MIGHTY FORMS: the Alps

6.6 David Cox (1783–1859). *Entrance to Calais Harbour,* 1829. Yale Center for British Art, Paul Mellon Collection. On summer break from Cambridge in 1790, Wordsworth and classmate Robert Jones began a three-month walking tour of France and the Alps. It "was our lot / To land at Calais on the very Eve / Of that great federal Day"—the eve of the Fête de la Fédération—the first anniversary of the storming of the Bastille.

■ *Landing at Calais, they soon witness and are greeted by revolutionary fervor.*

■ To land at Calais on the very Eve
Of that great federal Day;* and there we saw,
In a mean* City, and among a few,

How bright a face is worn when joy of one
Is joy of tens of millions. Southward thence
We took our way direct through Hamlets, Towns,

360

EVE . . . FEDERAL DAY: July 13, 1790: the next day was Bastille Day.
MEAN: common

Gaudy with reliques of that Festival,
Flowers left to wither on triumphal Arcs
And window Garlands. On the public roads,
And once three days successively, through paths
By which our toilsome journey was abridged,
Among sequestered villages we walked,
And found benevolence and blessedness
Spread like a fragrance everywhere, like Spring
That leaves no corner of the land untouched.   370
Where Elms, for many and many a league, in files,
With their thin umbrage,* on the stately roads

Their time is convivial,
pleasant . . .

Of that great Kingdom, rustled o'er our heads,
For ever near us as we paced along,
'Twas sweet at such a time, with such delights
On every side, in prime of youthful strength,
To feed a Poet's tender melancholy
And fond conceit of sadness, to the noise
And gentle undulations which they made.
Unhoused, beneath the Evening Star we saw   380
Dances of liberty, and in late hours
Of darkness, dances in the open air.
Among the vine-clad Hills of Burgundy,
Upon the bosom of the gentle Saone
We glided forward with the flowing stream:
Swift Rhone, thou wert the wings on which we cut
Between thy lofty rocks! Enchanting show
Those woods, and farms, and orchards did present,

umbrage: shade

And single Cottages, and lurking Towns,
Reach after reach,* procession without end   390
Of deep and stately Vales. A lonely Pair
Of Englishmen we were, and sailed along
Clustered together with a merry crowd
Of those emancipated, with a host
Of Travellers, chiefly Delegates, returning
From the great Spousals newly solemnized
At their chief City in the sight of Heaven.
Like bees they swarmed, gaudy and gay as bees;
Some vapoured* in the unruliness of joy
And flourished with their swords, as if to fight   400
The saucy air. In this blithe Company
We landed, took with them our evening Meal,
Guests welcome almost as the Angels were
To Abraham of old.* The Supper done,
With flowing cups elate, and happy thoughts,
We rose at signal giv'n, and formed a ring
And hand in hand danced round and round the Board;
All hearts were open, every tongue was loud
With amity and glee: we bore a name
Honoured in France, the name of Englishmen,   410
And hospitably did they give us hail*
As their forerunners in a glorious course,*
And round and round the board they danced again.
With this same Throng our voyage we pursued
At early dawn; the Monastery Bells

reach: stretch of river visible between bends
vapoured: talked or acted loosely or grandly
Angels . . . old: See Genesis 18:1–15.
hail: here, an open greeting of respect
forerunners . . . course: refers to the English Glorious or Bloodless Revolution, 1688–89

6.7 Charles Thevenin (1764–1838). *The Celebration of the Federation, Champs de Mars, Paris (14 July 1790)*, 1792. Musée de la Ville de Paris, Musée Carnavalet, Paris, France / Bridgeman Images. Almost all of Wordsworth's impressions of the festivities in France he recorded only years later. He had little "intimate concern" with the revolution during the summer of 1790.

Made a sweet jingling in our youthful ears,
The rapid River flowing without noise,
And every Spire we saw among the rocks
Spake with a sense of peace, at intervals
Touching the heart amid the boisterous Crew   420
With which we were environed. Having parted
From this glad Rout, the Convent of Chartreuse
Received us two days afterwards, and there

■ *... and soon they head   ■ We rested in an awful* Solitude;
towards Switzerland ...*   Thence onward to the Country of the Swiss.

'Tis not my present purpose to retrace
That variegated journey step by step:
A march it was of military speed,
And earth did change her images and forms
Before us, fast as clouds are changed in Heaven.   430
Day after day, up early and down late,
From vale to vale, from hill to hill we went
From Province on to Province did we pass,
Keen Hunters in a chace of fourteen weeks
Eager as birds of prey, or as a Ship
Upon the stretch when winds are blowing fair.
Sweet coverts did we cross of pastoral life,
Enticing Vallies, greeted them, and left
Too soon, while yet the very flash and gleam
Of salutation were not passed away.   440
Oh! sorrow for the Youth who could have seen

AWFUL: creating wonder or awe

6.8 Hercules Brabazon Brabazon (1821–1906). *Grande Chartreuse*, undated. Yale Center for British Art, Bequest of Joseph F. McCrindle. Before arriving at Mont Blanc, Wordsworth and Jones spent the night of August 4, 1790, at "the Convent of Chartreuse" in the French Alps.

Unchastened, unsubdued, unawed, unraised
To patriarchal* dignity of mind,
And pure simplicity of wish and will,
Those sanctified abodes of peaceful Man.
My heart leaped up when first I did look down
On that which was first seen of those deep haunts,
A green recess, an aboriginal vale
Quiet, and lorded over and possessed
By naked huts, wood-built, and sown like tents   450
Or Indian cabins over the fresh lawns,

PATRIARCHAL: here, venerable, most mature

■ ...then return to France, where Mont Blanc and Chamonix impress themselves upon the travelers.

■ And by the river side. That day we first
Beheld the summit of Mont Blanc,* and grieved
To have a soulless* image on the eye
Which had usurped upon a living thought
That never more could be: the wondrous Vale
Of Chamouny did on the following dawn,
With its dumb cataracts and streams of ice,
A motionless array of mighty waves,
Five rivers broad and vast, make rich amends,   460
And reconciled us to realities.
There small birds warble from the leafy trees,
The Eagle soareth in the element;
There doth the Reaper bind the yellow sheaf,
The Maiden spread the hay-cock in the sun,
While Winter like a tamèd Lion walks
Descending from the mountain to make sport
Among the cottages by beds of flowers.

Whate'er in this wide circuit we beheld,
Or heard, was fitted to our unripe state   470
Of intellect and heart. By simple strains

■ Again in Switzerland, they flourish in their freedom, read the Book of Nature, and find even sad fictions of their own devising pleasurable.

■ Of feeling, the pure breath of real life,
We were not left untouched. With such a book*
Before our eyes, we could not chuse but read
A frequent lesson of sound tenderness,
The universal reason of mankind,
The truth of Young and Old. Nor, side by side

Pacing, two brother Pilgrims, or alone
Each with his humour, could we fail to abound
(Craft this which hath been hinted at before)   480
In dreams and fictions pensively composed,
Dejection taken up for pleasure's sake,
And gilded sympathies; the willow wreath,*
Even among those solitudes sublime,
And sober posies of funereal flowers
Culled from the gardens of the Lady Sorrow
Did sweeten many a meditative hour.

Yet still in me, mingling with these delights
Was something of stern mood, an underthirst
Of vigour, never utterly asleep.   490
Far different dejection once was mine,
A deep and genuine sadness then I felt:
The circumstances I will here relate
Even as they were. Upturning with a Band
Of Travellers, from the Valais we had clomb*
Along the road that leads to Italy;
A length of hours making of these our Guides
Did we advance, and having reached an Inn
Among the mountains, we together ate
Our noon's repast, from which the Travellers rose,   500
Leaving us at the Board. Erelong we followed,
Descending by the beaten road that led
Right to a rivulet's edge, and there broke off.

MONT BLANC: highest Alpine peak, first scaled in 1786
SOULLESS: apparently lifeless, sterile
BOOK: the traditional Book of Nature

WILLOW WREATH: for grief or lost love
CLOMB: climbed

6.9 J. M. W. Turner (1775–1851). *Glacier and Source of the Arveiron, Chamonix*, 1803. Yale Center for British Art, Paul Mellon Collection. On the northern slopes of Mont Blanc, the Mer de Glace is the longest glacier in France (over four miles and almost 700 feet thick). Wordsworth and Jones trekked from the Chartreuse to that "wondrous Vale / Of Chamouny" on August 12, 1790.

6.10 John Singer Sargent (1856–1925). *Simplon Pass: Chalets*, 1911. Photograph © 2016, Museum of Fine Arts, Boston, the Hayden Collection. It was over the Simplon Pass that Wordsworth and Jones crossed the Alps. They had passed through "deep haunts, / A green recess, an aboriginal vale / Quiet, and lorded over and possessed / By naked huts."

The only track now visible was one
Upon the further side, right opposite,
And up a lofty Mountain. This we took
After a little scruple, and short pause,
And climbed with eagerness, though not, at length,
Without surprise, and some anxiety
On finding that we did not overtake   510
Our Comrades gone before. By fortunate chance,
While every moment now increased our doubts,
A Peasant met us, and from him we learned
That to the place which had perplexed us first

■ *One event leaves pro-
found feeling; unaware,
and without triumph of
any kind—even lost—
they are told that they
indeed have crossed the
Alps, the Simplon Pass.*

■ We must descend, and there should find the road
Which in the stony channel of the Stream
Lay a few steps, and then along its banks;
And further, that thenceforward all our course
Was downwards, with the current of that Stream.
Hard of belief,* we questioned him again,   520
And all the answers which the Man returned
To our inquiries, in their sense and substance,
Translated by the feelings which we had
Ended in this, *that we had crossed the Alps.*

■ *This brings consciousness
of invisible things,
greatness without bound,
hope and desire—and
of imagination itself.*

Imagination! lifting up itself
Before the eye and progress of my Song
Like an unfathered vapour; here that Power,
In all the might of its endowments, came
Athwart me; I was lost as in a cloud,

■ *They move through the
Gondo Gorge.*

HARD OF BELIEF: skeptical

■ Halted, without a struggle to break through.   530
And now recovering, to my Soul I say
I recognise thy glory; in such strength
Of usurpation, in such visitings
Of awful promise, when the light of sense
Goes out in flashes that have shewn to us
The invisible world, doth Greatness make abode,
There harbours* whether we be young or old.
Our destiny, our nature, and our home
Is with infinitude, and only there;
With hope it is, hope that can never die,   540
Effort, and expectation, and desire,
And something evermore about to be.
The mind beneath such banners militant
Thinks not of spoils or trophies,* nor of aught
That may attest its prowess, blest in thoughts
That are their own perfection and reward,
Strong in itself, and in the access of joy
Which hides it like the overflowing Nile.

The dull and heavy slackening which ensued
Upon those tidings by the Peasant given   550
Was soon dislodged; downwards we hurried fast
And entered with the road which we had missed
Into a narrow chasm:* the brook and road
■ Were fellow-travellers in this gloomy Pass,
And with them did we journey several hours

THERE HARBOURS: I.e., "in such strength" does Greatness find itself.
BANNERS . . . TROPHIES: W may distinguish himself from Napoleon, who crossed the Alps in 1800 and
built a road through the Simplon Pass as W wrote these lines.
CHASM: the Gondo Ravine or Gorge

At a slow step. The immeasurable height
Of woods decaying, never to be decayed,
The stationary blasts of water-falls,
And every where along the hollow rent*
Winds thwarting winds, bewildered and forlorn,   560
The torrents shooting from the clear blue sky,
The rocks that muttered close upon our ears,
Black drizzling crags that spake by the way-side
As if a voice were in them, the sick sight
And giddy prospect of the raving stream,
The unfettered clouds, and region of the Heavens,
Tumult and peace, the darkness and the light
Were all like workings of one mind, the features
Of the same face, blossoms upon one tree,
Characters* of the great Apocalypse,*   570
The types and symbols of Eternity,
Of first and last, and midst, and without end.

That night our lodging was an Alpine House,
An Inn, or Hospital,* as they are named,
Standing in that same valley by itself,
And close upon the confluence of two Streams,
A dreary Mansion, large beyond all need,
With high and spacious rooms, deafened and stunned
By noise of waters, making innocent Sleep
Lie melancholy among weary bones.   580

Upris'n betimes, our journey we renewed
Led by the Stream, ere noon-day magnified
Into a lordly River,* broad and deep,
Dimpling along in silent majesty,
With mountains for its neighbours, and in view
Of distant mountains and their snowy tops,
And thus proceeding to Locarno's Lake,*
Fit resting-place for such a Visitant.
—Locarno, spreading out in width like Heaven,
And Como, thou, a treasure by the earth   590
Kept to itself, a darling bosomed up
In Abyssinian* privacy, I spake
Of thee, thy chestnut woods, and garden plots
Of Indian corn tended by dark-eyed Maids,
Thy lofty steeps, and pathways roofed with vines
Winding from house to house, from town to town,
Sole link that binds them to each other, walks
League after league, and cloistral avenues
Where silence is, if music be not there:
While yet a Youth, undisciplined in Verse,   600
Through fond ambition of my heart, I told
Your praises;* nor can I approach you now
Ungreeted by a more melodious Song,
Where tones of learned Art and Nature mixed
May frame enduring language. Like a breeze
Or sunbeam over your domain I passed
In motion without pause; but ye* have left

■ *The pair walk along the southern edge of Lake Maggiore and on to Lake Como.*

■

RENT: a tear in the earth, a gorge or ravine
CHARACTERS: marks or symbols in writing or code
APOCALYPSE: literally an uncovering or revealing
HOSPITAL: place of hospitality or rest

RIVER: the River Toce
LOCARNO'S LAKE: Lake Maggiore
ABYSSINIAN: secluded or secret, even Edenic
I TOLD . . . PRAISES: in *Descriptive Sketches* (1793)
YE: Locarno (Lake Maggiore) and Lake Como

6.11 Unknown artist, formerly attributed to Thomas Charles Leeson Rowbotham (1823–1875). *Lake Maggiore*, 1850. Yale Center for British Art, Paul Mellon Collection. "Of distant mountains and their snowy tops": Wordsworth and Jones walked along Lake Maggiore, "Locarno's Lake," just south of the Alps, on August 19, 1790.

Your beauty with me, an impassioned sight
Of colours and of forms, whose power is sweet
And gracious, almost might I dare to say,   610
As virtue is, or goodness, sweet as love
Or the remembrance of a noble deed,
Or gentlest visitations of pure thought
When God, the Giver of all joy, is thanked
Religiously, in silent blessedness,
Sweet as this last itself; for such it* is.

Through those delightful pathways we advanced
Two days, and still in presence of the Lake,
Which winding up among the Alps now changed
Slowly its lovely countenance, and put on   620
A sterner character. The second night,
In eagerness, and by report* misled
Of those Italian clocks that speak the time
In fashion different from ours, we rose
By moonshine, doubting not that day was near,
And that, meanwhile, coasting the Water's edge

IT: the power of beauty of the two lakes

REPORT: the sound

6.12 William Callow (1812–1908). *Gravedona, Lake Como*, 1895. Bolton Museum and Art Gallery, Lancashire / Bridgeman Images. Wordsworth and Jones were misled by the chimes of Gravedona on August 21, 1790. The town is on the northwest shore of Lake Como.

As hitherto, and with as plain a track
To be our guide, we might behold the scene
In its most deep repose.—We left the Town

They trek north, up the western side of Lake Como.

Of Gravedona with this hope; but soon   630
Were lost, bewildered among woods immense,
Where having wandered for a while, we stopped
And on a rock sate down to wait for day.
An open place it was, and overlooked
From high the sullen water underneath,
On which a dull red image of the moon

Lay bedded, changing oftentimes its form
Like an uneasy snake: long time we sate,
For scarcely more than one hour of the night,
Such was our error, had been gone when we   640
Renewed our journey. On the rock we lay
And wished to sleep but could not for the stings
Of insects, which with noise like that of noon
Filled all the woods; the cry of unknown birds,
The mountains, more by darkness visible
And their own size than any outward light,
The breathless wilderness of clouds, the clock
That told with unintelligible voice
The widely-parted hours, the noise of streams
And sometimes rustling motions nigh at hand   650
Which did not leave us free from personal fear,
And lastly the withdrawing Moon, that set
Before us while she yet was high in heaven,
These were our food, and such a summer night
Did to that pair of golden days succeed,
With now and then a doze and snatch of sleep,
On Como's Banks, the same delicious Lake.

But here I must break off and quit at once,
Though loth, the record of these wanderings,
A theme which may seduce me else beyond   660
All reasonable bounds. Let this alone
Be mentioned as a parting word, that not

W reflects on what this trip meant for him and Jones.

Not fully cognizant at that time of convulsions surrounding him, W now recalls the journey as one of youth, adventure, and delight.

In hollow exultation, dealing forth
Hyperboles of praise comparative,
Not rich one moment to be poor for ever,
Not prostrate, overborn, as if the mind
Itself were nothing, a mean pensioner*
On outward forms, did we in presence stand
Of that magnificent region. On the front
Of this whole Song is written that my heart   670
Must in such temple needs have offered up
A different worship. Finally whate'er
I saw, or heard, or felt, was but a stream
That flowed into a kindred stream, a gale
That helped me forwards, did administer
To grandeur and to tenderness, to the one
Directly, but to tender thoughts, by means
Less often instantaneous in effect,
Conducted me to these along a path
Which in the main was more circuitous.   680

Oh! most belovèd Friend, a glorious time,
A happy time that was; triumphant looks
Were then the common language of all eyes:

As if awaked from sleep, the Nations hailed
Their great expectancy: the fife of War
Was then a spirit-stirring sound indeed,
A Blackbird's whistle in a vernal grove.*
We left the Swiss exulting in the fate
Of their near Neighbours, and when shortening fast
Our pilgrimage, nor distant far from home,   690
We crossed the Brabant Armies* on the fret
For battle in the cause of Liberty.
A Stripling, scarcely of the household then
Of social life, I looked upon these things
As from a distance, heard, and saw, and felt,
Was touched, but with no intimate concern;
I seemed to move among them as a bird
Moves through the air, or as a fish pursues
Its business, in its proper* element;
I needed not that joy,* I did not need   700
Such help; the ever-living Universe,
And independent spirit of pure youth
Were with me at that season, and delight
Was in all places spread around my steps
As constant as the grass upon the fields.

MEAN PENSIONER: living off of but with no power of its own

BLACKBIRD . . . GROVE: the Old World songbird, often a harbinger of spring
BRABANT ARMIES: Belgian republican forces
ITS PROPER: its own
THAT JOY: excitement of war and revolution

7.1 Delmar Harmood Banner (1896–1983). *Scafell from Birker Moor, Eskdale, Cumberland*, 1945. The Wordsworth Trust. Scafell Pike is the tallest mountain in England (3,209 feet). This massive red pyramid is located about seven miles west of Grasmere. Dorothy Wordsworth climbed Scafell in 1818.

Book Seventh
RESIDENCE IN LONDON

Five years are vanished since I first poured out,
Saluted by that animating breeze
Which met me issuing from the City's Walls,
A glad preamble to this Verse: I sang
Aloud in Dythyrambic* fervour, deep
But short-lived uproar, like a torrent sent
Out of the bowels of a bursting cloud
Down Scafell, or Blencathra's* rugged sides,
A water-spout from Heaven. But 'twas not long
Ere the interrupted stream broke forth once more   10
And flowed awhile in strength, then stopped for years,
Not heard again until a little space

■ Before last primrose-time.* Belovèd Friend,*
The assurances then given unto myself
Which did beguile me of some heavy thoughts
At thy departure to a foreign Land
Have failed; for slowly doth this work advance.
Through the whole summer* have I been at rest,
Partly from voluntary holiday

And part through outward hindrance. But I heard   20
After the hour of sunset yester even,
Sitting within doors betwixt light and dark,
A voice that stirred me. 'Twas a little Band,
A Quire* of Redbreasts gathered somewhere near
My threshold, Minstrels from the distant woods
And dells, sent in by Winter to bespeak
For the Old Man* a welcome, to announce
With preparation artful and benign,
Yea, the most gentle music of the year,
That their rough Lord had left the surly North   30
And hath begun his journey. A delight
At this unthought-of greeting unawares
Smote me, a sweetness of the coming time,
And listening, I half whispered, we will be,
Ye heartsome Choristers, ye and I will be
Brethren, and in the hearing of bleak winds
Will chaunt together. And, thereafter, walking
By later twilight on the hills, I saw
A Glow-worm from beneath a dusky shade
Or canopy of the yet unwithered fern,   40
Clear shining, like a Hermit's taper seen
Through a thick forest: silence touched me here
No less than sound had done before; the Child
Of Summer, lingering, shining by itself,
The voiceless Worm on the unfrequented hills,

■ *Composing this poem, W reflects on its interrupted progress and—stirred by a voice, a choir—its continuation.*

DYTHYRAMBIC: impassioned, unrestrained, from hymns to Dionysus
SCAFELL . . . BLENCATHRA: peaks in the Lake District
PRIMROSE-TIME: early spring
FRIEND: Coleridge
SUMMER: of 1804

QUIRE: Choir
OLD MAN: winter

Seemed sent on the same errand with the Quire
Of Winter that had warbled at my door,
And the whole year seemed tenderness and love.

The last Night's genial feeling overflowed
Upon this morning, and my favourite Grove,*   50
Now tossing its dark boughs in sun and wind,
Spreads through me a commotion like its own,
Something that fits me for the Poet's task,
Which we will now resume with chearful hope,
Nor checked by aught of tamer argument
That lies before us, needful to be told.

Returned from that excursion,* soon I bade
Farewell for ever to the private Bowers*
Of gownèd Students, quitted these, no more
To enter them, and pitched my vagrant tent,   60
A casual dweller and at large among
The unfenced regions of society.

Yet undetermined to what plan of life
I should adhere, and seeming thence to have
A little space of intermediate time
■ Loose and at full command, to London first
I turned, if not in calmness, nevertheless
In no disturbance of excessive hope,

At ease from all ambition personal,
Frugal as there was need, and though self-willed,   70
Yet temperate and reserved, and wholly free
From dangerous passions. 'Twas at least two years
Before this season when I first beheld
That mighty place, a transient visitant:
And now it pleased me my abode to fix
Single in the wide waste, to have a house
It was enough, what matter for a home,
That owned me, living chearfully abroad
With fancy on the stir from day to day,
And all my young affections out of doors.   80

There was a time when whatsoe'er is feigned
Of airy Palaces and Gardens built
By Genii of Romance, or hath in grave
Authentic History been set forth of Rome,
Alcairo,* Babylon, or Persepolis,
Or given upon report by Pilgrim Friars
Of golden Cities ten months' journey deep
Among Tartarian* wilds, fell short, far short,
Of that which I in simpleness believed
And thought of London, held me by a chain   90
Less strong of wonder and obscure delight.
I know not that herein I shot beyond
The common mark of childhood; but I well

■ *After graduating from Cambridge, he lives for a time in London, which earlier he had visited . . .*

FAVOURITE GROVE: "John's grove," where W's brother had walked
EXCURSION: the walking tour on the Continent (Book Sixth)
PRIVATE BOWERS: academic precincts of Cambridge

ALCAIRO: W may mean ancient Memphis, not Cairo.
TARTARIAN: hellish, from Tartarus, the deep underworld

7.2 William Marlow (1740–1813). *St. Paul's and Blackfriars Bridge*, 1770–1772. Yale Center for British Art, Paul Mellon Collection. Wordsworth, after graduating from Cambridge on January 21, 1791, "to London first / I turned." He remained there until late May, when he traveled to Wales and climbed Mount Snowdon (Book Thirteenth).

Remember that among our flock of Boys
Was one, a Cripple* from the birth, whom chance
Summoned from School to London, fortunate
And envied Traveller! and when he returned
After short absence, and I first set eyes
Upon his person, verily, though strange
The thing may seem, I was not wholly free   100
From disappointment to behold the same
Appearance, the same body, not to find
Some change, some beams of glory brought away
From that new region. Much I questioned him,
And every word he uttered on my ears
Fell flatter than a cagèd Parrot's note
That answers unexpectedly awry,

... and in childhood had dreamt of and wondered at.

■ And mocks the Prompter's listening. Marvellous things
My fancy had shaped forth of sights and shows,
Processions, Equipages, Lords and Dukes,   110
The King, and the King's Palace, and not last
Or least, heaven bless him! the renowned Lord Mayor,*
Dreams hardly less intense than those which wrought
A change of purpose in young Whittington

He had heard of London's famous sights...

When he in friendlessness, a drooping Boy,
Sate on a Stone and heard the Bells speak out
Articulate music.* Above all, one thought
Baffled my understanding, how men lived
Even next-door neighbours, as we say, yet still
Strangers, and knowing not each other's names.   120

CRIPPLE: Philip Braithwaite

LORD MAYOR: the Lord Mayor and his annual Show

WHITTINGTON . . . MUSIC: Dick Whittington heard bells call him Lord Mayor.

7.3 John S. Muller (1715–1792), After Samuel Wale (1721–1786). *Vauxhall Gardens shewing the Grand Walk at the Entrance of the Garden and the Orchestra with the Music Playing*, 1751. Yale Center for British Art, Paul Mellon Collection. "Vauxhall and Ranelagh": Vauxhall was loved by the well-dressed crowds for its 15,000 outdoor lamps, rotunda, music, fireworks, and magnificent garden.

Oh wondrous power of words, how sweet they are
According to the meaning which they bring,
Vauxhall and Ranelagh,* I then had heard
Of your green groves, and wilderness of lamps,
■ Your gorgeous Ladies, fairy cataracts,
And pageant fire-works; nor must we forget
Those other wonders, different in kind,
Though scarcely less illustrious in degree,
The River proudly bridged, the giddy top
And Whispering Gallery of St. Paul's, the Tombs   130

VAUXHALL AND RANELAGH: extensive pleasure gardens

7.4 Canaletto (1697–1768). *St. Paul's Cathedral*, 1754. Yale Center for British Art, Paul Mellon Collection. While in London Wordsworth lived alone ("Single in the wide waste") a short walk from St. Paul's.

7.5 William Hogarth (1697–1764). *A Rake's Progress VIII: The Rake in Bedlam*, 1733. The Trustees of Sir John Soane's Museum, London / Bridgeman Images. Bedlam, the archaic and outmoded Bethlehem Hospital, was sadly still a popular tourist attraction in 1791.

7.6 Frederick Nash (1782–1856). *The Monument and London Bridge*, 1825. Yale Center for British Art, Paul Mellon Collection. Sir Christopher Wren's monument to the 1666 Great Fire of London (far left, finished in 1677) stands 202 feet tall overlooking London Bridge.

7.7 Thomas Hearne (1744–1817). *The Tower of London*, 1801. Yale Center for British Art, Paul Mellon Collection. Wordsworth saw the "Armoury of the Tower" near the River Thames.

Of Westminster, the Giants* of Guildhall,
Bedlam, and the two figures* at its Gates,
Streets without end, and Churches numberless,
Statues, with flowery Gardens in vast Squares,
The Monument,* and Armoury of the Tower.

These fond imaginations of themselves
Had long before given way in season due,
Leaving a throng of others in their stead;
And now I looked upon the real scene,
Familiarly perused it day by day   140

GIANTS: statues of Gog and Magog
FIGURES: statues of Melancholy and Raving Madness
MONUMENT: column commemorating the Great Fire of 1666

With keen and lively pleasure, even there
Where disappointment was the strongest, pleased
Through courteous self-submission, as a tax
Paid to the object by prescriptive right,
A thing that ought to be. Shall I give way,
Copying the impression of the memory,
Though things remembered idly do half seem
The work of fancy, shall I, as the mood
Inclines me, here describe for pastime's sake
Some portion of that motley imagery,   150
A vivid pleasure of my Youth, and now

Among the lonely places that I love
A frequent day-dream for my riper mind?

■ . . . and now relates them from his own experience.

■ —And first the look and aspect of the place,
The broad high-way appearance, as it strikes
On Strangers of all ages, the quick dance
Of colours, lights and forms, the Babel din,
The endless stream of men, and moving things,
From hour to hour the illimitable walk
Still among Streets with clouds and sky above,   160
The wealth, the bustle and the eagerness,
The glittering Chariots* with their pampered Steeds,
Stalls, Barrows,* Porters; midway in the Street
The Scavenger, who begs with hat in hand,
The labouring Hackney Coaches, the rash speed
Of Coaches travelling far, whirled on with horn
Loud blowing, and the sturdy Drayman's Team
Ascending from some Alley of the Thames
And striking right across the crowded Strand*
Till the fore Horse veer round with punctual skill: 170

■ There are crowds, and faces in the crowd, motion and strange shapes.

■ Here, there, and every where a weary Throng,
The Comers and the Goers face to face,
Face after face, the string of dazzling Wares,
Shop after shop, with Symbols, blazoned Names,
And all the Tradesman's honours overhead;
Here, fronts of houses like a title-page

■ Entertainments and the cries of sellers wash over even less frequented spots.

With letters huge inscribed from top to toe;
Stationed above the door like guardian Saints,

CHARIOTS: various horse-drawn carriages
BARROWS: handcarts with flat trays, or wheelbarrows
STRAND: main thoroughfare roughly parallel to the Thames

There, allegoric shapes, female or male;
Or physiognomies of real men,   180
Land Warriors, Kings, or Admirals of the Sea,
Boyle,* Shakespear, Newton, or the attractive head
Of some Scotch doctor,* famous in his day.

Meanwhile the roar continues, till at length,
Escaped as from an enemy, we turn
Abruptly into some sequestered nook
Still as a sheltered place when winds blow loud.
At leisure thence, through tracts of thin resort
And sights and sounds that come at intervals
We take our way: a raree-show is here   190

■ With children gathered round, another Street
Presents a company of dancing Dogs,
Or Dromedary with an antic pair
Of Monkies on his back, a minstrel Band
Of Savoyards,* or single and alone,
An English Ballad-singer. Private Courts,
Gloomy as Coffins, and unsightly Lanes
Thrilled by some female Vender's scream, belike
The very shrillest of all London Cries,
May then entangle us awhile,   200
Conducted through those labyrinths unawares
To privileged Regions* and inviolate,
Where from their airy lodges studious Lawyers
Look out on waters, walks, and gardens green.

BOYLE: Robert Boyle, famous scientist
SCOTCH DOCTOR: James Graham, a quack
SAVOYARDS: people from Savoy in southeastern France
PRIVILEGED REGIONS: Inns of Court, where lawyers have offices

7.8 John Collet (1725–1780). *Scene in a London Street*, 1770. Yale Center for British Art, Paul Mellon Collection. From 1760 to 1815 the population of London doubled to 1.4 million, at that time the largest city in the western world: "the Babel din, / The endless stream of men, and moving things."

Thence back into the throng until we reach,
Following the tide that slackens by degrees,
Some half-frequented scene where wider Streets
Bring straggling breezes of suburban air:
Here files of ballads dangle from dead walls;*
Advertisements of giant size from high   210
Press forward in all colours on the sight,

■ *The catalogue of notices
and people continues . . .*
■ These, bold in conscious merit; lower down
That, fronted with a most imposing word,
Is, peradventure, one in masquerade.*
As on the broadening Causeway we advance,
Behold a Face turned up towards us, strong
In lineaments, and red with over-toil;
'Tis one, perhaps, already met elsewhere,
A travelling Cripple, by the trunk cut short,
And stumping with his arms: in Sailor's garb   220
Another lies at length beside a range
Of written characters, with chalk inscribed
Upon the smooth flat stones: the Nurse is here,
The Bachelor that loves to sun himself,
The military Idler, and the Dame
That field-ward takes her walk in decency.

Now homeward through the thickening hubbub, where
See, among less distinguishable Shapes,

■ *. . . including men and
women exotic and for-
eign to a rural youth.*
■ The Italian with his frame of Images*
Upon his head; with Basket at his waist   230

DEAD WALLS: walls with no openings of any kind
IN MASQUERADE: false or misleading
FRAME OF IMAGES: tray or box of statuettes, likely saints

The Jew; the stately and slow-moving Turk
With freight of slippers piled beneath his arm.
Briefly we find, if tired of random sights
And haply to that search our thoughts should turn,
Among the crowd, conspicuous less or more,
As we proceed, all specimens of Man
Through all the colours which the sun bestows,
And every character of form and face,
The Swede, the Russian; from the genial South
The Frenchman and the Spaniard; from remote   240
America the hunter Indian; Moors,
Malays, Lascars,* the Tartar and Chinese,
And Negro Ladies in white muslin gowns.

At leisure let us view from day to day,
As they present themselves, the Spectacles
Within doors, troops of wild Beasts, birds and beasts
Of every nature from all climes convened,
And, next to these, those mimic sights that ape
The absolute presence of reality,
Expressing, as in mirror, sea and land,   250
And what earth is, and what she hath to shew;
I do not here allude to subtlest craft,
By means refined attaining purest ends,
But imitations fondly made in plain
Confession of Man's weakness, and his loves.
Whether the Painter fashioning a work

LASCARS: East Indian sailors

■ *Panoramas and models*
  represent in minute
  detail yet other places
  and cities.

To Nature's circumambient scenery,

And with his greedy pencil* taking in

A whole horizon on all sides,* with power

Like that of Angels or commissioned Spirits,   260

Plant us upon some lofty Pinnacle,

Or in a Ship on Waters, with a world

Of life, and life-like mockery, to East,

To West, beneath, behind us, and before;

Or more mechanic Artist represent

By scale exact, in Model, wood or clay,

From shading colours also borrowing help,

Some miniature of famous spots and things

Domestic, or the boast of foreign Realms;

The Firth of Forth, and Edinburgh throned   270

On crags, fit empress of that mountain Land;

Saint Peter's Church, or more aspiring aim,

In microscopic vision, Rome itself,

Or else perhaps some rural haunt, the Falls

Of Tivoli*

And high upon the Steep that mouldering Fane,

■ *Theatrical shows at*
  Sadler's Wells present
  lively if common recre-
  ation.

The Temple of the Sibyl,* every tree

Through all the landscape, tuft, stone, scratch minute,

And every Cottage lurking in the rocks,

All that the Traveller sees when he is there.   280

Add to these exhibitions mute and still

Others of wider scope, where living men,

PENCIL: here, an artist's brush

WHOLE . . . SIDES: a panorama on the wall of a circular room

TIVOLI: In 1805 W left this line unfinished.

TEMPLE OF THE SIBYL: dedicated to a Roman nymph of oracular power

7.9 J. M. W. Turner (1775–1851). *Tivoli with the Temple of the Sybil and the Cascades,*
1796–97. Yale Center for British Art, Paul Mellon Collection. Wordsworth later visited
"the Falls / Of Tivoli / And . . . that mouldering Fane, / The Temple of the Sibyl" (upper
right), fifteen miles east of Rome in the Apennine Mountains, on his Italian tour of 1837.

Music, and shifting pantomimic scenes

Together joined their multifarious aid

■ To heighten the allurement. Need I fear

To mention by its name, as in degree

Lowest of these, and humblest in attempt,

Yet richly graced with honours of its own,

Half-rural Sadler's Wells?* Though at that time

Intolerant, as is the way of Youth   290

Unless itself be pleased, I more than once

SADLER'S WELLS: entertainment theater in Islington, near London

Here took my seat, and maugre* frequent fits
Of irksomeness, with ample recompense
Saw Singers, Rope-dancers, Giants and Dwarfs,
Clowns, Conjurors, Posture-masters, Harlequins,*
Amid the uproar of the rabblement,
Perform their feats. Nor was it mean delight
To watch crude nature work in untaught minds,
To note the laws and progress of belief;
Though obstinate in this way, yet on that   300
How willingly we travel, and how far!
To have, for instance, brought upon the scene
The Champion Jack the Giant-killer, lo!
He dons his Coat of Darkness; on the Stage
Walks and atchieves his wonders, from the eye
Of living mortal safe as is the moon
'Hid in her vacant interlunar cave'*.
Delusion bold! and faith must needs be coy;*
How is it wrought? His garb is black, the word
Invisible flames forth upon his Chest.   310

There he sees a troupe of actors, the "daring Brotherhood," perform Edward and Susan, a play about Mary Robinson. W and Coleridge had met her in Buttermere. Mary not long afterward had been entrapped in a bigamous marriage, which Coleridge helped expose.

Nor was it unamusing here to view
Those samples as of the ancient Comedy
And Thespian times,* dramas of living Men
And recent things, yet warm with life, a Sea-fight,
Shipwreck, or some domestic incident,
The fame of which is scattered through the Land;
Such as the daring Brotherhood of late

7.10 James Bourne (1773–1854). *Buttermere Lake*, 1802. The Wordsworth Trust. Mary Robinson, the "Maid of Buttermere," was the "artless Daughter" of the innkeeper at the Fish Inn in Buttermere. In 1802, Mary was "wooed" and married "in cruel mockery" to the unscrupulous bigamist John Hatfield. Coleridge met with this "'bold bad Man'" in prison before Hatfield was hanged on September 3, 1803.

Set forth, too holy theme for such a place,
And doubtless treated with irreverence
Albeit with their very best of skill,   320
I mean, O distant Friend!* a Story drawn
From our own ground, the Maid of Buttermere,*
And how the Spoiler came, 'a bold bad Man'*
To God unfaithful, Children, Wife, and Home,
And wooed the artless Daughter of the hills,
And wedded her in cruel mockery
Of love and marriage bonds. O Friend! I speak

MAUGRE: despite (maw′ger)
POSTURE-MASTERS, HARLEQUINS: contortionists, clown-like characters
'HID . . . CAVE': a line from Milton's *Samson Agonistes*
COY: susceptible, resisting but willing to be won
THESPIAN TIMES: sixth century B.C.E., from Greek tragedian Thespis

DISTANT FRIEND: Coleridge was now in Malta.
MAID OF BUTTERMERE: Mary Robinson, born 1778
'A BOLD BAD MAN': a phrase from Spenser's *Faerie Queene*

W recounts the story that
Mary's new-born child
had died.

With tender recollection of that time
When first we saw the Maiden, then a name
By us unheard of, in her cottage Inn   330
Were welcomed and attended on by her,
Both stricken with one feeling of delight,
An admiration of her modest mien
And carriage, marked by unexampled grace.
Not unfamiliarly we since that time
Have seen her, her discretion have observed,
Her just opinions, female modesty,
Her patience and retiredness of mind
Unsoiled by commendation and the excess
Of public notice. This memorial Verse   340
Comes from the Poet's heart, and is her due.
For we were nursed, as almost might be said,
On the same mountains,* Children at one time

This brings to mind
another child in different
circumstances, innocent
amid indecency.

Must haply often on the self-same day
Have from our several dwellings gone abroad
To gather daffodils on Coker's Stream.*

These last words uttered, to my argument
I was returning, when with sundry Forms
Mingled, that in the way which I must tread
Before me stand, thy image rose again,   350
Mary of Buttermere! She lives in peace
Upon the spot where she was born and reared;
Without contamination does she live

In quietness, without anxiety:
Beside the mountain Chapel sleeps in earth
Her new-born Infant, fearless as a lamb
That thither comes from some unsheltered place
To rest beneath the little rock-like Pile
When storms are blowing. Happy are they both,
Mother and Child! These feelings, in themselves   360
Trite,* do yet scarcely seem so when I think
Of those ingenuous moments of our youth
Ere yet by use we have learned to slight the crimes
And sorrows of the world. Those days are now
My theme, and 'mid the numerous scenes which they
Have left behind them, foremost I am crossed
Here by remembrance of two figures, one
A rosy Babe, who for a twelvemonth's space
Perhaps had been of age to deal about
Articulate prattle, Child as beautiful   370
As ever sate upon a Mother's knee;
The other was the Parent of that Babe,
But on the Mother's cheek the tints were false,
A painted bloom.* 'Twas at a Theatre
That I beheld this Pair; the Boy had been
The pride and pleasure of all lookers-on
In whatsoever place; but seemed in this
A sort of Alien scattered from the clouds.
Of lusty vigour, more than infantine,
He was in limbs, in face a Cottage rose   380

SAME MOUNTAINS: W and the Maid grew up just miles apart.
COKER'S STREAM: The River Cocker flows from Buttermere to Cockermouth.

TRITE: commonplace (here, no sense of worthlessness)
PAINTED BLOOM: makeup that suggests prostitution

Just three parts blown;* a Cottage Child, but ne'er
Saw I, by Cottage or elsewhere, a Babe
By Nature's gifts so honoured. Upon a Board
Whence an attendant of the Theatre
Served out refreshments, had this Child been placed
And there he sate, environed* with a ring
Of chance Spectators, chiefly dissolute men
And shameless women, treated and caressed,
Ate, drank, and with the fruit and glasses played,
While oaths, indecent speech, and ribaldry   390
Were rife about him as are songs of birds
In spring-time after showers. The Mother too
Was present! but of her I know no more
Than hath been said, and scarcely at this time

■ *W wonders now what might have happened to this other child—a fate perhaps no better than Mary's nameless infant.*

■ Do I remember her. But I behold
The lovely Boy as I beheld him then,
Among the wretched and the falsely gay,
Like one of those* who walked with hair unsinged
Amid the fiery furnace. He hath since
Appeared to me oft-times as if embalmed   400
By Nature; through some special privilege
Stopped at the growth he had, destined to live,
To be, to have been, come and go a Child
And nothing more, no partner in the years

■ *He reflects on the degradation, pain, and grief he witnessed first on his way to Cambridge.*

That bear us forward to distress and guilt,
Pain and abasement, beauty in such excess
Adorned him in that miserable place.

BLOWN: blossomed
ENVIRONED: surrounded
THOSE: Shadrach, Meshach, Abednego (Daniel 3:12–27)

So have I thought of him a thousand times,
And seldom otherwise. But he perhaps
Mary! may now have lived till he could look   410
With envy on thy nameless Babe that sleeps
Beside the mountain Chapel undisturbed.

It was but little more than three short years
Before the season which I speak of now*
■ When first, a Traveller from our pastoral hills,
Southward two hundred miles I had advanced,
And for the first time in my life did hear
The voice of Woman utter blasphemy,
Saw Woman as she is to open shame
Abandoned and the pride of public vice.   420
Full surely from the bottom of my heart
I shuddered; but the pain was almost lost,
Absorbed and buried in the immensity
Of the effect: a barrier seemed at once
Thrown in, that from humanity divorced
The human Form, splitting the race of Man
In twain, yet leaving the same outward shape.
Distress of mind ensued upon this sight
And ardent meditation: afterwards
A milder sadness on such spectacles   430
Attended; thought, commiseration, grief
For the individual, and the overthrow
Of her soul's beauty: farther at that time

IT . . . NOW: W left for Cambridge in late 1787 and first lived in London in 1791.

Than this I was but seldom led; in truth
The sorrow of the passion stopped me here.

I quit this painful theme; enough is said
To shew what thoughts must often have been mine
At theatres, which then were my delight,
A yearning made more strong by obstacles

■ *The novelty and pleasure of the stage capture his attention, but only for a while.*

■ Which slender funds imposed. Life then was new,   440
The senses easily pleased; the lustres,* lights,
The carving and the gilding, paint and glare,
And all the mean upholstery* of the place
Wanted not animation in my sight:
Far less the living Figures on the Stage,
Solemn or gay: whether some beauteous Dame
Advanced in radiance through a deep recess
Of thick-entangled forest, like the Moon
Opening the clouds; or sovereign King, announced
With flourishing Trumpets, came in full-blown State   450
Of the world's greatness, winding round with Train
Of Courtiers, Banners, and a length of Guards;
Or Captive led in abject weeds,* and jingling
His slender manacles; or romping Girl
Bounced, leapt, and pawed the air; or mumbling Sire,
A scare-crow pattern of old Age, patched up
Of all the tatters of infirmity,
All loosely put together, hobbled in,
Stumping upon a Cane, with which he smites,

LUSTRES: chandeliers or bright glass reflectors
MEAN UPHOLSTERY: common furniture and room decoration
ABJECT WEEDS: poor, humiliating clothes

From time to time, the solid boards, and makes them   460
Prate* somewhat loudly of the whereabout
Of one so overloaded with his years.
But what of this! the laugh, the grin, grimace,
And all the antics and buffoonery,
The least of them not lost, were all received
With charitable pleasure. Through the night
Between the show, and many-headed mass
Of the Spectators, and each little nook
That had its fray or brawl, how eagerly,
And with what flashes, as it were, the mind   470
Turned this way, that way, sportive and alert
And watchful as a kitten when at play,
While winds are blowing round her, among grass
And rustling leaves. Enchanting age and sweet!
Romantic almost, looked at through a space
How small of intervening years. For then,
Though surely no mean progress had been made
In meditations holy and sublime,
Yet something of a girlish child-like gloss
Of novelty survived for scenes like these;   480
Pleasure that had been handed down from times
When, at a Country Play-house, having caught
In summer, through the fractured wall, a glimpse
Of day-light, at the thought of where I was
I gladdened more than if I had beheld
Before me some bright Cavern of Romance,

PRATE: talk on, chatter

Or than we do when on our beds we lie
At night, in warmth, when rains are beating hard.

The matter which detains me now will seem
To many neither dignified enough   490
Nor arduous, and is, doubtless, in itself
Humble and low, yet not to be despised
By those who have observed the curious props
By which the perishable hours of life
Rest on each other, and the world of thought
Exists and is sustained. More lofty Themes,
Such as at least do wear a prouder face,
Might here be spoken of: but when I think
Of these I feel the imaginative Power
Languish within me; even then it slept   500
When, wrought upon by tragic sufferings,
The heart was full; amid my sobs and tears
It slept, even in the season of my youth:
For though I was most passionately moved
And yielded to the changes of the scene
With most obsequious* feeling, yet all this
Passed not beyond the suburbs of the mind.
If aught there were of real grandeur here
'Twas only then when gross realities,
The incarnation of the Spirits that moved   510
Amid the Poet's beauteous world, called forth,
With that distinctness which a contrast gives

■ *W's imagination sleeps during such diversion, though by contrast this reminds him of a higher poetry, a more serious calling.*

■ *In London he hears lawyers, orators, even the Prime Minister . . .*

OBSEQUIOUS: easily led, obedient

Or opposition, made me recognise
As by a glimpse, the things which I had shaped
And yet not shaped, had seen and scarcely seen,
Had felt and thought of in my solitude.

Pass we from entertainments that are such
Professedly to others titled higher,
Yet in the estimate of youth, at least,
More near akin to those than names imply,   520
I mean the brawls* of Lawyers in their Courts
Before the ermined* Judge, or that great Stage
Where Senators, tongue-favoured Men, perform,
Admired and envied. Oh! the beating heart
When one among the prime* of these rose up,
One, of whose name from Childhood we had heard
Familiarly, a household term, like those,
The Bedfords, Glocesters, Salisburys of old,
Which the fifth Harry* talks of. Silence! hush!
This is no trifler, no short-flighted Wit,   530
No stammerer of a minute, painfully
Delivered. No! the Orator hath yoked
The Hours, like young Aurora, to his Car;*
O Presence of delight, can patience e'er
Grow weary of attending on a track
That kindles with such glory? Marvellous!
The enchantment spreads and rises; all are rapt
Astonished; like a Hero in Romance

BRAWLS: arguments
ERMINED: robes graced with white and black-tipped ermine fur
ONE . . . PRIME: William Pitt the Younger, Prime Minister
FIFTH HARRY: Henry V in Shakespeare's play by that name
AURORA . . . CAR: goddess of the dawn, her chariot pulled by the Hours

■ . . . though finally all
these fail to cast their
spell.

■ Elaborate pulpit rhetoric,
full of allusions, seems
too a passing show.

7.11 Studio of Thomas Gainsborough (1727–1788). *William Pitt*, 1787 to 1789.
Yale Center for British Art, Paul Mellon Collection. "Oh! the beating heart / When one
among the prime of these rose up" to speak before parliament.

He winds away his never-ending horn,
Words follow words, sense seems to follow sense;   540

■ What memory and what logic! till the Strain,
Transcendant, superhuman as it is,
Grows tedious even in a young Man's ear.

These are grave follies: other public Shows
The capital City teems with, of a kind
More light, and where but in the holy Church?
There have I seen a comely Bachelor,
Fresh from a toilette of two hours, ascend
The Pulpit, with seraphic glance look up,
And, in a tone elaborately low   550
■ Beginning, lead his voice through many a maze,
A minuet course, and winding up his mouth
From time to time into an orifice
Most delicate, a lurking eyelet, small
And only not invisible, again
Open it out, diffusing thence a smile
Of rapt irradiation exquisite.
Meanwhile the Evangelists, Isaiah, Job,
Moses, and he who penned* the other day
The Death of Abel, Shakespear, Doctor Young,*   560
And Ossian* (doubt not, 'tis the naked truth),
Summoned from streamy Morven,* each and all
Must in their turn lend ornament and flowers
To entwine the Crook of eloquence with which
This pretty Shepherd, pride of all the Plains,
Leads up and down his captivated Flock.*

HE WHO PENNED: Salomon Gessner

DOCTOR YOUNG: Edward Young

OSSIAN: James Macpherson claimed to have translated an ancient poet, Ossian.

MORVEN: northwestern coast of Scotland in Ossianic poetry

CROOK . . . FLOCK: preachers as shepherds (e.g., 3.414–18)

I glance but at a few conspicuous marks,
Leaving ten thousand others that do each,
In Hall or Court, Conventicle,* or Shop,
In public Room or private, Park or Street,   570
With fondness reared on his own Pedestal,*
Look out for admiration. Folly, vice,
Extravagance in gesture, mien, and dress,
And all the strife of singularity,
Lies to the ear, and lies to every sense,
Of these and of the living shapes they wear
There is no end. Such Candidates for regard,
Although well pleased to be where they were found,
I did not hunt after or greatly prize,
Nor made unto myself a secret boast   580
Of reading them with quick and curious eye,
But as a common produce, things that are
Today, tomorrow will be, took of them
Such willing note as, on some errand bound
■ Of pleasure or of love, some Traveller might,
Among a thousand other images,
Of sea-shells that bestud the sandy beach,
Or daisies swarming through the fields in June.

But foolishness, and madness in parade,
Though most at home in this their dear domain,   590
Are scattered every where, no rarities
Even to the rudest novice of the Schools.

■ *He noted, read, and heard such a great deal, yet never were these urban things highly prized.*

■ *Among the many faces, all mysteries, one face that could not see him yet remains, an unforgettable vision.*

O Friend! one feeling was there which belonged
To this great City by exclusive right:
How often in the overflowing Streets
Have I gone forwards with the Crowd and said
Unto myself, the face of every one
That passes by me is a mystery.
Thus have I looked, nor ceased to look, oppressed
By thoughts of what, and whither, when and how   600
Until the shapes before my eyes became
A second-sight procession,* such as glides
Over still mountains, or appears in dreams;
And all the ballast of familiar life,
The present, and the past, hope, fear, all stays,
All laws of acting, thinking, speaking Man
Went from me, neither knowing me nor known.
And once, far-travelled in such mood, beyond
The reach of common indications, lost
■ Amid the moving pageant, 'twas my chance   610
Abruptly to be smitten with the view
Of a blind Beggar, who, with upright face
Stood propped against a Wall, upon his Chest
Wearing a written paper to explain
The Story of the Man and who he was.
My mind did at this spectacle turn round
As with the might of waters, and it seemed
To me that in this Label was a type
Or emblem of the utmost that we know

CONVENTICLE: place of worship, especially for dissenters
WITH . . . PEDESTAL: i.e., each fondly placed on its own pedestal

SECOND-SIGHT PROCESSION: of visionary clairvoyance, here related to a Lake District legend

Both of ourselves and of the universe;   620

And on the shape of this unmoving Man,

His fixèd face and sightless eyes, I looked

As if admonished from another world.

The city yields strange ■ Though reared upon the base of outward things,
times of pause and
calm—silence, beauty . . . ■ These chiefly are such structures as the mind

Builds for itself. Scenes different there are,

Full formed, which take, with small internal help,

Possession of the faculties, the peace

Of night, for instance, the solemnity

Of nature's intermediate hours of rest,   630

When the great tide of human life stands still,

The business of the day to come unborn,

Of that gone by locked up as in the grave;

The calmness, beauty of the spectacle,

Sky, stillness, moonshine, empty streets, and sounds

Unfrequent as in desarts: at late hours

Of winter evenings when unwholesome rains

. . . yet violence, too,   Are falling hard, with people yet astir,
action crazed . . .
The feeble salutation from the voice

Of some unhappy Woman,* now and then   640

Heard as we pass; when no one looks about,

Nothing is listened to. But these I fear

Are falsely catalogued, things that are, are not

Even as we give them welcome, or assist,

Are prompt, or are remiss. What say you then

UNHAPPY WOMAN: an unfortunate prostitute

7.12 John Bluck (active 1791–1831), Thomas Rowlandson (1756–1827), after Augustus Charles Pugin (1762–1832). *Bartholomew Fair*, 1808. Yale Center for British Art, Paul Mellon Collection. Wordsworth describes in detail the annual Fair with its "far-fetched, perverted things, / All freaks of Nature."

To times when half the City shall break out

■ Full of one passion, vengeance, rage, or fear,

To executions,* to a Street on fire,

Mobs, riots,* or rejoicings? From these sights

Take one, an annual Festival, the Fair*   650

Holden where Martyrs suffered in past time,

And named of Saint Bartholomew; there see

A work that's finished to our hands, that lays,

If any spectacle on earth can do,

EXECUTIONS: Public hangings were common.

RIOTS: W may be recalling the Gordon Riots of 1780.

FAIR: Bartholomew Fair, held every September

The whole creative powers of man asleep!
For once the Muse's help will we implore,
And she shall lodge us, wafted on her wings,
Above the press and danger of the Crowd,
Upon some Show-man's platform: what a hell

■ . . . and the varied spec-
tacles of Bartholomew
Fair that put creative
power to sleep.

■ For eyes and ears! what anarchy and din   660
Barbarian and infernal! 'tis a dream
Monstrous in colour, motion, shape, sight, sound.
Below, the open space, through every nook
Of the wide area, twinkles, is alive
With heads; the midway region and above
Is thronged with staring pictures, and huge scrolls,
Dumb proclamations of the prodigies,
And chattering monkeys dangling from their poles,
And children whirling in their roundabouts,
With those that stretch the neck, and strain the eyes,   670
And crack the voice in rivalship, the crowd

■ The Fair seems a version
of London's very self.

Inviting, with buffoons against buffoons
Grimacing, writhing, screaming, him who grinds
The hurdy-gurdy, at the fiddle weaves,*
Rattles the salt-box,* thumps the kettle-drum,
And him who at the trumpet puffs his cheeks,
The silver-collared Negro* with his timbrel,*
Equestrians, Tumblers, Women, Girls and Boys,
Blue-breeched, pink-vested, and with towering plumes.
—All moveables of wonder from all parts   680
Are here, Albinos, painted Indians, Dwarfs,

WEAVES: moves his bow across the strings
SALT-BOX: used as a small percussion or rhythm instrument
SILVER-COLLARED NEGRO: suggesting slavery, still legal
TIMBREL: older type of tambourine

The Horse of Knowledge, and the learned Pig,
The Stone-eater, the Man that swallows fire,
Giants, Ventriloquists, the Invisible Girl,
The Bust that speaks, and moves its goggling eyes,
The Wax-work, Clock-work, all the marvellous craft
Of modern Merlins,* wild Beasts, Puppet Shews,
All out-o'-th'-way, far-fetched, perverted things,
All freaks of Nature, all Promethean* thoughts
Of Man, his dullness, madness, and their feats,   690
All jumbled up together to make up
This Parliament of Monsters: Tents and Booths,
Meanwhile, as if the whole were one vast Mill,*
Are vomiting, receiving, on all sides,
Men, Women, three years' Children, Babes in arms.

Oh! blank confusion, and a type* not false
Of what the mighty City is itself
■ To all except a Straggler here and there,
To the whole swarm of its inhabitants;
An undistinguishable world to men,   700
The slaves* unrespited of low pursuits,
Living amid the same perpetual flow
Of trivial objects, melted and reduced
To one identity, by differences
That have no law, no meaning, and no end,
Oppression under which even highest minds
Must labour, whence the strongest are not free.

MODERN MERLINS: fortunetellers, from the figure in Arthurian legend
PROMETHEAN: inventive, but here meaning misguided, imprudent
MILL: place of mechanical production, factory
TYPE: image or symbol, here as a microcosm
SLAVES: those trapped by their own coarse desires

But though the picture weary out the eye,

By nature an unmanageable sight,

It is not wholly so to him who looks   710

In steadiness, who hath among least things

An under sense of greatest, sees the parts

As parts, but with a feeling of the whole.

This, of all acquisitions first, awaits

On sundry and most widely different modes

Of education; nor with least delight

On that through which I passed. Attention comes,

And comprehensiveness, and memory,

From early converse with the works of God

Among all regions: chiefly where appear   720

Most obviously simplicity and power.

By influence habitual to the mind

The mountain's outline and its steady form

Gives a pure grandeur, and its presence shapes

■ The measure and the prospect of the soul

To majesty; such virtue have the forms

Perennial of the ancient hills; nor less

The changeful language of their countenances

Gives movement to the thoughts, and multitude,

With order and relation. This, if still,   730

As hitherto, with freedom I may speak,

And the same perfect openness of mind,

7.13 Francis Towne (1740–1816). *The Entrance into Borrowdale*, undated. Yale Center for British Art, Paul Mellon Collection. "By influence habitual to the mind / The mountain's outline and its steady form / Gives a pure grandeur." This is the language of the sublime: "simplicity and power."

Not violating any just restraint,

As I would hope, of real modesty,

This did I feel in that vast receptacle:

The Spirit of Nature was upon me here,

The Soul of Beauty and enduring life

Was present as a habit and diffused,

Through meagre lines and colours, and the press

Of self-destroying, transitory things,   740

Composure and ennobling Harmony.

■ *What shapes a comprehensive mind best emanates from the spirit of natural forms and the soul of beauty. Such habitual presence turns to harmony poor arts and even passing shows that otherwise would corrode the self.*

Book Eighth

RETROSPECT—LOVE OF NATURE
LEADING TO LOVE OF MANKIND

What sounds are those, Helvellyn, which are heard
Up to thy summit? Through the depth of air
Ascending, as if distance had the power
To make the sounds more audible: what Crowd
Is yon, assembled in the gay green field?
Crowd seems it, solitary Hill! to thee,
Though but a little Family of Men,
Twice twenty, with their Children and their Wives,
And here and there a Stranger interspersed.

■ *Sounds of a summer fair held in the fields reach even higher peaks.*

■ It is a summer Festival, a Fair,   10
Such as, on this side now, and now on that,
Repeated through his tributary Vales,
Helvellyn, in the silence of his rest,
Sees annually, if storms be not abroad
And mists have left him an unshrouded head.
Delightful day it is for all who dwell
In this secluded Glen, and eagerly
They give it welcome. Long ere heat of noon
Behold the cattle are driven down; the sheep
That have for traffic* been culled out are penned   20

TRAFFIC: trade, selling

In cotes* that stand together on the Plain
Ranged side by side; the chaffering* is begun.
The Heifer lows uneasy at the voice
Of a new Master, bleat the Flocks aloud;
Booths are there none; a Stall or two is here,
A lame Man, or a blind, the one to beg,
The other to make music; hither, too,
From far, with Basket slung upon her arm
Of Hawker's wares, books, pictures, combs, and pins,
Some agèd Woman finds her way again,   30
Year after year a punctual Visitant!
The Show-man with his Freight upon his Back,
And once, perchance, in lapse of many years,
Prouder Itinerant, Mountebank,* or He
Whose Wonders in a covered Wain* lie hid.
But One is here, the loveliest of them all,
Some sweet Lass of the Valley, looking out
For gains, and who that sees her would not buy?
Fruits of her Father's Orchard, apples, pears,
(On that day only to such office stooping)   40
She carries in her Basket, and walks round
Among the crowd half pleased with, half ashamed
Of her new calling, blushing restlessly.
The Children now are rich, the old Man now
Is generous; so gaiety prevails
Which all partake of, Young and Old. Immense
Is the Recess, the circumambient World

COTES: structures protecting animals, e.g., dovecote
CHAFFERING: haggling
MOUNTEBANK: seller of dubious medicine, a trickster
WAIN: large uncovered wagon

8.1 Attributed to Luke Clennell (1781–1840). *A Village Fair*, unknown date. National Trust, Upton House, Warwickshire / National Trust Images / Angelo Hornak / Art Resource, NY. Grasmere's annual "summer Festival, a Fair," occurred in early September: "Fruits of her Father's Orchard, apples, pears . . . She carries in her Basket."

8.2 Charles Leslie (1835–1890). *Thirlmere Looking towards Helvellyn*, 1882. National Trust, Grasmere, Cumbria / National Trust Photographic Library / Bridgeman Images. In her *Grasmere Journals*, Dorothy wrote in 1800 that she and William talked of building "a house on Helvellyn"—never fulfilled. He and Coleridge climbed "thy summit" on November 5, 1799.

Magnificent, by which they are embraced.

They move about upon the soft green field:

■ *While seeming insigni -*
ficant, the people there,
bonded with their
surroundings, become
naturally great.

■ How little They, they and their doings seem,   50

Their herds and flocks about them, they themselves,

And all which they can further or obstruct!

Through utter weakness pitiably dear,

As tender Infants are: and yet how great!

For all things serve them; them the Morning-light

Loves as it glistens on the silent rocks,

And them the silent Rocks which now from high

Look down upon them; the reposing Clouds,

The lurking Brooks from their invisible haunts,

And Old Helvellyn, conscious of the stir,   60

And the blue sky that roofs their calm abode.

With deep devotion, Nature, did I feel

In that great City* what I owed to thee,

High thoughts of God and Man, and love of Man,

Triumphant over all those loathsome sights

Of wretchedness and vice; a watchful eye,

Which with the outside of our human life

Not satisfied, must read the inner mind;

■ *Love of Nature comes*
closely bound with love
of humankind.

■ For I already had been taught to love

My Fellow-beings, to such habits trained   70

Among the woods and mountains, where I found

In thee* a gracious Guide, to lead me forth

Beyond the bosom of my Family,

My Friends and youthful Playmates. 'Twas thy power

That raised the first complacency* in me,

And noticeable kindliness of heart,

Love human to the Creature in himself

As he appeared, a Stranger in my path,

Before my eyes a Brother of this world;

Thou first didst with those motions of delight   80

Inspire me.—I remember, far from home

Once having strayed, while yet a very Child,

I saw a sight, and with what joy and love!

It was a day of exhalations spread

Upon the mountains, mists and steam-like fogs

Redounding every-where, not vehement,

But calm and mild, gentle and beautiful,

With gleams of sunshine on the eyelet spots

And loopholes of the hills, wherever seen,

Hidden by quiet process, and as soon   90

Unfolded, to be huddled up again:

Along a narrow Valley and profound

I journeyed, when, aloft above my head,

Emerging from the silvery vapours, lo!

A Shepherd and his Dog! in open day:

Girt round with mists they stood and looked about

From that enclosure small, inhabitants

Of an aerial Island floating on,

CITY: London
THEE: Nature

COMPLACENCY: contented or calm pleasure (no negative sense)

A Shepherd in the bottom of a Vale
Towards the centre standing, who with voice,
And hand waved to and fro as need required,
Gave signal to his Dog, thus teaching him
To chace along the mazes of steep crags
The Flock he could not see: and so the Brute,   110
Dear Creature! with a Man's intelligence
Advancing, or retreating on his steps,
Through every pervious strait,* to right or left,
Thridded* away unbaffled; while the Flock
Fled upwards from the terror of his bark
Through rocks and seams of turf with liquid gold
Irradiate, that deep farewell light by which
The setting sun proclaims the love he bears
To mountain regions.

               B eauteous the domain
Where to the sense of beauty first my heart   120
Was opened, tract more exquisitely fair
Than is that Paradise of ten thousand Trees,
Or Gehol's famous Gardens,* in a Clime
Chosen from widest Empire, for delight
Of the Tartarian Dynasty composed;
(Beyond that mighty Wall,* not fabulous,
China's stupendous mound!) by patient skill
Of myriads, and boon Nature's lavish help:
Scene linked to scene, an ever growing change,

PERVIOUS STRAIT: narrow passage
THRIDDED: threaded
GEHOL'S . . . GARDENS: created by a Chinese emperor in Zhe-hol, Tartary
WALL: Great Wall of China

8.3 Edmund Bristow (1787–1876). *A Traveller and a Shepherd in a Landscape*, 1825. Yale Center for British Art, Paul Mellon Collection. "I beheld . . . A Shepherd in the bottom of a Vale . . . who with voice . . . Gave signal to his Dog."

As seemed, with that Abode in which they were,
A little pendant area of grey rocks,
By the soft wind breathed forward. With delight   100
As bland almost, one Evening I beheld,
And at as early age (the spectacle
Is common, but by me was then first seen)

Soft, grand, or gay! with Palaces and Domes   130
Of Pleasure spangled over, shady Dells
For Eastern Monasteries, sunny Mounds
With Temples crested, Bridges, Gondolas,
Rocks, Dens, and Groves of foliage taught to melt
Into each other their obsequious* hues
Going and gone again, in subtile chace,*
Too fine to be pursued; or standing forth
In no discordant opposition, strong
And gorgeous as the colours side by side
Bedded among the plumes of Tropic Birds;   140
And mountains over all embracing all;
And all the landscape endlessly enriched
With waters running, falling, or asleep.

But lovelier far than this the Paradise
Where I was reared; in Nature's primitive gifts
Favored no less, and more to every sense
■ Delicious, seeing that the sun and sky,
The elements and seasons in their change
Do find their dearest Fellow-labourer there,
The heart of Man; a district on all sides   150
The fragrance breathing of humanity,
Man free, man working for himself, with choice
Of time, and place, and object; by his wants,
His comforts, native occupations, cares,
Conducted on to individual ends

OBSEQUIOUS: here, easily blended and successive

SUBTILE CHACE: fine mixture

8.4 Charles Towne (1763–1840). *Landscape with a Shepherd*, c. 1800. Yale Center for British Art, Paul Mellon Collection. The delicious "Paradise / Where I was reared"— a landscape with "The fragrance breathing of humanity, / Man free, man working for himself."

Or social, and still followed by a train
Unwooed, unthought-of even, simplicity
And beauty, and inevitable grace.

Yea, doubtless, at an age when but a glimpse
Of those resplendent Gardens, with their frame   160
Imperial, and elaborate ornaments,
Would to a Child be transport over-great,
When but a half-hour's roam through such a place

■ *W believes he was raised in a place blessed to bring its elements in contact with the human heart . . .*

Would leave behind a dance of images
That shall break in upon his sleep for weeks;
Even then the common haunts of the green earth
With the ordinary human interests
■ Which they embosom, all without regard
As both may seem, are fastening on the heart
Insensibly, each with the other's help,   170
So that we love, not knowing that we love,
And feel, not knowing whence our feeling comes.

S uch league have these two principles of joy
In our affections. I have singled out
Some moments, the earliest that I could, in which
Their several currents blended into one,
Weak yet, and gathering imperceptibly,
Flowed in by gushes. My first human love,
As hath been mentioned, did incline to those
Whose occupations and concerns were most   180
Illustrated by Nature and adorned,
And Shepherds were the Men who pleased me first.
■ Not such as in Arcadian Fastnesses*
Sequestered, handed down among themselves,
So ancient Poets sing, the golden Age;
Nor such, a second Race, allied to these,
As Shakespeare in the Wood of Arden placed
Where Phoebe sighed for the false Ganymede,
Or there where Florizel and Perdita*

■ *. . . and it impresses itself on the young inhabitant more perhaps than some exotic scene or famous garden.*

■ *True shepherds of his day hold more of worth and authenticity than storied ones of old.*

8.5 Francis Towne (1740–1816). *Ambleside*, 1786. Yale Center for British Art, Paul Mellon Collection. With its "common haunts of the green earth," Ambleside, three miles southeast of Grasmere, was in Wordsworth's time one of the most picturesque locations in Great Britain.

FASTNESSES: remote areas, strongholds
PHOEBE . . . PERDITA: characters in Shakespeare's pastoral settings

8.6 Joshua Cristall (1768–1847). *Arcadian Landscape with Shepherds*, 1814. Yale Center for British Art, Paul Mellon Collection. "And Shepherds were the Men who pleased me first. / Not such as in Arcadian Fastnesses / Sequestered . . . So ancient Poets sing, the golden Age." Wordsworth questioned such older accounts of pastoral life.

Together danced, Queen of the Feast and King;
Nor such as Spenser fabled. True it is
That I had heard what he perhaps had seen,

190

Of maids at sunrise bringing in from far
Their May-bush,* and along the Streets, in flocks,
Parading with a Song of taunting rhymes,

MAY-BUSH: hawthorn

8.7 J. M. W. Turner (1775–1851). *Slave Ship (Slavers Throwing Overboard the Dead and Dying, Typhoon Coming On)*, 1840. Museum of Fine Arts, Boston / Bridgeman Images. "But images of danger and distress, / And suffering, these took deepest hold of me, / Man suffering among awful Powers, and Forms."

Aimed at the Laggards slumbering within doors,
Had also heard, from those who yet remembered,
Tales of the May-pole dance, and flowers that decked
The Posts and the Kirk-pillars,* and of Youths
That each one with his Maid at break of day   200
By annual custom issued forth in troops
To drink the waters of some favourite Well
And hang it round with Garlands. This, alas,
Was but a dream; the times had scattered all
These lighter graces, and the rural ways
And manners, which it was my chance to see
In childhood, were severe and unadorned,
The unluxuriant produce of a life
Intent on little but substantial* needs,
Yet beautiful, and beauty that was felt.   210
But images of danger and distress,
And suffering, these took deepest hold of me,
Man suffering among awful Powers, and Forms:
Of this I heard and saw enough to make
The imagination restless; nor was free

■ *Their work will call to mind tales of risk and danger.*
■ Myself from frequent perils; nor were tales
Wanting, the tragedies of former times,
Or hazards and escapes, which in my walks
I carried with me among crags and woods
And mountains; and of these may here be told   220
One, as recorded by my Household Dame.*

KIRK-PILLARS: church pillars, often decorative
SUBSTANTIAL: subsistence, and hard to secure
HOUSEHOLD DAME: Ann Tyson

8.8 George Morland (1763–1804). *Winter Landscape*, 1790. Yale Center for British Art, Paul Mellon Collection. "At the first falling of autumnal snow / A Shepherd and his Son one day went forth / (Thus did the Matron's Tale begin) to seek / A Straggler of their Flock."

At the first falling of autumnal snow
A Shepherd and his Son one day went forth
(Thus did the Matron's Tale begin) to seek
A Straggler of their Flock. They both had ranged
Upon this service the preceding day
All over their own pastures and beyond,
And now, at sun-rise sallying out again
Renewed their search, begun where from Dove Crag,*
Ill home for bird so gentle, they looked down   230

DOVE CRAG: northeast of Grasmere

On Deep-dale Head, and Brothers-water, named
From those two Brothers that were drowned therein.

■ *One such tale, heard from Ann Tyson, he now recounts.*

■ Thence northward, having passed by Arthur's Seat,
To Fairfield's highest summit, on the right
Leaving St. Sunday's Pike, to Grisedale Tarn
They shot, and over that cloud-loving hill,
Seat Sandal, a fond lover of the clouds;
Thence up Helvellyn, a superior Mount
With prospect underneath of Striding-edge,
And Grisedale's houseless Vale, along the brink   240
Of Russet Cove,* and those two other Coves,
Huge skeletons of crags, which from the trunk
Of old Helvellyn spread their arms abroad,
And make a stormy harbour for the winds.
Far went those Shepherds in their devious* quest,
From mountain ridges peeping as they passed
Down into every Glen: at length the Boy
Said, 'Father, with your leave I will go back,
And range the ground which we have searched before.'
So speaking, southward down the hill the Lad   250
Sprang like a gust of wind, crying aloud,
'I know where I shall find him.' 'For take note,'
Said here my grey-haired Dame, 'that tho' the storm
Drive one of these poor Creatures miles and miles,
If he can crawl he will return again
To his own hills, the spots where, when a Lamb,
He learned to pasture at his Mother's side.'

RUSSET COVE: now called Brown Cove
DEVIOUS: changing, turning from a regular path

After so long a labour, suddenly
Bethinking him of this, the Boy
Pursued his way towards a brook whose course   260
Was through that unfenced tract of mountain-ground
Which to his Father's little Farm belonged,
The home and ancient Birth-right of their Flock.
Down the deep channel of the Stream he went,
Prying through every nook; meanwhile the rain
Began to fall upon the mountain tops,
Thick storm and heavy which for three hours' space
Abated not; and all that time the Boy
Was busy in his search until at length
He spied the Sheep upon a plot of grass,   270
An Island in the Brook. It was a place
Remote and deep, piled round with rocks where foot
Of man or beast was seldom used to tread;
But now, when every where the summer grass
Had failed, this one Adventurer, hunger-pressed,
Had left his Fellows, and made his way alone
To the green plot of pasture in the Brook.
Before the Boy knew well what he had seen
He leapt upon the Island with proud heart
And with a Prophet's joy. Immediately   280
The Sheep sprang forward to the further Shore
And was borne headlong by the roaring flood.
At this the Boy looked round him, and his heart
Fainted with fear; thrice did he turn his face

To either brink; nor could he summon up

The courage that was needful to leap back

Cross the tempestuous torrent; so he stood,

A Prisoner on the Island, not without

More than one thought of death and his last hour.

Meanwhile the Father had returned alone   290

To his own house; and now at the approach

Of evening he went forth to meet his Son,

Conjecturing vainly for what cause the Boy

Had stayed so long. The Shepherd took his way

Up his own mountain grounds, where, as he walked

Along the Steep that overhung the Brook,

He seemed to hear a voice, which was again

Repeated, like the whistling of a kite.*

At this, not knowing why, as oftentimes

Long afterwards he has been heard to say,   300

Down to the Brook he went, and tracked its course

Upwards among th' o'erhanging rocks; nor thus

Had he gone far, ere he espied the Boy

Where on that little plot of ground he stood

Right in the middle of the roaring Stream,

Now stronger every moment and more fierce.

The sight was such as no one could have seen

Without distress and fear. The Shepherd heard

The outcry of his Son, he stretched his Staff

Towards him, bade him leap, which word scarce said   310

The Boy was safe within his Father's arms.

KITE: a bird of prey

Smooth life had Flock and Shepherd in old time,

Long Springs and tepid Winters on the Banks

Of delicate Galesus;* and no less

Those scattered along Adria's* myrtle Shores:

Smooth life the herdsman and his snow-white Herd

To Triumphs and to sacrificial Rites

Devoted, on the inviolable Stream

Of rich Clitumnus;* and the Goatherd lived

As sweetly, underneath the pleasant brows   320

Of cool Lucretilis,* where the Pipe was heard

Of Pan, the invisible God, thrilling the rocks

With tutelary* music, from all harm

The Fold protecting. I myself, mature

In manhood then, have seen a pastoral Tract

Like one of these where Fancy might run wild,

Though under skies less generous and serene;

Yet there, as for herself, had Nature framed

A Pleasure-ground, diffused a fair expanse

Of level Pasture, islanded with Groves   330

And banked with woody risings; but the plain

Endless, here opening widely out, and there

Shut up in lesser lakes or beds of lawn

And intricate recesses, creek or bay

Sheltered within a shelter, where at large

The Shepherd strays, a rolling hut his home:

Thither he comes with spring-time, there abides

All summer; and at sunrise ye may hear

GALESUS: pastoral river in southern Italy

ADRIA'S: the Adriatic Sea's

CLITUMNUS: pastoral river in central Italy

LUCRETILIS: a mountain near Horace's Sabine farm

TUTELARY: guardian or protecting

Such stories of his own land lead to pastoral thoughts of other times and places . . .

His flute or flagelet* resounding far;
There's not a Nook or Hold of that vast Space,   340
Nor Strait where passage is, but it shall have
In turn its Visitant, telling there his hours
In unlaborious pleasure, with no task
More toilsome than to carve a beechen bowl
For Spring or Fountain, which the Traveller finds
When through the region he pursues at will

■ *. . . including what he
saw in Germany.*

■ His devious course. A glimpse of such sweet life
I saw, when from the melancholy Walls
Of Goslar,* once Imperial! I renewed
My daily walk along that chearful Plain,   350
Which reaching to her Gates, spreads East and West
And Northwards, from beneath the mountainous verge
Of the Hercynian forest. Yet hail to You,
Your rocks and precipices, Ye that seize
The heart with firmer grasp! your snows and streams
Ungovernable, and your terrifying winds
That howled so dismally when I have been

■ *The shepherd's difficult
task yet brings dignity,
and freedom.*

Companionless among your solitudes.
There 'tis the Shepherd's task the winter long
To wait upon the storms: of their approach   360
Sagacious,* from the height he drives his Flock
Down into sheltering coves, and feeds them there
Through the hard time, long as the storm is locked,
(So do they phrase it) bearing from the stalls
A toilsome burthen* up the craggy ways,

FLAGELET: pipe or recorder
GOSLAR: city near Harz (Hercynian) forest in Germany
SAGACIOUS: aware, even predicting
BURTHEN: a load of hay or fodder

To strew it on the snow. And when the Spring
Looks out, and all the mountains dance with lambs,
He through the enclosures won from the steep Waste,
And through the lower Heights hath gone his rounds;
And when the Flock with warmer weather climbs   370
Higher and higher, him his office leads
To range among them, through the hills dispersed,
And watch their goings, whatsoever track
Each Wanderer chuses for itself; a work
That lasts the summer through. He quits his home
At day-spring, and no sooner doth the sun
Begin to strike him with a fire-like heat
Than he lies down upon some shining place
And breakfasts with his Dog: when he hath stayed,   380
As for the most he doth, beyond his time,
He springs up with a bound, and then away!
Ascending fast with his long Pole in hand,
Or winding in and out among the crags.
What need to follow him through what he does

■ Or sees in his day's march? He feels himself
In those vast regions where his service is
A Freeman; wedded to his life of hope
And hazard, and hard labour interchanged
With that majestic indolence so dear
To native Man.* A rambling School-boy, thus   390
Have I beheld him, without knowing why
Have felt his presence in his own domain

NATIVE MAN: natural or original human nature

As of a Lord and Master; or a Power

Or Genius,* under Nature, under God

Presiding; and severest solitude

Seemed more commanding oft when he was there.

Seeking the raven's nest, and suddenly

Surprized with vapours, or on rainy days

When I have angled up the lonely brooks

Mine eyes have glanced upon him, few steps off,   400

In size a Giant, stalking through the fog,

His Sheep like Greenland Bears: at other times,

When round some shady promontory turning,

His Form hath flashed upon me, glorified

By the deep radiance of the setting sun:

Or him have I descried in distant sky,

A solitary object and sublime,

Above all height! like an aerial Cross,

As it is stationed on some spiry Rock

■ *Seeing such simple, hard work in nature elevates W's sense of humankind.*

■ Of the Chartreuse,* for worship. Thus was Man   410

Ennobled outwardly before mine eyes,

And thus my heart at first was introduced

To an unconscious love and reverence

Of human Nature; hence the human form

To me was like an index of delight,

Of grace and honour, power and worthiness.

■ *Those who think such reverence false will miss the spirit holding man and nature joined as one.*

Meanwhile this Creature, spiritual almost

As those of Books, but more exalted far,

Far more of an imaginative form,

GENIUS: presiding spirit, here of a particular place

CHARTREUSE: mountains in southeastern France

Was not a Corin of the groves, who lives   420

For his own fancies, or to dance by the hour

In coronal,* with Phillis* in the midst,

But for the purposes of kind,* a Man

With the most common, Husband, Father; learned,

Could teach, admonish, suffered with the rest

From vice and folly, wretchedness and fear;

Of this I little saw, cared less for it,

But something must have felt.

               Call ye these appearances

Which I beheld of Shepherds in my youth,

This sanctity of Nature given to Man   430

A shadow, a delusion, ye who are fed

By the dead letter, miss the spirit* of things,

Whose truth is not a motion or a shape

Instinct with vital functions, but a Block

Or waxen Image which yourselves have made,

And ye adore. But blessèd be the God

Of Nature and of Man that this was so,

That Men did at the first present themselves

Before my untaught eyes thus purified,

■ Removed, and at a distance that was fit.   440

And so we all of us in some degree

Are led to knowledge, whencesoever led,

And howsoever; were it otherwise,

And we found evil fast as we find good

CORIN . . . PHILLIS: common names from classical pastorals

IN CORONAL: in a circle or ring (from crown or wreath)

OF KIND: of real human activity

LETTER . . . SPIRIT: 2 Corinthians 3:6

In our first years, or think that it is found,
How could the innocent heart bear up and live!
But doubly fortunate my lot; not here
Alone, that something of a better life
Perhaps was round me than it is the privilege
Of most to move in, but that first I looked   450
At Man through objects that were great and fair,
First communed with him by their help. And thus
Was founded a sure safeguard and defence
Against the weight of meanness,* selfish cares,
Coarse manners, vulgar passions that beat in
On all sides from the ordinary world
In which we traffic. Starting from this point,
I had my face towards the truth, began
With an advantage; furnished with that kind
Of prepossession without which the soul   460
Receives no knowledge that can bring forth good,
No genuine insight ever comes to her:
Happy in this, that I with nature walked,
Not having a too early intercourse
With the deformities of crowded life,
And those ensuing laughters and contempts
Self-pleasing, which if we would wish to think
With admiration and respect of man
Will not permit us; but pursue the mind
That to devotion willingly would be raised   470
Into the Temple and the Temple's heart.

■ *What first was implanted by these experiences has later deepened and matured.*

MEANNESS: what is trivial, low, insignificant

Yet do not deem, my Friend, though thus I speak
Of Man as having taken in my mind
A place thus early which might almost seem
Preeminent, that this was really so.
Nature herself was at this unripe time,
But secondary to my own pursuits
And animal activities, and all
Their trivial pleasures: and long afterwards
■ When these had died away and Nature did   480
For her own sake become my joy, even then
And upwards through late youth, until not less
Than three and twenty summers had been told
Was man in my affections and regards
Subordinate to her; her awful forms
And viewless agencies: a passion she!
A rapture often, and immediate joy,
Ever at hand; he distant, but a grace
Occasional, an accidental thought,
His hour being not yet come. Far less had then   490
The inferior Creatures, beast or bird, attuned
My spirit to that gentleness of love,
Won from me those minute obeisances
Of tenderness which I may number now
With my first blessings. Nevertheless, on these
The light of beauty did not fall in vain,
Or grandeur circumfuse them to no end.

8.9 James Ward (1769–1859). *A Harvest Scene with Workers Loading Hay on to a Farm Wagon,* 1800. Yale Center for British Art, Paul Mellon Collection. "Men and Boys / In festive summer busy with the rake."

Why should I speak of Tillers of the soil?
The Ploughman and his Team; or Men and Boys
In festive summer busy with the rake,   500
Old Men and ruddy Maids, and Little-ones
All out together, and in sun and shade

Dispersed among the hay-grounds alder-fringed,
The Quarry-man, far heard! that blasts the rocks,
The Fishermen in pairs, the one to row
And one to drop the Net, plying their trade
"Mid tossing lakes and tumbling boats' and winds

8.10 James Ward (1769–1859). *The Reapers*, 1800. Yale Center for British Art, Paul Mellon Collection. "The Ploughman and his Team . . . Old Men and ruddy Maids, and Little-ones / All out together."

Whistling;* the Miner, melancholy Man!
That works by taper light, while all the hills
Are shining with the glory of the day.   510

But when that first poetic Faculty
Of plain imagination and severe,
No longer a mute Influence of the soul,
An Element of the Nature's inner self,

■ *Fanciful impulses
worked on these common
elements of human life
an instinct of exagger-
ation . . .*

■ Began to have some promptings to put on
A visible shape, and to the works of art,
The notions and the images of books
Did knowingly conform itself, by these
Enflamed, and proud of that her new delight,
There came among those shapes of human life   520
A wilfulness of fancy and conceit
Which gave them new importance to the mind;
And Nature and her objects beautified
These fictions, as in some sort in their turn
They burnished her. From touch of this new power
Nothing was safe: the Elder-tree that grew
Beside the well-known Charnel-house* had then
A dismal look; the Yew-tree had its Ghost

■ *. . . or embellishment . . .*

That took its station there for ornament:
Then common death was none, common mishap,   530
But matter for this humour every where,
The tragic super-tragic, else left short.
Then, if a Widow staggering with the blow

"'Mid . . . boats' and winds Whistling: a line and phrase from the poet James Graham
Charnel-house: where bones from old graves are kept

Of her distress was known to have made her way
To the cold grave in which her Husband slept
One night, or haply more than one, through pain
Or half-insensate impotence of mind
The fact was caught at greedily, and there
She was a Visitant the whole year through,
Wetting the turf with never-ending tears,   540
And all the storms of Heaven must beat on her.

Through wild obliquities could I pursue
Among all objects of the fields and groves
These cravings: when the Fox-glove, one by one,
Upwards through every stage of its tall stem
Had shed its bells, and stood by the way-side
Dismantled, with a single one perhaps
Left at the ladder's top, with which the Plant
Appeared to stoop, as slender blades of grass
Tipped with a bead of rain or dew, behold!   550
If such a sight were seen, would Fancy bring
Some Vagrant thither with her Babes, and seat her
Upon the turf beneath the stately flower
Drooping in sympathy, and making so
■ A melancholy Crest above the head
Of the lorn Creature, while her Little-ones,
All unconcerned with her unhappy plight,
Were sporting with the purple cups that lay
Scattered upon the ground.

There was a Copse,

An upright bank of wood and woody rock   560

That opposite our rural Dwelling* stood,

In which a sparkling patch of diamond light

Was in bright weather duly to be seen

On summer afternoons within the wood

At the same place. 'Twas doubtless nothing more

Than a black rock, which wet with constant springs

Glistered far seen from out its lurking-place

As soon as ever the declining sun

Had smitten it. Beside our Cottage hearth,

Sitting with open door, a hundred times   570

■ Upon this lustre have I gazed, that seemed

To have some meaning which I could not find;

And now it was a burnished shield, I fancied,

Suspended over a Knight's Tomb, who lay

Inglorious, buried in the dusky wood;

An entrance now into some magic cave

Or Palace for a Fairy of the rock;

Nor would I, though not certain whence the cause

Of the effulgence, thither have repaired

Without a precious bribe, and day by day   580

And month by month I saw the spectacle,

Nor ever once have visited the spot

Unto this hour. Thus sometimes were the shapes

Of wilful fancy grafted upon feelings

Of the imagination, and they rose

RURAL DWELLING: Ann Tyson's cottage at Colthouse

In worth accordingly. My present Theme

Is to retrace the way that led me on

Through Nature to the love of Human Kind;

Nor could I with such object overlook

The influence of this Power* which turned itself   590

Instinctively to human passions, things

Least understood; of this adulterate Power,*

For so it may be called, and without wrong,

When with that first compared. Yet in the midst

Of these vagaries, with an eye so rich

As mine was, through the chance, on me not wasted

Of having been brought up in such a grand

And lovely region, I had forms distinct

To steady me; these thoughts did oft revolve

About some centre palpable which at once   600

Incited them to motion, and controled,

And whatsoever shape the fit might take,

■ And whencesoever it might come, I still

At all times had a real solid world

Of images about me; did not pine

As one in cities bred might do; as Thou,

Belovèd Friend! hast told me that thou didst,

Great Spirit as thou art, in endless dreams

Of sickliness, disjoining, joining things

Without the light of knowledge. Where the harm,   610

If when the Woodman languished with disease

From sleeping night by night among the woods

THIS POWER: imagination
ADULTERATE POWER: "wilful fancy" mixed ("grafted") with imagination

■ *. . . so much so that to the lustre rock he never walked, but kept in mind all its associations, invented and dear.*

■ *Yet there remained a steadying presence of natural forms and real life images . . .*

Within his sod-built Cabin, Indian-wise,
I called the pangs of disappointed love
And all the long Etcetera of such thought
To help him to his grave. Meanwhile the Man,
If not already from the woods retired
To die at home, was haply, as I knew,
Pining alone among the gentle airs,

■ *. . . to counterbalance*
fancied things.

■ Birds, running Streams, and Hills so beautiful   620
On golden evenings, while the charcoal Pile
Breathed up its smoke, an image of his ghost
Or spirit that was soon to take its flight.

■ *His creative power*
growing, it brings, too,
thoughts of human trial
and suffering . . .

There came a time of greater dignity
Which had been gradually prepared, and now
Rushed in as if on wings, the time in which
The pulse of Being every where was felt,
When all the several frames of things, like stars
Through every magnitude distinguishable,
Were half confounded in each other's blaze,   630
One galaxy of life and joy. Then rose
Man, inwardly contemplated, and present
In my own being, to a loftier height;
As of all visible natures crown; and first
In capability of feeling what
Was to be felt; in being rapt away
By the divine effect of power and love,
As more than any thing we know instinct

With Godhead, and by reason and by will
Acknowledging dependency sublime.   640

Erelong transported hence as in a dream
I found myself begirt with temporal shapes
Of vice and folly thrust upon my view,
Objects of sport, and ridicule, and scorn,

■ Manners and characters discriminate,
And little busy passions that eclipsed,
As well they might, the impersonated thought,
The idea or abstraction of the Kind.*
An Idler among academic Bowers,
Such was my new condition, as at large   650
Has been set forth: yet here the vulgar light
Of present actual superficial life,
Gleaming through colouring of other times,
Old usages and local privilege,
Thereby was softened, almost solemnized,
And rendered apt and pleasing to the view;
This notwithstanding, being brought more near,
As I was now, to guilt and wretchedness,
I trembled, thought of human life at times
With an indefinite terror and dismay   660
Such as the storms and angry elements
Had bred in me, but gloomier far, a dim
Analogy to uproar and misrule,
Disquiet, danger, and obscurity.

THE KIND: humankind

—It might be told (but wherefore speak of things
Common to all?) that seeing, I essayed
To give relief, began to deem myself
A moral agent, judging between good
And evil, not as for the mind's delight

■ . . . a moral conscious-
ness, sympathy, and love.

■ But for her safety, one who was to *act*,   670
As sometimes, to the best of my weak means,
I did, by human sympathy impelled;
And through dislike and most offensive pain
Was to the truth conducted; of this faith
Never forsaken, that by acting well
And understanding, I should learn to love,
The end* of life and every thing we know.

Preceptress stern, that did instruct me next,
London! to thee I willingly return.
Erewhile my Verse played only with the flowers   680
Enwrought upon thy mantle,* satisfied
With this amusement, and a simple look
Of childlike inquisition, now and then
Cast upwards on thine eye to puzzle out
Some inner meanings, which might harbour there.
Yet did I not give way to this light mood
Wholly beguiled, as one incapable

■ He reflects on lessons
that London taught,
and his first entrance
into that city.

■ Of higher things, and ignorant that high things
Were round me. Never shall I forget the hour,
The moment rather say, when having thridded   690

END: goal, final meaning
MANTLE: outward covering

The labyrinth of suburban Villages,
At length I did unto myself first seem
To enter the great City. On the roof
Of an itinerant Vehicle I sate
With vulgar Men about me, vulgar* forms
Of houses, pavement, streets, of men and things,
Mean* shapes on every side: but at the time
When to myself it fairly might be said,
The very moment that I seemed to know
The threshold now is overpassed, Great God!   700
That aught *external* to the living mind
Should have such mighty sway! yet so it was
A weight of Ages did at once descend
Upon my heart, no thought embodied, no
Distinct remembrances; but weight and power,
Power growing with the weight: alas! I feel
That I am trifling: 'twas a moment's pause.
All that took place within me came and went
As in a moment, and I only now
Remember that it was a thing divine.   710

As when a Traveller hath from open day
With torches passed into some Vault of Earth,
The Grotto of Antiparos,* or the Den
Of Yordas* among Craven's mountain tracts,
He looks and sees the Cavern spread and grow,
Widening itself on all sides, sees, or thinks

VULGAR: common, ordinary
MEAN: undistinguished, not special
GROTTO OF ANTIPAROS: famous cavern on that Greek isle
DEN OF YORDAS: northern Yorkshire cave (from Norse "earth stream")

He sees, erelong, the roof above his head,
Which instantly unsettles and recedes
Substance and shadow, light and darkness, all
Commingled, making up a Canopy   720
Of Shapes and Forms, and Tendencies to Shape
That shift and vanish, change and interchange
Like Spectres, ferment quiet, and sublime;
Which after short space works less and less

■ *The transforming view
of London he compares,
in a great simile, to the
process of discerning
shadows, shapes, and
substances in some great
cave.*

■ Till every effort, every motion gone,
The scene before him lies in perfect view,
Exposed and lifeless, as a written book.
But let him pause awhile, and look again
And a new quickening* shall succeed, at first
Beginning timidly, then creeping fast   730
Through all which he beholds: the senseless mass
In its projections, wrinkles, cavities,
Through all its surface, with all colours streaming,
Like a magician's airy pageant, parts,
Unites, embodying every where some pressure*

■ *In early manhood this
had pleased him, though
as yet he had not gained
a deeper sense of human
nature.*

Or image recognised or new, some type*
Or picture of the world, forests and lakes,
Ships, Rivers, Towers, the Warrior clad in Mail,
The prancing Steed, the Pilgrim with his Staff,
The mitred Bishop and the thronèd King,   740
A Spectacle to which there is no end.

QUICKENING: enlivening, animating
PRESSURE: stamp, imprint
TYPE: representation

No otherwise had I at first been moved
With such a swell of feeling followed soon
By a blank sense of greatness passed away
And afterwards continued to be moved
In presence of that vast Metropolis,
The Fountain of my Country's destiny
And of the destiny of Earth itself,
That great Emporium, Chronicle at once
And Burial-place of passions and their home   750
Imperial, and chief living residence.

With strong Sensations, teeming as it did
Of past and present, such a place must needs
Have pleased me in those times; I sought not then
Knowledge but craved for power, and power I found
In all things; nothing had a circumscribed
And narrow influence; but all objects, being
Themselves capacious, also found in me
Capaciousness and amplitude of mind:
■ Such is the strength and glory of our Youth.   760
The Human-nature unto which I felt
That I belonged, and which I loved and reverenced,
Was not a punctual* Presence, but a Spirit
Living in time and space, and far diffused.
In this my joy, in this my dignity
Consisted: the external universe,
By striking upon what is found within,

PUNCTUAL: specific to a time and place

Had given me this conception, with the help
Of Books, and what they picture and record.

'Tis true the History of my native Land   770
With those of Greece compared and popular Rome,
Events not lovely nor magnanimous,
But harsh and unaffecting in themselves
And in our high-wrought modern narratives
Stript of their harmonising soul, the life
Of manners and familiar incidents,
Had never much delighted me. And less
Than other minds I had been used to owe
The pleasure which I found in place or thing
To extrinsic transitory accidents,   780
To records or traditions; but a sense
Of what had been here done, and suffered here
Through ages, and was doing, suffering, still
Weighed with me, could support the test of thought,
■ Was like the enduring majesty and power
Of independent nature; and not seldom
Even individual remembrances,
By working on the shapes before my eyes,
Became like vital functions of the soul:
And out of what had been, what was, the place   790
Was thronged with impregnations, like those wilds
In which my early feelings had been nursed,
And naked valleys, full of caverns, rocks

And audible seclusions, dashing lakes,
Echoes and Waterfalls, and pointed crags
That into music touch the passing wind.

Thus here Imagination also found
An element that pleased her, tried her strength,
Among new objects simplified, arranged,
Impregnated my knowledge, made it live,   800
And the result was elevating thoughts
Of human Nature. Neither guilt nor vice,
Debasement of the body, or the mind,
■ Nor all the misery forced upon my sight,
Which was not lightly passed, but often scanned
Most feelingly, could overthrow my trust
In what we may become, induce belief
That I was ignorant, had been falsely taught,
A Solitary, who with vain conceits
Had been inspired, and walked about in dreams.   810
When from that rueful prospect, overcast
And in eclipse, my meditations turned,
Lo! every thing that was indeed divine
Retained its purity inviolate
And unencroached upon, nay, seemed brighter far
For this deep shade in counterview, this gloom
Of opposition, such as shewed itself
To the eyes of Adam, yet in Paradise,
Though fallen from bliss, when 'in the East he saw

■ *Not broad or abstract histories, but specific human events and individual experiences worked most on him, rooted often in familiar places where he was reared.*

■ *Even in London, amid human misery, his creative power could hold a trust in "what we may become."*

8.11 Thomas Cole (1801–1848). *Expulsion from the Garden of Eden*, 1828. Museum of Fine Arts, Boston, Gift of Martha C. Karolik for the M. and M. Karolik Collection of American Paintings, 1815–65 / Bridgeman Images. Here is "this gloom / Of opposition, such as shewed itself / To the eyes of Adam, yet in Paradise, / Though fallen from bliss."

Darkness ere day's mid course, and morning light   820
More orient in the western cloud, that drew
O'er the blue firmament a radiant white,
Descending slow, with something heavenly fraught.'*

■ *The city could be a crucible for deeper hope of human goodness and community . . .*

■ Add also that among the multitudes
Of that great City oftentimes was seen
Affectingly set forth, more than elsewhere
Is possible, the unity of Man,
One spirit over ignorance and vice
Predominant, in good and evil hearts
One sense for moral judgements, as one eye   830
For the sun's light. When strongly breathed upon
By this sensation, whencesoe'er it comes
Of union or communion doth the soul
Rejoice as in her highest joy: for there,
There chiefly hath she feeling whence she is,
And passing through all Nature rests with God.

■ *. . . where its crowds hold countless single acts of tenderness and love.*

■ And is not, too, that vast Abiding-place
Of human Creatures, turn where'er we may,
Profusely sown with individual sights
Of courage, and integrity, and truth,   840
And tenderness, which here set off by foil*
Appears more touching. In the tender scenes
Chiefly was my delight, and one of these
Never will be forgotten. 'Twas a Man

'IN . . . FRAUGHT': lines from Milton's *Paradise Lost*
BY FOIL: by surrounding contrasts

8.12 Benjamin Robert Haydon (1786–1846). *Wordsworth on Helvellyn*, 1843. The Wordsworth Trust. Helvellyn (3,118 feet) offers one of the finest views of Cumbria, including Grasmere below, four miles to the south.

The love of nature that
will lead to love of
humankind evolves
from personal growth.

Whom I saw sitting in an open Square

Close to an iron paling that fenced in

The spacious Grass-plot: on the corner stone

Of the low wall in which the pales were fixed

Sate this one Man, and with a sickly Babe

Upon his knee, whom he had thither brought   850

For sunshine, and to breathe the fresher air.

Of those who passed and me who looked at him

He took no note; but in his brawny Arms

(The Artificer was to the elbow bare

And from his work this moment had been stolen)

He held the Child, and bending over it,

As if he were afraid both of the sun

And of the air which he had come to seek,

He eyed it with unutterable love.

Thus from a very early age, O Friend!   860

My thoughts had been attracted more and more

By slow gradations towards human kind

And to the good and ill of human life:

Nature had led me on, and now I seemed

To travel independent of her help,

As if I had forgotten her; but no,

My Fellow-beings still were unto me

Far less than she was, though the scale of love

Were filling fast, 'twas light, as yet, compared

With that in which her mighty objects lay.   870

Book Ninth

RESIDENCE IN FRANCE

As oftentimes a River, it might seem,
Yielding in part to old remembrances,
Part swayed by fear to tread an onward road
That leads direct to the devouring sea,
Turns, and will measure back his course, far back,
Towards the very regions which he crossed
In his first outset; so have we long time
Made motions retrograde, in like pursuit

■ *The poem launches afresh.*

■ Detained. But now we start afresh; I feel
An impulse to precipitate* my Verse.   10
Fair greetings to this shapeless eagerness
Whene'er it comes, needful in work so long,
Thrice needful to the argument* which now
Awaits us; oh! how much unlike the past!

■ *Returning to France, W passes through the political ferment of Paris.*

One which, though bright the promise, will be found
Ere far we shall advance, ungenial, hard
To treat of, and forbidding in itself.

Free as a colt at pasture on the hills,
I ranged at large through the Metropolis*

PRECIPITATE: move forward, hasten
ARGUMENT: theme or story
METROPOLIS: London

Month after month. Obscurely did I live,   20
Not courting the society of Men
By literature, or elegance, or rank
Distinguished; in the midst of things, it seemed,
Looking as from a distance on the world
That moved about me; yet insensibly
False preconceptions were corrected thus
And errors of the fancy rectified,
Alike with reference to men and things,
And sometimes from each quarter were poured in
Novel imaginations and profound.   30
A year* thus spent, this field (with small regret
Save only for the Book-stalls in the streets,
Wild produce, hedge-row fruit, on all sides hung
To tempt the sauntering traveller aside)
I quitted, and betook myself to France,
Led thither chiefly by a personal wish
To speak the language more familiarly,
With which intent I chose for my abode
A City* on the Borders of the Loire.

■ Through Paris lay my readiest path, and there   40
I sojourned a few days, and visited
In haste each spot of old and recent fame,
The latter chiefly, from the Field of Mars*
Down to the Suburbs of St. Anthony,
And from Mont Martyr* southward, to the Dome

YEAR: actually, about four months in 1791
CITY: Orléans
FIELD OF MARS: site of political action, strife, and violence
MONT MARTYR: Montmartre

9.1 William Callow (1812–1908). *View of the Pont Royal*, 1833. Yale Center for British Art, Paul Mellon Collection. Wordsworth arrived in Paris from Rouen on the evening of November 30, 1791. The city was quiet but tense, stirred up by radical publications including Jean-Paul Marat's newspaper *L'Ami du Peuple* ("The Friend of the People"). Wordsworth remained in the city until he departed for Orléans on December 5.

9.2 Thomas Girtin (1775–1802). *View of the Pantheon from the Arsenal*, 1802. Yale Center for British Art, Paul Mellon Collection. Originally finished in 1791 as a church, "the Dome of Geneviève" became instead the Panthéon, a mausoleum for the remains of great French citizens including Voltaire (1694–1778), who was reinterred there on July 11, 1791.

Of Geneviève. In both her clamorous Halls,
The National Synod* and the Jacobins,*
I saw the revolutionary Power
Toss like a Ship at anchor, rocked by storms;
The Arcades I traversed in the Palace huge   50
Of Orleans, coasted round and round the line
Of Tavern, Brothel, Gaming-house, and Shop,
Great rendezvous of worst and best, the walk
Of all who had a purpose, or had not;
I stared and listened with a stranger's ears
To Hawkers and Haranguers, hubbub wild!

And hissing Factionists with ardent eyes,
In knots, or pairs, or single, ant-like swarms
Of Builders and Subverters, every face
That hope or apprehension could put on,   60
Joy, anger, and vexation in the midst
Of gaiety and dissolute idleness.

Where silent zephyrs sported with the dust
Of the Bastille,* I sate in the open sun,
And from the rubbish gathered up a stone
And pocketed the relick in the guise

NATIONAL SYNOD: short-lived legislature
JACOBINS: anti-royalist revolutionaries

BASTILLE: royal prison, symbol of tyranny, demolished 1789

9.3 Joseph Navlet (1821–1889). *Camille Desmoulins (1760–1794) au Palais Royal*, unknown date. Private collection. Christie's Images / Bridgeman Images. "The Arcades I traversed in the Palace huge / Of Orleans"—a primary site of political and social activity in 1791. The "hissing Factionists . . . Of Builders and Subverters," including Desmoulins, called for the deposition of the king. Desmoulins later grew alarmed at the extremities of violence and was himself guillotined by the Revolutionary Tribunal on April 5, 1794, with his political ally Georges Jacques Danton (1759–1794).

Of an Enthusiast, yet, in honest truth

Though not without some strong incumbences;

And glad (could living man be otherwise?)

I looked for something which I could not find,   70

Affecting more emotion than I felt,

For 'tis most certain that the utmost force

Of all these various objects which may shew

The temper of my mind as then it was

Seemed less to recompense the Traveller's pains,

Less moved me, gave me less delight than did

A single Picture merely, hunted out

Among other sights, the Magdalene of le Brun,

A Beauty exquisitely wrought, fair face
And rueful, with its ever-flowing tears.   80

■ But hence to my more permanent residence*
I hasten: there, by novelties in speech,
Domestic manners, customs, gestures, looks,
And all the attire of ordinary life,
Attention was at first engrossed; and thus,
Amused and satisfied, I scarcely felt
The shock of these concussions, unconcerned,
Tranquil, almost, and careless as a flower
Glassed in a Green-house, or a Parlour shrub
While every bush and tree, the country through,   90
Is shaking to the roots; indifference this
Which may seem strange; but I was unprepared
With needful knowledge, had abruptly passed
Into a theatre, of which the stage
Was busy with an action far advanced.
Like others I had read, and eagerly
Sometimes, the master Pamphlets* of the day;
Nor wanted such half-insight as grew wild
Upon that meagre soil, helped out by Talk
And public News; but having never chanced   100
To see a regular Chronicle which might shew
(If any such indeed existed then)
Whence the main Organs of the public Power
Had sprung, their transmigrations when and how

RESIDENCE: Orléans
MASTER PAMPHLETS: major pamphlets or books debating revolution

■ *He settles for a time in Orléans.*

9.4 Charles Le Brun (1619–1690). *Saint Mary Magdalen renounces all pleasures of life,* 1655. Musée du Louvre, Paris. Photo: Erich Lessing / Art Resource, NY. "I looked for something which I could not find, / Affecting more emotion than I felt." In early December 1791, Wordsworth seemed "moved" more by Le Brun's painting at the Carmelite Convent in the Rue d'Enfer than by the revolution: "A Beauty exquisitely wrought, fair face / And rueful, with its ever-flowing tears."

Accomplished, giving thus unto events
A form and body, all things were to me
Loose and disjointed, and the affections left

Without a vital interest. At that time,
Moreover, the first storm was overblown,
And the strong hand of outward violence   110
Locked up in quiet. For myself, I fear
Now in connection with so great a Theme
To speak (as I must be compelled to do)
Of one so unimportant: a short time
I loitered, and frequented night by night
Routs,* card-tables, the formal haunts of Men,
Whom in the City privilege of birth
Sequestered from the rest, societies
Where through punctilios of elegance
And deeper causes, all discourse, alike   120
Of good and evil of the time, was shunned
With studious care: but 'twas not long ere this
Proved tedious, and I gradually withdrew
Into a noisier world; and thus did soon
Become a Patriot, and my heart was all
Given to the People, and my love was theirs.

A knot of military Officers
That to a Regiment appertained which then
Was stationed in the City were the chief
Of my associates: some of these wore Swords   130

■ *Growing more aware, he finds his feelings side with the populace and with their cause.*

■ *He notes one officer who shows, unlike his fellows, courage and sympathy for the revolution.*

Routs: parties, often convivial or wild

Which had been seasoned in the Wars,* and all
Were men well born, at least laid claim to such
Distinction, as the Chivalry of France.
In age and temper differing, they had yet
One spirit ruling in them all alike
(Save only one, hereafter to be named),
Were bent upon undoing what was done:
This was their rest, and only hope, therewith
No fear had they of bad becoming worse,
For worst to them was come, nor would have stirred,   140
Or deemed it worth a moment's while to stir,
In any thing, save only as the act
Looked thitherward. One, reckoning by years,
Was in the prime of manhood, and erewhile
He had sate Lord in many tender hearts,
Though heedless of such honours now, and changed:
His temper was quite mastered by the times,
And they had blighted him, had eat away
The beauty of his person, doing wrong
Alike to body and to mind: his port,*   150
Which once had been erect and open, now
Was stooping and contracted, and a face
By nature lovely in itself expressed
As much as any that was ever seen,
A ravage out of season, made by thoughts
Unhealthy and vexatious. At the hour,
The most important of each day, in which

Wars: Seven Years' War, American Revolution
port: stature, bearing

9.5 Léon Cogniet (1794–1880). *The Garde Nationale de Paris Leaves to Join the Army in September 1792*, c. 1835. Château de Versailles / Bridgeman Images. "'Twas in truth an hour / Of universal ferment; mildest men / Were agitated." The French Republic was proclaimed on September 22, 1792. That day in Orléans Wordsworth attended its celebration.

The public News was read, the fever came,
A punctual visitant, to shake this Man,
Disarmed his voice, and fanned his yellow cheek 160
Into a thousand colours; while he read,
Or mused, his sword was haunted by his touch
Continually, like an uneasy place
In his own body. 'Twas in truth an hour
Of universal ferment; mildest men
Were agitated, and commotions, strife
Of passion and opinion filled the walls
Of peaceful houses with unquiet sounds.
The soil of common life was at that time

*Complex unrest and
great extremes cover
the land.*

■ Too hot to tread upon: oft said I then, 170
And not then only, 'what a mockery this
Of history, the past, and that to come!
Now do I feel how I have been deceived,
Reading of Nations and their works, in faith,
Faith given to vanity and emptiness;

*Other officers try to
persuade W to the
royalist side.*

Oh! laughter for the Page that would reflect
To future times the face of what now is!'
The land all swarmed with passion like a Plain
Devoured by locusts, Carra, Gorsas,* add
A hundred other names, forgotten now, 180
Nor to be heard of more, yet were they Powers
Like earthquakes, shocks repeated day by day,
And felt through every nook of town and field.

CARRA, GORSAS: Jean-Louis Carra, Antoine-Joseph Gorsas, radicals later guillotined

The Men already spoken of as chief
Of my Associates were prepared for flight
To augment the band of Emigrants in Arms
Upon the Borders of the Rhine, and leagued
With foreign Foes* mustered for instant war.
This was their undisguised intent, and they
Were waiting with the whole of their desires 190
The moment to depart.

                    An Englishman,
Born in a Land, the name of which appeared
To license some unruliness of mind,
A Stranger, with Youth's further privilege,
And that indulgence which a half-learned speech
Wins from the courteous, I who had been else
Shunned and not tolerated freely lived
■ With these Defenders of the Crown, and talked
And heard their notions, nor did they disdain
The wish to bring me over to their cause. 200

But though untaught by thinking or by books
To reason well of polity or law
And nice distinctions, then on every tongue,
Of natural rights and civil, and to acts
Of Nations, and their passing interests,
(I speak comparing these with other things)
Almost indifferent, even the Historian's Tale

FOREIGN FOES: Austria and Prussia

Prizing but little otherwise than I prized
Tales of the Poets, as it made my heart
Beat high and filled my fancy with fair forms,   210
Old Heroes and their sufferings and their deeds;
Yet in the regal Sceptre and the pomp
Of Orders and Degrees I nothing found
Then, or had ever, even in crudest youth,
That dazzled me; but rather what my soul
Mourned for, or loathed, beholding that the best
Ruled not, and feeling that they ought to rule.

For, born in a poor District, and which yet
Retaineth more of ancient homeliness,
Manners erect, and frank simplicity   220
Than any other nook of English Land,
It was my fortune scarcely to have seen
Through the whole tenor of my School-day time
The face of one, who, whether Boy or Man,
Was vested with attention or respect
Through claims of wealth or blood; nor was it least
Of many debts which afterwards I owed
To Cambridge and an academic life
That something there was holden up to view
Of a Republic, where all stood thus far   230
Upon equal ground, that they were brothers all
In honour, as in one community,
Scholars and Gentlemen, where furthermore

Distinction lay open to all that came,
And wealth and titles were in less esteem
Than talents and successful industry.
Add unto this, subservience from the first
To God and Nature's single sovereignty,
Familiar presences of awful Power
And fellowship with venerable books   240
To sanction* the proud workings of the soul,
And mountain liberty. It could not be
But that one tutored thus, who had been formed
To thought and moral feeling in the way
This Story hath described, should look with awe
Upon the faculties of Man, receive
Gladly the highest promises, and hail
As best the government of equal rights
And individual worth. And hence, O Friend!*
If at the first great outbreak I rejoiced   250
Less than might well befit my youth, the cause
In part lay here, that unto me the events
Seemed nothing out of nature's certain course,
A gift that rather was come late than soon.
No wonder then if advocates like these
Whom I have mentioned, at this riper day
Were impotent to make my hopes put on
The shape of theirs, my understanding bend
In honour to their honour; zeal which yet
Had slumbered now in opposition burst   260

SANCTION: validate
FRIEND: The friend addressed directly remains Coleridge.

■ But background and
conviction lend him
counterblasts.

■ Though Cambridge was
in fact no meritocracy,
still it knew what a
republic meant and
proved more equal than
rights of birth alone.

■ His words appear
to vanquish royalist
officers.

Forth like a Polar Summer; every word
They uttered was a dart by counter-winds
Blown back upon themselves, their reason seemed
Confusion-stricken by a higher power
Than human understanding, their discourse
Maimed, spiritless, and in their weakness strong
I triumphed.

Now at Blois, he describes Michel Beaupuy and that man's character.

       Meantime, day by day the roads
(While I consorted with these Royalists)
Were crowded with the bravest Youth of France
And all the promptest of her Spirits, linked   270
In gallant Soldiership and posting on
To meet the War upon her Frontier Bounds.
Yet at this very moment do tears start
Into mine eyes; I do not say I weep,
I wept not then, but tears have dimmed my sight,
In memory of the farewells of that time,
Domestic severings, female fortitude
At dearest separation, patriot love
And self-devotion, and terrestrial hope
Encouraged with a martyr's confidence;   280
Even files of Strangers merely seen but once
And for a moment, men from far with sound
Of music, martial tunes, and banners spread
Entering the City,* here and there a face
Or person singled out among the rest,

CITY: Blois

Yet still a Stranger and beloved as such,
Even by these passing spectacles my heart
Was oftentimes uplifted, and they seemed
Like arguments from Heaven that 'twas a cause
Good, and which no one could stand up against   290
Who was not lost, abandoned, selfish, proud,
Mean, miserable, wilfully depraved,
Hater perverse of equity and truth.

       Among that band of Officers was one*
Already hinted at, of other mold,
A Patriot, thence rejected by the rest
And with an oriental loathing spurned,
As of a different Cast.* A meeker Man
Than this lived never, or a more benign,
Meek, though enthusiastic to the height   300
Of highest expectation. Injuries
Made him more gracious, and his nature then
Did breathe its sweetness out most sensibly
As aromatic flowers on Alpine turf
When foot hath crushed them. He through the events
Of that great change wandered in perfect faith
As through a Book, an old Romance or Tale
Of Fairy, or some dream of actions wrought
Behind the summer clouds. By birth he ranked
With the most noble, but unto the poor   310
Among mankind he was in service bound

ONE: Michel Beaupuy
CAST: caste, (lower) rank

As by some tie invisible, oaths professed
To a religious Order. Man he loved
As Man; and to the mean and the obscure
And all the homely in their homely works
Transferred a courtesy which had no air
Of condescension, but did rather seem
A passion and a gallantry, like that
Which he, a Soldier, in his idler day
Had payed to Woman; somewhat vain he was,   320
Or seemed so, yet it was not vanity

■ *They speak about a new,
more equal world, and
see around them signs
of it.*

But fondness, and a kind of radiant joy
That covered him about when he was bent
On works of love or freedom, or revolved
Complacently* the progress of a cause
Whereof he was a part; yet this was meek
And placid, and took nothing from the Man
That was delightful: oft in solitude
With him did I discourse about the end
Of civil government, and its wisest forms,   330
Of ancient prejudice, and chartered rights,
Allegiance, faith, and laws by time matured,
Custom and habit, novelty and change,
Of self-respect and virtue in the Few
For patrimonial honour set apart,
And ignorance in the labouring Multitude.
For he, an upright Man and tolerant,
Balanced these contemplations in his mind

REVOLVED COMPLACENTLY: reflected on with satisfaction

And I, who at that time was scarcely dipped
Into the turmoil, had a sounder judgment   340
Than afterwards, carried about me yet
With less alloy to its integrity
The experience of past ages, as through help
Of Books and common life it makes its way
To youthful minds, by objects over near
Not pressed upon, nor dazzled or misled
By struggling with the crowd for present ends.

■ But though not deaf and obstinate to find
Error without apology on the side
Of those who were against us, more delight   350
We took, and let this freely be confessed,
In painting to ourselves the miseries
Of royal Courts, and that voluptuous life
Unfeeling, where the Man who is of soul
The meanest* thrives the most, where dignity,
True personal dignity, abideth not,
A light and cruel world, cut off from all
The natural inlets of just sentiment,
From lowly sympathy, and chastening truth,
Where good and evil never have that name,   360
That which they ought to have, but wrong prevails,
And vice at home. We added dearest themes,
Man and his noble nature, as it is
The gift of God and lies in his own power,

MEANEST: lowest, least worthy

His blind desires and steady faculties
Capable of clear truth, the one to break
Bondage, the other to build liberty
On firm foundations, making social life,
Through knowledge spreading and imperishable,
As just in regulation, and as pure   370
As individual in the wise and good.
We summoned up the honourable deeds
Of ancient Story, thought of each bright spot
That could be found in all recorded time
Of truth preserved, and error passed away,
Of single Spirits that catch the flame from Heaven,
And how the multitude of men will feed
And fan each other, thought of Sects, how keen
They are to put the appropriate nature on,
Triumphant over every obstacle   380
Of custom, language, country, love and hate,
And what they do and suffer for their creed,
How far they travel, and how long endure,
How quickly mighty Nations have been formed
From least beginnings, how, together locked
By new opinions, scattered tribes have made
One body spreading wide as clouds in heaven.
To aspirations then of our own minds
Did we appeal; and finally beheld
A living confirmation of the whole   390
Before us in a People risen up

9.6 Louisa Anne Beresford, Lady Waterford (1818–1891). *View from Clappersgate*, un-
dated. The Wordsworth Trust. "Our Rotha's Stream," the River Rothay, flows gently
through Grasmere a few yards from the churchyard where Wordsworth is buried. It
joins the River Brathway near the tiny village of Clappersgate two miles south before
flowing into the northern waters of Windermere.

Fresh as the morning Star: elate we looked
Upon their virtues, saw in rudest* men
Self-sacrifice the firmest, generous love
And continence* of mind, and sense of right
Uppermost in the midst of fiercest strife.

Oh! sweet it is in academic Groves
Or such retirement, Friend! as we have known
Among the mountains, by our Rotha's Stream,

RUDEST: least well educated or polished
CONTINENCE: control or restraint

Greta or Derwent,* or some nameless Rill   400
To ruminate with interchange of talk
On rational liberty, and hope in Man,
Justice and peace: but far more sweet such toil,
Toil say I, for it leads to thoughts abstruse
If Nature then be standing on the brink
Of some great trial, and we hear the voice
Of One devoted, one whom circumstance
Hath called upon to embody his deep sense
In action, give it outwardly a shape,
And that of benediction to the world: 410
Then doubt is not, and truth is more than truth,
A hope it is and a desire, a creed
Of zeal by an authority divine
Sanctioned of danger, difficulty or death.

■ *Their conversation recalls how Plato's student Dion and philosopher friends fought against the tyrant Dionysius of Syracuse.*

■ Such conversation under Attic shades
Did Dion hold with Plato, ripened thus
For a Deliverer's glorious task, and such,
He, on that ministry already bound,
Held with Eudemus and Timonides,
Surrounded by Adventurers in Arms   420
When those two Vessels with their daring Freight
For the Sicilian Tyrant's overthrow
Sailed from Zacynthus, philosophic war
Led by Philosophers. With harder fate,
Though like ambition, such was he, O Friend!
Of whom I speak, so Beaupuis (let the Name

ROTHA . . . DERWENT: favorite rivers in the Lake District

9.7 Alexandre Bloch (1860–1919). *The Death of General Beaupuy*, 1888. Musée des Beaux-Arts, Rennes / Bridgeman Images. Wordsworth met Beaupuy (1755–1796) in Blois in early 1792. He believed that Beaupuy "perished fighting in supreme command / Upon the Borders of the unhappy Loire" in a losing battle against royalists at Entrammes (on the River Mayenne, a tributary of the Loire) in western France on October 26, 1793. However, fighting against Austrian forces in what is now southwestern Germany, the general died at the battle of Emmendingen on October 19, 1796. Under the same mistaken impression that Wordsworth was, Bloch depicted Beaupuy dying in 1793 at the battle of Entrammes, when in fact he was only wounded there.

Stand near the worthiest of antiquity)
Fashioned his life, and many a long discourse
With like persuasion honoured we maintained,
He on his part accoutred* for the worst.   430
He perished* fighting in supreme command
Upon the Borders of the unhappy Loire
For Liberty against deluded Men,
His Fellow-countrymen, and yet most blessed
In this, that he the fate of later times
Lived not to see, nor what we now behold
Who have as ardent hearts as he had then.

Along that very Loire, with Festivals
Resounding at all hours, and innocent yet
Of civil slaughter, was our frequent walk   440
Or in wide Forests of the neighbourhood,
High woods and over-arched with open space
On every side, and footing many a mile,
Inwoven roots and moss smooth as the sea,
■ A solemn region. Often in such place
From earnest dialogues I slipped in thought
And let remembrance steal to other times
When Hermits from their sheds and caves forth strayed,
Walked by themselves, so met in shades like these,
And if a devious Traveller was heard   450
Approaching from a distance, as might chance,
With speed and echoes loud of trampling hoofs

■ *In interludes W fancies
he hears not present-day
riders but princesses
Angelica and Erminia,
virgins in epic poems
who escape pursuers
and then pursue their
own true loves.*

ACCOUTRED: prepared, armed
PERISHED: For his death see illustration 9.7.

9.8 J. M. W. Turner (1775–1851). *Banks of the Loire*, 1829. Worcester Art Museum,
Massachusetts / Bridgeman Images. Wordsworth and Beaupuy had often walked
"Along that very Loire, with Festivals / Resounding at all hours, and innocent yet /
Of civil slaughter."

From the hard floor reverberated, then
It was Angelica thundering through the woods
Upon her Palfrey, or that gentler Maid
Erminia, fugitive as fair as She.
Sometimes I saw, methought, a pair of Knights
Joust underneath the trees, that, as in storm,
Did rock above their heads: anon the din   460
Of boisterous merriment and music's roar,
With sudden Proclamation! burst from haunt
Of Satyrs in some viewless glade, with dance
Rejoicing o'er a Female in the midst,
A mortal Beauty their unhappy Thrall;
The width of those huge Forests, unto me
A novel scene, did often in this way
Master my fancy, while I wandered on
With that revered Companion. And sometimes
When to a Convent in a meadow green
By a brook side we came, a roofless Pile*   470
And not by reverential touch of Time
Dismantled, but by violence abrupt,
In spite of those heart-bracing colloquies,
In spite of real fervour, and of that
Less genuine and wrought up within myself
I could not but bewail a wrong so harsh,
And for the matin Bell to sound no more
Grieved, and the evening Taper, and the Cross

■ *Beaupuy shows W sites of history . . .*

High on the topmost Pinnacle, a sign
Admonitory, by the Traveller   480
First seen above the woods.

            And when my Friend
Pointed upon occasion to the Site
■ Of Romorantin,* home of ancient Kings,
To the imperial Edifice of Blois
Or to that rural Castle, name now slipped
From my remembrance, where a Lady lodged
By the first Francis wooed, and bound to him
In chains of mutual passion; from the Tower,
As a Tradition of the Country tells,
Practised to commune with her Royal Knight   490
By cressets* and love-beacons, intercourse
'Twixt her high-seated Residence and his
Far off at Chambord on the Plain beneath.
Even here, though less than with the peaceful House
Religious, 'mid those frequent monuments
Of Kings, their vices or their better deeds,
Imagination, potent to enflame
At times with virtuous wrath and noble scorn,
Did also often mitigate the force
Of civic prejudice, the bigotry,   500
So call it, of a youthful Patriot's mind,
And on these spots with many gleams I looked

PILE: large stone building

ROMORANTIN: site of a château home to François I's mother
CRESSETS: metal cups of burning oil often hung on poles

9.9 Thomas Shotter Boys (1803–1874). *Le Chateau de Blois*, undated. Yale Center for British Art, Paul Mellon Collection. "To the imperial Edifice of Blois": the royal château, begun in the 13th century, was home to many French kings and the spot where, in 1429, Joan of Arc was blessed before she began at Orléans her campaign to rid France of the English.

9.10 Pierre-Denis Martin (1663–1742). *The Chateau de Chambord*, 1722. Château de Versailles / Bridgeman Images. "Far off at Chambord on the Plain beneath" and eight miles east of Blois lies the never completed château, begun in the 16th century by François I.

Of chivalrous delight. Yet not the less,
Hatred of absolute rule, where will of One
Is law for all, and of that barren pride
In those who by immunities unjust
Betwixt the Sovereign and the People stand,

His helpers and not theirs, laid stronger hold
Daily upon me, mixed with pity too,
And love; for where hope is there love will be   510
■ For the abject multitude. And when we chanced
One day to meet a hunger-bitten Girl
Who crept along, fitting her languid self
Unto a Heifer's motion, by a cord
Tied to her arm, and picking thus from the lane
Its sustenance, while the Girl with her two hands
Was busy knitting, in a heartless* mood
Of solitude, and at the sight my Friend
In agitation said, "'Tis against *that*
Which we are fighting,' I with him believed   520
Devoutly that a Spirit was abroad
Which could not be withstood, that poverty
At least like this, would in a little time
Be found no more, that we should see the earth
Unthwarted in her wish to recompense
The industrious, and the lowly Child of Toil,
All institutes for ever blotted out
That legalized exclusion, empty pomp
Abolished, sensual state and cruel power
Whether by edict of the one or few,   530
And finally, as sum and crown of all,
Should see the People having a strong hand
In making their own Laws, whence better days

HEARTLESS: dejected, resigned

To all mankind. But, these things set apart,
Was not the single confidence enough
To animate the mind that ever turned
A thought to human welfare, that henceforth
Captivity by mandate without law*
Should cease, and open accusation lead
To sentence in the hearing of the world 540
And open punishment, if not the air
Be free to breathe in, and the heart of Man
Dread nothing. Having touched this argument
I shall not, as my purpose was, take note
Of other matters which detained us oft
In thought or conversation, public acts,
And public persons, and the emotions wrought
Within our minds by the ever-varying wind
Of Record or Report which day by day

■ Beaupuy and others tell
the tale of Vaudracour
and Julia.

■ That pair love each other
almost from birth, yet his
father rejects all thought
of it. She is too low.

■ Swept over us: but I will here instead 550
Draw from obscurity a tragic Tale,
Not in its spirit singular indeed
But haply worth memorial, as I heard
The events related by my patriot Friend
And others who had borne a part therein.

Oh! happy time of youthful Lovers! thus
My Story may begin, Oh! balmy time
In which a Love-knot* on a Lady's brow

Is fairer than the fairest Star in heaven!
To such inheritance of blessedness 560
Young Vaudracour was brought by years that had
A little overstepped his stripling prime.
A Town of small repute in the heart of France
Was the Youth's Birth-place: there he vowed his love
To Julia, a bright Maid, from Parents sprung
Not mean in their condition; but with rights
Unhonoured of Nobility, and hence
The Father of the young Man, who had place
Among that order, spurned the very thought
■ Of such alliance. From their cradles up 570
With but a step between their several homes,
The pair had thriven together year by year
Friends, Playmates, Twins in pleasure, after strife
And petty quarrels had grown fond again,
Each other's advocate, each other's help,
Nor ever happy if they were apart:
A basis this for deep and solid love,
And endless constancy, and placid truth;
But whatsoever of such treasures might
Beneath the outside* of their youth have lain 580
Reserved for mellower years, his present mind
Was under fascination; he beheld
A vision, and he loved the thing he saw.
Arabian Fiction never filled the world

CAPTIVITY . . . LAW: *lettres de cachet*, imprisonment without process
LOVE-KNOT: ribbon tied and worn to show favor or fidelity

OUTSIDE: appearance, surface

With half the wonders that were wrought for him;
Earth lived in one great presence of the spring,
Life turned the meanest of her implements
Before his eyes to price above all gold,
The house she dwelt in was a sainted shrine,
Her chamber window did surpass in glory   590
The portals of the East, all paradise
Could by the simple opening of a door
Let itself in upon him, pathways, walks,
Swarmed with enchantment till his spirits sank
Beneath the burthen, overblessed for life.
This state was theirs, till whether through effect
Of some delirious hour, or that the Youth,
Seeing so many bars betwixt himself
And the dear haven where he wished to be

■ *The lovers conceive*   ■ In honourable wedlock with his love   600
a child, and Julia's
family remove her   Without a certain knowledge of his own,
for the birth.   Was inwardly prepared to turn aside
From law and custom, and entrust himself

■ *Vaudracour secures*   To Nature for a happy end of all,
a way to find her . . .   And thus abated of that pure reserve
Congenial to his loyal heart, with which
It would have pleased him to attend the steps

■ *. . . and they reunite.*   Of Maiden so divinely beautiful
I know not, but reluctantly must add
That Julia, yet without the name of Wife   610

Carried about her for a secret grief
The promise of a Mother.

To conceal

The threatened shame the Parents of the Maid
Found means to hurry her away by night
And unforewarned, that in a distant Town
She might remain shrouded in privacy,
Until the Babe was born. When morning came
The Lover thus bereft, stung with his loss
And all uncertain whither he should turn,
Chafed like a wild beast in the toils:* at length,   620
■ Following as his suspicions led, he found
O joy! sure traces of the fugitives,
Pursued them to the Town where they had stopped,
And lastly to the very House itself
Which had been chosen for the Maid's retreat.
The sequel may be easily divined:
Walks backwards, forwards, morning, noon and night,
When decency and caution would allow
And Julia, who, whenever to herself
She happened to be left a moment's space,   630
Was busy at her casement, as a Swallow
■ About its nest, ere long did thus espy
Her Lover, thence a stolen interview
By night accomplished, with a ladder's help.

TOILS: long nets for catching game

I pass the raptures of the Pair; such theme
Hath by a hundred Poets been set forth
In more delightful verse than skill of mine
Could fashion, chiefly by that darling Bard*
Who told of Juliet and her Romeo,   640
And of the Lark's note heard before its time,
And of the streaks that laced the severing clouds
In the unrelenting East. 'Tis mine to tread
The humbler province of plain history,
And without choice of circumstance submissively
Relate what I have heard. The Lovers came
To this resolve, with which they parted, pleased
And confident, that Vaudracour should hie
Back to his Father's house, and there employ
Means aptest to obtain a sum of gold,
A final portion,* even, if that might be,   650
Which done, together they could then take flight
To some remote and solitary place
Where they might live with no one to behold
Their happiness, or to disturb their love.
Immediately, and with this mission charged,

■ *Their plan meets more resistance from his father's house.*

■ Home to his Father's House the Youth returned
And there remained a while without hint given
Of his design; but if a word were dropped
Touching the matter of his passion, still
In hearing of his Father, Vaudracour   660

■ *Through intrigue and temper, Vaudracour is drawn to fight, then sent to prison.*

Persisted openly that nothing less
Than death should make him yield up hope to be
A blessèd Husband of the Maid he loved.

Incensed at such obduracy and slight
Of exhortations and remonstrances,
The Father threw out threats that by a mandate
Bearing the private signet of the State
He should be baffled in his mad intent,
And that should cure him. From this time the Youth
Conceived a terror, and by night or day   670
Stirred nowhere without Arms. Soon afterwards
His Parents to their Country Seat withdrew
Upon some feigned occasion; and the Son
Was left with one Attendant in the house.
■ Retiring to his Chamber for the night,
While he was entering at the door, attempts
Were made to seize him by three armed Men,
The instruments of ruffian power; the Youth,
In the first impulse of his rage, laid one
Dead at his feet, and to the second gave   680
A perilous wound, which done, at sight
Of the dead Man he peacefully resigned
His Person to the Law, was lodged in prison,
And wore the fetters of a Criminal.

BARD: Shakespeare, with allusions to *Romeo and Juliet*
FINAL PORTION: settlement from his family

Through three week's space, by means which love devised,
The Maid in her seclusion had received
Tidings of Vaudracour, and how he sped
Upon his enterprize. Thereafter came
A silence, half a circle did the moon
Complete, and then a whole, and still the same   690
Silence; a thousand thousand fears and hopes
Stirred in her mind; thoughts waking, thoughts of sleep

■ *Released, he makes his*
way to Julia again . . .

Entangled in each other, and at last
Self-slaughter seemed her only resting-place.
So did she fare in her uncertainty.

At length, by interference of a Friend,
One who had sway at Court, the Youth regained
His liberty, on promise to sit down
Quietly in his Father's House, nor take
One step to reunite himself with her   700
Of whom his Parents disapproved: hard law
To which he gave consent only because
His freedom else could no wise be procured.
Back to his Father's house he went, remained
Eight days, and then his resolution failed:
He fled to Julia, and the words with which
He greeted her were these. 'All right is gone,
Gone from me. Thou no longer now art mine,
I thine; a Murderer, Julia, cannot love

An innocent Woman; I behold thy face,   710
I see thee, and my misery is complete.'
She could not give him answer; afterwards
She coupled with his Father's name some words
Of vehement indignation; but the Youth
Checked her, nor would he hear of this; for thought
Unfilial, or unkind, had never once
■ Found harbour in his breast. The Lovers thus
United once again together lived
For a few days, which were to Vaudracour
Days of dejection, sorrow and remorse   720
For that ill deed of violence which his hand
Had hastily committed: for the Youth
Was of a loyal spirit, a conscience nice*
And over tender for the trial which
His fate had called him to. The Father's mind
Meanwhile remained unchanged, and Vaudracour
Learned that a mandate had been newly issued
To arrest him on the spot. Oh pain it was
To part! he could not—and he lingered still
To the last moment of his time, and then,   730
At dead of night with snow upon the ground,
He left the City, and in Villages
The most sequestered of the neighbourhood*
Lay hidden for the space of several days
Until the horseman bringing back report

NICE: scrupulous, carefully judged
NEIGHBOURHOOD: surrounding region

That he was nowhere to be found, the search
Was ended. Back returned the ill-fated Youth,
And from the House where Julia lodged (to which
He now found open ingress, having gained
The affection of the family, who loved him   740
Both for his own, and for the Maiden's sake)

■ . . . but once again is
seized, released, and
told he must go home.

■ One night retiring, he was seized.—But here
A portion of the Tale may well be left
In silence, though my memory could add
Much how the Youth, and in short space of time,
Was traversed* from without, much, too, of thoughts
By which he was employed in solitude
Under privation and restraint, and what
Through dark and shapeless fear of things to come,
And what through strong compunction for the past   750
He suffered, breaking down in heart and mind.
Such grace, if grace it were, had been vouchsafed,
Or such effect had through the Father's want
Of power, or through his negligence, ensued

■ He rejoins Julia prior
to the birth.

That Vaudracour was suffered to remain,
Though under guard and without liberty,
In the same City with the unhappy Maid
From whom he was divided. So they fared
Objects of general concern, till, moved
With pity for their wrongs, the Magistrate,   760
The same who had placed the Youth in custody,

TRAVERSED: crossed or blocked

By application to the Minister
Obtained his liberty upon condition
That to his Father's house he should return.

He left his Prison almost on the eve
Of Julia's travail;* she had likewise been
As from the time, indeed, when she had first
Been brought for secresy to this abode,
Though treated with consoling tenderness,
Herself a Prisoner, a dejected one,   770
Filled with a Lover's and a Woman's fears,
And whensoe'er the Mistress of the House
Entered the Room for the last time at night
And Julia with a low and plaintive voice
Said, 'You are coming then to lock me up,'
The Housewife when these words, always the same,
Were by her Captive languidly pronounced
Could never hear them uttered without tears.

■ A day or two before her Child-bed time
Was Vaudracour restored to her, and soon   780
As he might be permitted to return
Into her Chamber after the Child's birth
The Master of the Family begged that all
The household might be summoned, doubting not
But that they might receive impressions then

TRAVAIL: birth labor

■ *They live a short while together. Vaudracour believes the infant's presence will change his own father, who might relent.*

9.11 Unknown artist. *Presumed Image of Annette Vallon*, unknown date. The Wordsworth Trust. In early December 1791, Wordsworth met Annette Vallon (1766–1841) in Orléans. The unmarried couple soon had one daughter, Caroline (1792–1862), with whom Wordsworth had little contact but later helped to support. The story of Vaudracour and Julia seems prompted in some respects by William and Annette's own love affair.

9.12 Robert Hancock (1730–1817). Engraved by Nathan Cooper Branwhite (1775–1857). *William Wordsworth*, 1798, engraved at unknown date. The Wordsworth Trust. In June 1798 at Bristol, Wordsworth sat for Hancock's pencil and chalk drawing. At that time the daughter he had with Annette would have been five years old.

Friendly to human kindness. Vaudracour
(This heard I from one present at the time)
Held up the new-born Infant in his arms
And kissed and blessed, and covered it with tears,
Uttering a prayer that he might never be   790
As wretched as his Father; then he gave
The Child to her who bare it, and she too
Repeated the same prayer, took it again

And muttering something faintly afterwards
He gave the Infant to the Standers-by,
And wept in silence upon Julia's neck.

■ Two months did he continue in the House,
And often yielded up himself to plans
Of future happiness. 'You shall return,
Julia,' said he, 'and to your Father's House   800
Go with your Child, you have been wretched, yet
It is a Town where both of us were born,
None will reproach you, for our loves are known,
With ornaments the prettiest you shall dress
Your Boy, as soon as he can run about,
And when he thus is at his play my Father
Will see him from the window, and the Child
Will by his beauty move his Grandsire's heart,
So that it will be softened, and our loves
End happily as they began.' These gleams   810
Appeared but seldom, oftener was he seen
Propping a pale and melancholy face
Upon the Mother's bosom, resting thus
His head upon one breast, while from the other
The Babe was drawing in its quiet food.
At other times when he, in silence, long
And fixedly had looked upon her face,
He would exclaim, 'Julia, how much thine eyes
Have cost me!' During day-time when the Child

Lay in its cradle, by its side he sate,   820

Not quitting it an instant. The whole Town

In his unmerited misfortunes now

Took part, and if he either at the door

Or window for a moment with his Child

Appeared, immediately the Street was thronged

While others frequently without reserve

Passed and repassed before the house to steal

A look at him. Oft at this time he wrote

Requesting, since he knew that the consent

Of Julia's Parents never could be gained   830

To a clandestine marriage, that his Father

Would from the birth-right of an eldest Son

Exclude him, giving but, when this was done,

■ *But that hope fails, and Julia's mother sends her to a convent without term of time.*

■ A sanction to his nuptials: vain request,

To which no answer was returned. And now

From her own home the Mother of his Love

Arrived to apprise the Daughter of her fixed

■ *Vaudracour arranges for his son to be nursed . . .*

And last resolve, that since all hope to move

The old Man's heart proved vain, she must retire

Into a Convent, and be there immured.*   840

Julia was thunderstricken by these words,

And she insisted on a Mother's rights

To take her Child along with her, a grant

Impossible, as she at last perceived;

The Persons of the house no sooner heard

Of this decision upon Julia's fate

BE THERE IMMURED: live inside its walls permanently

Than every one was overwhelmed with grief

Nor could they frame a manner soft enough

To impart the tidings to the Youth; but great

Was their astonishment when they beheld him   850

Receive the news in calm despondency,

Composed and silent, without outward sign

Of even the least emotion; seeing this

When Julia scattered some upbraiding words

Upon his slackness, he thereto returned

No answer, only took the Mother's* hand

Who loved him scarcely less than her own Child

And kissed it without seeming to be pressed

By any pain that 'twas the hand of one

Whose errand was to part him from his Love   860

For ever. In the City he remained

A season after Julia had retired

And in the Convent taken up her home,

To the end that he might place his Infant Babe

■ With a fit Nurse, which done, beneath the roof

Where now his little One was lodged, he passed

The day entire, and scarcely could at length

Tear himself from the cradle to return

Home to his Father's House, in which he dwelt

A while, and then came back that he might see   870

Whether the Babe had gained sufficient strength

To bear removal. He quitted this same Town

For the last time attendant by the side

MOTHER'S: Julia's mother's

Of a close chair, a Litter or Sedan,*

In which the Child was carried. To a hill

Which rose at a league's distance from the Town

The Family of the house where he had lodged

Attended him, and parted from him there,

Watching below till he had disappeared

On the hill top. His eyes he scarcely took,   880

Through all that journey, from the Chair in which

The Babe was carried; and at every Inn

Or place at which they halted or reposed

Laid him upon his knees, nor would permit

The hands of any but himself to dress

The Infant or undress. By one of those

Who bore the Chair these facts at his return

Were told; and in relating them he wept.

■ . . . and makes a last
request, his own retreat.

■ This was the manner in which Vaudracour

Departed with his Infant; and thus reached   890

His Father's House, where to the innocent Child

Admittance was denied. The young Man spake

No words of indignation or reproof,

But of his Father begged, a last request,

■ After a terrible event,
Vaudracour, silent and
alone, lives out his days.

That a retreat might be assigned to him,

A house where in the Country he might dwell

With such allowance as his wants required

And the more lonely that the Mansion was

'Twould be more welcome. To a lodge that stood

LITTER OR SEDAN: closed bed or chair carried by two men

Deep in a Forest, with leave given, at the age   900

Of four and twenty summers he retired

And thither took with him his Infant Babe

And one Domestic for their common needs,

An agèd woman. It consoled him here

To attend upon the Orphan* and perform

The office of a Nurse to his young Child,

Which after a short time, by some mistake

Or indiscretion of the Father, died.

The Tale I follow to its last recess

Of suffering or of peace, I know not which;   910

Theirs be the blame who caused the woe, not mine.

From that time forth he never uttered word

To any living. An Inhabitant

Of that same Town in which the Pair had left

So lively a remembrance of their griefs

By chance of business coming within reach

Of his retirement to the spot repaired

With the intent to visit him: he reached

The House and only found the Matron there,

Who told him that his pains were thrown away,   920

■ For that her Master never uttered word

To living soul, not even to her. Behold

While they were speaking Vaudracour approached,

But seeing some one there, just as his hand

Was stretched towards the garden gate, he shrunk

ORPHAN: at that time, loss of even one parent

And like a shadow glided out of view.
Shocked at his savage outside,* from the place
The Visitor retired.

                    Thus lived the Youth
Cut off from all intelligence* with Man,

And shunning even the light of common day,   930
Nor could the voice of Freedom which through France
Soon afterwards resounded, public hope,
Or personal memory of his own deep wrongs
Rouze him; but in those solitary shades
His days he wasted, an imbecile* mind.

SAVAGE OUTSIDE: appearing like a wild creature of the forest
INTELLIGENCE: communication, contact

IMBECILE: enfeebled, having lost all support

10.1 Jean Duplessis-Bertaux (1747–1819). *Taking of the Tuileries, Court of the Carrousel, 10th August 1792*. Château de Versailles, France / Bridgeman Images. "From his Throne / The King had fallen." Louis XVI (1754–1793) was deposed and imprisoned on this day. The mob murdered and burned more than 700 members of the Swiss Guard protecting him and his family. Many in the mob also fell. The Republic was soon proclaimed on September 22, 1792.

Book Tenth
RESIDENCE IN FRANCE AND FRENCH REVOLUTION

It was a beautiful and silent day
That overspread the countenance of earth,
Then fading, with unusual quietness,
When from the Loire I parted, and through scenes
Of vineyard, orchard, meadow-ground and tilth,
Calm waters, gleams of sun, and breathless trees,
Towards the fierce Metropolis* turned my steps

■ *The allied armies seek to encircle the French but, once confronted, flee.*

Their homeward way to England. From his Throne
The King had fallen; the congregated Host,*
Dire cloud upon the front of which was written   10
The tender mercies of the dismal wind
That bore it, on the Plains of Liberty
Had burst innocuously, say more, the swarm
That came elate and jocund, like a Band
Of Eastern Hunters, to enfold in ring
Narrowing itself by moments and reduce
To the last punctual spot of their despair
A race of victims, so they seemed, themselves
Had shrunk from sight of their own task, and fled
In terror; desolation and dismay   20

■ *W reflects on the September Massacres and the state of Paris now.*

METROPOLIS: Paris
CONGREGATED HOST: armies allied against France

Remained for them whose fancies had grown rank
With evil expectations, confidence
And perfect triumph to the better cause.
The State, as if to stamp the final seal
On her security, and to the world
Shew what she was, a high and fearless soul,
Or rather in a spirit of thanks to those
Who had stirred up her slackening faculties
To a new transition, had assumed with joy
The body and the venerable name   30
■ Of a Republic: lamentable crimes*
'Tis true had gone before this hour,* the work
Of massacre in which the senseless sword
Was prayed to as a judge; but these were past,
Earth free from them for ever, as was thought,
Ephemeral monsters, to be seen but once,
Things that could only shew themselves and die.

This was the time in which enflamed with hope,
To Paris I returned. Again I ranged
More eagerly than I had done before   40
Through the wide City, and in progress passed
The Prison* where the unhappy Monarch lay
Associate with his Children and his Wife
In bondage; and the Palace* lately stormed
With roar of cannon, and a numerous Host.
I crossed (a blank and empty area then)

LAMENTABLE CRIMES: executions of the September Massacres
BEFORE THIS HOUR: from September 2 to 7, 1792
PRISON: the Temple, an old fortress
PALACE: Tuileries Palace

10.2 Léon-Maxime Faivre (1856–1941). *Death of the Princess de Lamballe, in front of the door of the prison by the people, Paris, September 3, 1792*, 1908. Châteaux de Versailles et de Trianon, Versailles. Photo: Gérard Blot / Art Resource, NY. "I thought of those September Massacres": in the few days following the mutilation, murder, and beheading of the princess, over 1,400 priests, nuns, monks, children, and prisoners were butchered—100 hours of "substantial dread" and slaughter—"lamentable crimes . . . the work / Of massacre."

The Square of the Carousel,* few weeks back*
Heaped up with dead and dying, upon these
And other sights looking as doth a Man
Upon a volume whose contents he knows   50
Are memorable, but from him locked up,
Being written in a tongue he cannot read,
So that he questions the mute leaves with pain
And half upbraids their silence. But that night
When on my bed I lay, I was most moved
And felt most deeply in what world I was;
My room was high and lonely, near the roof
Of a large Mansion or Hotel,* a spot
That would have pleased me in more quiet times,
Nor was it wholly without pleasure then.   60
With unextinguished taper I kept watch,
Reading at intervals; the fear gone by
Pressed on me almost like a fear to come;
I thought of those September Massacres,
Divided from me by a little month,
And felt and touched them, a substantial dread;
The rest was conjured up from tragic fictions
And mournful Calendars* of true history,
Remembrances and dim admonishments.
'The horse is taught his manage,* and the wind   70
Of heaven wheels round and treads in his own steps,
Year follows year, the tide returns again,
Day follows day, all things have second birth;

10.3 George Fennell Robson (1788–1833). *Macbeth and Banquo on the Heath*, 1830. Yale Center for British Art, Paul Mellon Collection. Destruction of hope and the cyclical return of death and murder: from "tragic fictions" and "true history" Wordsworth conjures up the sense that, "Year follows year . . . Day follows day" until, in words from *Macbeth*, a voice seems to cry to Paris, "'Sleep no more,'" and the city becomes "Defenceless as a wood where tigers roam."

The earthquake is not satisfied at once.'
And in such way I wrought upon myself
Until I seemed to hear a voice that cried
To the whole City, 'Sleep no more.' To this
Add comments of a calmer mind, from which
I could not gather full security,
But at the best it seemed a place of fear   80
Unfit for the repose of night,
Defenceless as a wood where tigers roam.

Square of the Carousel: Place du Carrousel
few weeks back: in early August 1792
Mansion or Hotel: dwelling or lodging house
Calendars: chronicles, chronological accounts
manage: gaits and movements

He recounts how Robespierre was denounced yet flourished.

Betimes next morning to the Palace Walk
Of Orleans* I repaired and entering there
Was greeted, among divers other notes,
By voices of the Hawkers in the crowd
Bawling, *Denunciation of the crimes*
Of Maximilian Robespierre: the speech
Which in their hands they carried was the same
Which had been recently pronounced the day   90
When Robespierre, well knowing for what mark
Some words of indirect reproof had been
Intended, rose in hardihood and dared
The Man* who had an ill surmise of him
To bring his charge in openness, whereat
When a dead pause ensued, and no one stirred,
In silence of all present, from his seat
Louvet walked singly through the avenue*
And took his station in the Tribune, saying,
'I, Robespierre, accuse thee!' 'Tis well known   100
What was the issue of that charge, and how
Louvet was left alone without support
Of his irresolute Friends: but these are things
Of which I speak only as they were storm
Or sunshine to my individual mind,

The Girondins, in W's estimate the best of all the revolutionaries, lack decisive action.

No further. Let me then relate that now
In some sort seeing with my proper* eyes
That Liberty, and Life and Death would soon
To the remotest corners of the land

PALACE WALK OF ORLEANS: arcades of the Palais Royal (9.50)
MAN: Jean-Baptiste Louvet de Couvray
AVENUE: aisle, way cleared by people parting
PROPER: own

10.4 A. Demarle (19th century). *Jean-Baptiste Louvet de Couvrai*, engraved by Hippolyte de la Charlerie (1827–1869), from *Histoire de la Révolution Française* (1847–1869) by Louis Blanc (1811–1882). Private Collection / Ken Welsh / Bridgeman Images. On October 29, 1792, in *"Denunciation of the crimes / Of Maximilian Robespierre,"* Louvet (1760–1797) declared, "I, Robespierre, accuse thee!" Wordsworth most likely arrived in Paris from Orléans that same day.

On the edge of events, he feels yet attracted to them, part of some greater spirit.

Lie in the arbitrement* of those who ruled   110
The capital City, what was struggled for,
And by what Combatants victory must be won,
The indecision on their* part whose aim
Seemed best, and the straight-forward path of those
Who in attack or in defence alike
Were strong through their impiety, greatly I
Was agitated; yea, I could almost
Have prayed that throughout earth upon all souls
Worthy of liberty, upon every soul
Matured to live in plainness and in truth,   120
The gift of tongues* might fall, and men arrive
From the four quarters of the winds to do
For France what without help she could not do,
A work of honour; think not that to this
I added work of safety; from such thought
And the least fear about the end of things
I was as far as Angels are from guilt.

Yet did I grieve, nor only grieved, but thought
Of opposition and of remedies,
An insignificant Stranger, and obscure,   130
Mean* as I was, and little graced with powers
Of eloquence even in my native speech,
And all unfit for tumult and intrigue,
Yet would I willingly have taken up
A service at this time for cause so great,

However dangerous. Inly I revolved*
How much the destiny of man had still
Hung upon single persons, that there was,
Transcendent to all local patrimony,*
One Nature as there is one Sun in heaven,   140
That objects, even as they are great, thereby
Do come within the reach of humblest eyes,
That Man was only weak through his mistrust
And want of hope, where evidence divine
Proclaimed to him that hope should be most sure;
That with desires heroic and firm sense,
A Spirit thoroughly faithful to itself,
Unquenchable, unsleeping, undismayed,
Was as an instinct among Men, a stream
That gathered up each petty straggling rill   150
And vein of water, glad to be rolled on
In safe obedience; that a mind whose rest
Was where it ought to be, in self-restraint,
In circumspection and simplicity,
Fell rarely in entire discomfiture
Below its aim, or met with from without
A treachery that defeated it, or foiled.

On the other side I called to mind those truths
Which are the common-places* of the Schools,*
A theme for Boys, too trite even to be felt,   160
Yet, with a revelation's liveliness

ARBITREMENT: power of decision
THEIR: the Girondins
GIFT OF TONGUES: from the Holy Spirit, Acts 2:3–4
MEAN: common, undistinguished

REVOLVED: considered, reflected on
LOCAL PATRIMONY: national or more confined attachments and loyalties
COMMON-PLACES: traditional topics
SCHOOLS: schools of philosophic thought or of rhetoric

In all their comprehensive bearings known
And visible to Philosophers of old,

■ *W thinks of two ancient Greeks who fought tyranny, and of opposition to Julius Caesar by Brutus, who regarded justice and equity as natural goods.*

■ Men who, to business of the world untrained,
Lived in the Shade, and to Harmodius known
And his Compeer Aristogiton, known
To Brutus, that tyrannic Power is weak,
Hath neither gratitude, nor faith, nor love,
Nor the support of good or evil men
To trust in, that the Godhead which is ours   170
Can never utterly be charmed or stilled,*
That nothing hath a natural right to last
But equity and reason, that all else
Meets foes irreconcilable, and at best
Doth live but by variety of disease.

Well might my wishes be intense, my thoughts
Strong and perturbed, not doubting at that time
Creed which ten shameful years* have not annulled,
But that the virtue of one paramount mind

■ *He hopes, despite disappointment in immediate results of the revolution, that it has laid a foundation for future liberty.*

■ Would have abashed those impious crests,* have quelled   180
Outrage and bloody power, and in despite
Of what the People were through ignorance
And immaturity, and in the teeth
Of desperate opposition from without,
Have cleared a passage for just government,
And left a solid birth-right to the State,

CHARMED OR STILLED: tricked or defeated
TEN SHAMEFUL YEARS: 1793–1803, Reign of Terror, then rise of Napoleon
IMPIOUS CRESTS: radical Jacobins

10.5 Laurent Blanchard (1767–1819). *Homage to the Girondins*, 1793. Musée de la Ville de Paris, Musée Carnavalet, Paris / Bridgeman Images. When Wordsworth arrived in Paris from Orléans in late October 1792, he made acquaintances among the Girondins, including the writers Jean-Antoine Gorsas (1752–1793) and Jacques Pierre Brissot (1754–1793). He might have remained with them longer, but within a month was "Compelled by nothing less than absolute want / Of funds" to return to England.

Redeemed according to example given
By ancient Lawgivers.

           In this frame of mind
Reluctantly to England I returned,
Compelled by nothing less than absolute want   190
Of funds for my support, else,* well assured
That I both was and must be of small worth,
No better than an alien in the Land,
■ I doubtless should have made a common cause
With some who perished, haply* perished too,
A poor mistaken and bewildered offering,
Should to the breast of Nature have gone back
With all my resolutions, all my hopes,
A Poet only to myself, to Men
Useless, and even, belovèd Friend! a soul   200
To thee unknown.

           When to my native Land
(After a whole year's absence) I returned,
I found the air yet busy with the stir
Of a contention which had been raised up
Against the Traffickers* in Negro blood,
An effort, which though baffled, nevertheless
Had called back old forgotten principles
Dismissed from service, had diffused some truths
And more of virtuous feeling through the heart

ELSE: or otherwise
HAPLY: by chance or accident
TRAFFICKERS: slave traders

■ *Had he stayed in France, W might have met the fate of many Girondins, execution, and never would have known Coleridge.*

■ *Abolitionists, though then blocked, rally to the cause of French liberty. W later will support ending the slave trade and slavery.*

10.6 James Hayllar (1829–1920). *Granville Sharp (1735–1813), The Abolitionist, Rescuing a Slave from The Hands of His Master,* 1874. Victoria and Albert Museum. V&A Images / Art Resource, NY. When Wordsworth returned to England, he found that prominent citizens, among them Sharp and William Wilberforce (1759–1833) had "raised up / Against the Traffickers in Negro blood."

■ Of the English People. And no few of those   210
So numerous (little less in verity
Than a whole Nation crying with one voice)
Who had been crossed in this their just intent
And righteous hope, thereby were well prepared
To let that journey sleep awhile and join
Whatever other Caravan appeared
To travel forward towards Liberty

With more success. For me that strife* had ne'er
Fastened on my affections, nor did now
Its unsuccessful issue much excite   220
My sorrow, having laid this faith to heart,
That if France prospered good Men would not long
Pay fruitless worship to humanity,
And this most rotten branch of human shame,*
Object, as seemed, of a superfluous pains
Would fall together with its parent tree.

■ *He is aghast to see England move against France.*

■ Such was my then belief, that there was one,
And only one solicitude for all.
And now the strength of Britain was put forth
In league with the confederated Host,*   230
Not in my single self alone I found,
But in the minds of all ingenuous Youth,

■ *A leaf on the tree of his own country, he is now by his own convictions detached, blown off.*

Change and subversion from this hour. No shock
Given to my moral nature had I known
Down to that very moment; neither lapse
Nor turn of sentiment that might be named
A revolution, save at this one time,
All else was progress on the self-same path
On which with a diversity of pace

■ *Alienated from his country's entry into war, he feels inner conflict and seems alone.*

I had been travelling; this a stride at once   240
Into another region. True it is,
'Twas not concealed with what ungracious eyes
Our native Rulers from the very first

THAT STRIFE: abolition
ROTTEN . . . SHAME: slavery and the slave trade
HOST: Britain, Austria, Prussia, Spain, and others

Had looked upon regenerated France,
Nor had I doubted that this day would come.
But in such contemplation I had thought
Of general interests only, beyond this
Had never once foretasted the event.
Now had I other business, for I felt
The ravage of this most unnatural strife   250
In my own heart; there lay it like a weight
At enmity with all the tenderest springs
Of my enjoyments. I, who with the breeze
Had played, a green leaf on the blessèd tree
Of my belovèd Country; nor had wished
For happier fortune than to wither there,

■ Now from my pleasant station* was cut off
And tossed about in whirlwinds. I rejoiced,
Yes, afterwards truth painful to record!
Exulted in the triumph of my soul   260
When Englishmen by thousands were o'erthrown,*
Left without glory on the Field, or driven,

■ Brave hearts, to shameful flight. It was a grief,
Grief call it not, 'twas any thing but that,
A conflict of sensations without name,
Of which he only who may love the sight
Of a Village Steeple as I do can judge
When in the Congregation, bending all
To their great Father, prayers were offered up,
Or praises for our Country's Victories,   270

PLEASANT STATION: place on that tree, point of view
WHEN . . . o'ERTHROWN: in battles fought in late 1793

10.7 Charles Benazech (1767–1794). *Louis XVI (1754–1793) at the Foot of the Scaffold, 21st January 1793*, c. 1793. Château de Versailles / Giraudon / Bridgeman Images. France declared war on England on February 1, 1793, three days after Wordsworth's two volumes of verse, *An Evening Walk* and *Descriptive Sketches*, were published.

10.8 John Glover (1767–1849). *Sandown Bay, from near Shanklin Chine, Isle of Wight*, 1827. Yale Center for British Art, Paul Mellon Collection. In late June 1793, Wordsworth and his friend William Calvert stayed "Through a whole month of calm and glassy days / In that delightful island," the Isle of Wight, able to witness the British Fleet preparing for war against France.

And 'mid the simple worshippers, perchance,
I only, like an uninvited Guest
Whom no one owned,* sate silent, shall I add,
Fed on the day of vengeance yet to come?

Oh! much have they to account for, who could tear
By violence at one decisive rent
From the best Youth in England their dear pride,

■ *A new, false patriotism prevails. It claims that misguided ventures against the French republicans are victories. These acts betray the youth of England and mock the pretense to wisdom in decisions of older men.*

■ Their joy in England; this too, at a time
In which worst losses easily might wear
The best of names, when patriotic love   280
Did of itself in modesty give way
Like the Precursor when the Deity
Is come whose Harbinger he is, a time
In which apostacy from ancient faith
Seemed but conversion to a higher creed,
Withal a season dangerous and wild,
A time in which Experience would have plucked
Flowers out of any hedge to make thereof
A Chaplet,* in contempt of his grey locks.

Ere yet the Fleet of Britain had gone forth   290
On this unworthy service, whereunto
The unhappy counsel of a few weak Men

■ *He witnesses terrible instruments of war as they gather.*

■ Had doomed it, I beheld the Vessels lie,
A brood of gallant Creatures, on the Deep
I saw them in their rest, a sojourner

OWNED: acknowledged, welcomed
CHAPLET: wreath for the head

10.9 Dominic Serres (1722–1793). *Warships Preparing to Sail from their Anchorage*, 1782. Yale Center for British Art, The U Collection. "I beheld the Vessels lie, / A brood of gallant Creatures . . . thought of woes to come, / And sorrow for mankind, and pain of heart."

Through a whole month of calm and glassy days
In that delightful Island* which protects
Their place of convocation;* there I heard
Each evening, walking by the still sea-shore,
A monitory sound which never failed,   300
The sunset Cannon. While the Orb went down
In the tranquillity of Nature, came
That voice, ill requiem! seldom heard by me
Without a spirit overcast, a deep
Imagination, thought of woes to come,
And sorrow for mankind, and pain of heart.

ISLAND: the Isle of Wight
PLACE OF CONVOCATION: gathering place, Portsmouth

In France, the Men who for their desperate ends
Had plucked up mercy by the roots were glad
Of this new enemy. Tyrants,* strong before
In devilish pleas, were ten times stronger now,   310
And thus beset with Foes on every side
The goaded Land waxed mad; the crimes of few
Spread into madness of the many, blasts
From hell came sanctified like airs from heaven;
The sternness of the Just, the faith of those
Who doubted not that Providence had times
Of anger and of vengeance, theirs who throned
The human understanding* paramount
And made of that their God, the hopes of those
Who were content to barter short-lived pangs   320
For a paradise of ages, the blind rage
Of insolent tempers, the light vanity
Of intermeddlers, steady purposes
Of the suspicious, slips of the indiscreet,
And all the accidents of life were pressed
Into one service, busy with one work;

■ *Bowing to the mob, the National Convention arrests the Girondins. The Reign of Terror begins, the guillotine falls faster, more often, like a whirling toy windmill urged on by a child's running.*

■ The Senate was heart-stricken,* not a voice
Uplifted, none to oppose or mitigate:
Domestic carnage now filled all the year
With Feast-days; the old Man from the chimney-nook,   330
The Maiden from the bosom of her Love,
The Mother from the cradle of her Babe,
The Warrior from the field, all perished, all,

TYRANTS: men such as Robespierre
UNDERSTANDING: here, a narrowed, irreligious rationale
HEART-STRICKEN: lifeless, inert

Friends, enemies, of all parties, ages, ranks,
Head after head, and never heads enough
For those that bade them fall: they found their joy,
They made it, ever thirsty as a Child,
If light desires of innocent little Ones
May with such heinous appetites be matched,
Having a toy, a wind-mill, though the air   340
Do of itself blow fresh, and make the vane
Spin in his eyesight, he is not content,
But with the play-thing at arm's length he sets
His front against the blast, and runs amain
To make it whirl the faster.

                    In the depth
Of those enormities, even thinking minds
Forgot at seasons whence they had their being,
Forgot that such a sound was ever heard
As Liberty upon earth; yet all beneath
Her innocent authority was wrought,   350
Nor could have been, without her blessèd name.
The illustrious Wife of Roland,* in the hour
Of her composure, felt that agony
And gave it vent in her last words. O Friend!
It was a lamentable time for man
Whether a hope had e'er been his or not;
A woeful time for them whose hopes did still
Outlast the shock; most woeful for those few,

WIFE OF ROLAND: See illustration 10.11.

10.10 Pierre-Antoine Demachy (1723–1807). *An Execution, Place de la Révolution, between August 1793 and June 1794*, c. 1794. Musée de la Ville de Paris, Musée Carnavalet, Paris / Bridgeman Images. "Domestic carnage now filled all the year." The Reign of Terror and its "unjust Tribunals" accelerated in September 1793 and lasted until Robespierre himself was guillotined on July 28, 1794. Thousands perished. In 1840 Wordsworth stated that he had witnessed the execution of Antoine-Joseph Gorsas on October 7, 1793.

■ *Having repulsed their enemies, the French occupy Belgium, parts of Holland, and the Rhineland.*

■ *W dreams himself entangled in the Terror, wrongly accused yet wracked by inner guilt.*

10.11 Johann Ernst Heinsius (1740–1812). *Madame Jeanne-Marie Roland de La Platière, née Philippon (1754–1793)*, 1792. Château de Versailles / Bridgeman Images. Favored hostess to the doomed Girondins, "the illustrious Wife of Roland" was guillotined on November 8, 1793. On the way to the guillotine she is reported to have cried out, "O liberty, how many crimes are committed in thy name!"

They had the deepest feeling of the grief,
Who still were flattered,* and had trust in man.   360
■ Meanwhile the Invaders* fared as they deserved;
The Herculean Commonwealth* had put forth her arms
And throttled with an infant Godhead's might
The snakes about her cradle: that was well
And as it should be, yet no cure for those
Whose souls were sick with pain of what would be
Hereafter brought in charge against mankind.
Most melancholy at that time, O Friend!
Were my day thoughts, my dreams were miserable:
Through months, through years, long after the last beat   370
Of those atrocities (I speak bare truth,
As if to thee alone in private talk)
■ I scarcely had one night of quiet sleep,
Such ghastly visions had I of despair
And tyranny and implements of death,
And long orations which in dreams I pleaded
Before unjust Tribunals with a voice
Labouring, a brain confounded, and a sense
Of treachery and desertion in the place
The holiest that I knew of, my own soul.   380

When I began at first in early youth
To yield myself to Nature, when that strong
And holy passion overcame me first,
Neither day nor night, evening or morn

FLATTERED: deceived into hope or optimism
INVADERS: the British and their allies
HERCULEAN COMMONWEALTH: the young republic, like infant Hercules

Were free from the oppression: but Great God!
Who send'st thyself into this breathing world
Through Nature and through every kind of life,
And mak'st Man what he is, Creature divine,
In single or in social eminence
Above all these raised infinite ascents,   390
When reason, which enables him to be,
Is not sequestered,* what a change is here!
How different ritual for this after worship,

■ *Love of humanity, once a secure joy, is tested by the Terror, which outrages reason yet invokes its very name.*

■ What countenance* to promote this second love!*
That first was service but to things which lie
At rest, within the bosom of thy will:
Therefore to serve was high beatitude;
The tumult was a gladness, and the fear
Ennobling, venerable; sleep secure,
And waking thoughts more rich than happiest dreams.   400

But as the ancient Prophets were enflamed*
Nor wanted consolations of their own

■ *The abuses of the revolution seem bitter overflow from a reservoir filled by long ages of fear and loathing.*

And majesty of mind when they denounced
On Towns and Cities, wallowing in the abyss
Of their offences, punishment to come;
Or saw like other men with bodily eyes
Before them in some desolated place
The consummation of the wrath of Heaven,
So did some portions of that spirit fall
On me, to uphold me through those evil times,   410

SEQUESTERED: here, kept from encroachment, protected
COUNTENANCE: encouragement or support
SECOND LOVE: love of humanity
ENFLAMED: impassioned, inspired

And in their rage and dog-day heat I found
Something to glory in, as just and fit,
And in the order of sublimest laws;
And even if that were not, amid the awe
Of unintelligible chastisement*
I felt a kind of sympathy with power,
Motions raised up within me, nevertheless,
Which had relationship to highest things.
Wild blasts of music thus did find their way
Into the midst of terrible events,   420
So that worst tempests might be listened to:
Then was the truth received into my heart
That under heaviest sorrow earth can bring,
Griefs bitterest of ourselves or of our Kind,
If from the affliction somewhere do not grow
Honour which could not else have been, a faith,
An elevation, and a sanctity,
If new strength be not given, or old restored,
The blame is ours not Nature's. When a taunt
■ Was taken up by Scoffers in their pride,   430
Saying, 'Behold the harvest which we reap
From popular Government and Equality,'
I saw that it was neither these, nor aught
Of wild belief engrafted on their names
By false philosophy, that caused the woe,
But that it was a reservoir of guilt
And ignorance, filled up from age to age,

UNINTELLIGIBLE CHASTISEMENT: senseless punishments or executions

That could no longer hold its loathsome charge*
But burst, and spread in deluge through the Land.

And as the desart hath green spots, the sea   440
Small islands in the midst of stormy waves,
So that disastrous period did not want*
Such sprinklings of all human excellence
As were a joy to hear of. Yet (nor less
For those bright spots, those fair examples given
Of fortitude, and energy, and love,
And human nature faithful to itself
Under worst trials), was I impelled to think

■ *Of the glad time when first I traversed France,*
A youthful Pilgrim, above all remembered   450
That day when through an Arch that spanned the street,
A rainbow made of garish ornaments,
Triumphal pomp for Liberty confirmed,
We* walked, a pair of weary Travellers,
Along the Town of Arras, place from which
Issued* that Robespierre, who afterwards
Wielded the sceptre of the Atheist* crew.
When the calamity spread far and wide,
And this same City, which had then appeared
To outrun the rest in exultation, groaned   460
Under the vengeance of her cruel Son,
As Lear reproached the winds,* I could almost
Have quarreled with that blameless spectacle

For being yet an image in my mind
To mock me under such a strange reverse.

O Friend! few happier moments have been mine
Through my whole life than that when first I heard
That this foul Tribe of Moloch* was o'erthrown,
And their chief Regent levelled with the dust.
The day was one which haply* may deserve   470
A separate chronicle. Having gone abroad
From a small Village* where I tarried then,
To the same far-secluded privacy
■ I was returning. Over the smooth Sands
Of Leven's ample Æstuary lay
My journey, and beneath a genial sun
With distant prospect among gleams of sky
And clouds, and intermingled mountain tops,
In one inseparable glory clad,
Creatures of one ethereal substance, met   480
In Consistory, like a diadem
Or crown of burning Seraphs, as they sit
In the Empyrean. Underneath this show
Lay, as I knew, the nest of pastoral Vales
Among whose happy* fields I had grown up
From childhood. On the fulgent* spectacle
Which neither changed, nor stirred, nor passed away,
I gazed, and with a fancy more alive
On this account, that I had chanced to find

■ *The first he was in France is recollected now and compared with present tumult and imminent departure.*

■ *Returned to the Lake District, W visits the resting place of his dear teacher, who introduced him to the honorable labor of poetry.*

CHARGE: here, liquid contents (used metaphorically)
WANT: lack
WE: W and Robert Jones in July 1790 (Book Sixth)
ISSUED: came, was born
As . . . WINDS: *King Lear* 3.2.14–24

MOLOCH: a fallen angel in *Paradise Lost*
HAPLY: in this instance
VILLAGE: probably Rampside
HAPPY: fortunate, blessed
FULGENT: shining or flashing brilliantly

That morning, ranging through the churchyard graves   490
Of Cartmel's rural Town, the place in which
An honoured Teacher* of my youth was laid.
While we were School-boys he had died among us
And was borne hither, as I knew, to rest
With his own Family. A plain Stone, inscribed
With name, date, office, pointed out the spot,
To which a slip of verses was subjoined*
(By his desire, as afterwards I learned),
A fragment from the Elegy of Gray.*
A week, or little less, before his death   500
He had said to me, 'my head will soon lie low,'
And when I saw the turf that covered him,
After the lapse* of full eight years, those words,
With sound of voice and countenance of the Man,
Came back upon me; so that some few tears
Fell from me in my own despite. And now,
Thus travelling smoothly o'er the level Sands,
I thought with pleasure of the Verses graven
Upon his Tomb-stone, saying to myself,
He loved the Poets, and if now alive   510
Would have loved me, as one not destitute
Of promise, nor belying the kind hope
That he had formed when I, at his command,
Began to spin, at first, my toilsome* Song.

Crossing great tidal sands, a passing traveler offers W stunning news.

Without me and within, as I advanced,
All that I saw, or felt, or communed with
Was gentleness and peace. Upon a small
And rocky Island near, a fragment stood
(Itself like a sea rock) of what had been
A Romish* Chapel, where in ancient times   520
Masses were said at the hour which suited those
Who crossed the Sands with ebb of morning tide:
Not far from this still Ruin all the Plain
Was spotted with a variegated crowd
Of Coaches, Wains,* and Travellers, horse and foot,
Wading, beneath the conduct of their Guide
In loose procession, through the shallow Stream
Of inland water: the great Sea, meanwhile,
Was at safe distance, far retired. I paused,
Unwilling to proceed, the scene appeared   530
So gay and chearful, when a Traveller
Chancing to pass, I carelessly inquired
If any news were stirring: he replied
In the familiar language of the day
That 'Robespierre was dead.' Nor was a doubt,
On further question, left within my mind
But that the tidings were substantial truth,
That He and his Supporters all were fallen.*

Great was my glee of spirit, great my joy
In vengeance, and eternal justice, thus   540

TEACHER: William Taylor (1754–1786)

SUBJOINED: added beneath

ELEGY OF GRAY: Thomas Gray's "Elegy in a Country Churchyard"

LAPSE: from 1786 to 1794

TOILSOME: composed with effort or labor

ROMISH: Roman Catholic

WAINS: large uncovered wagons

HE . . . FALLEN: He and more than eighty were guillotined.

W rejoices, a new beginning may be at hand . . .

. . . and he recalls his happy boyhood ventures there.

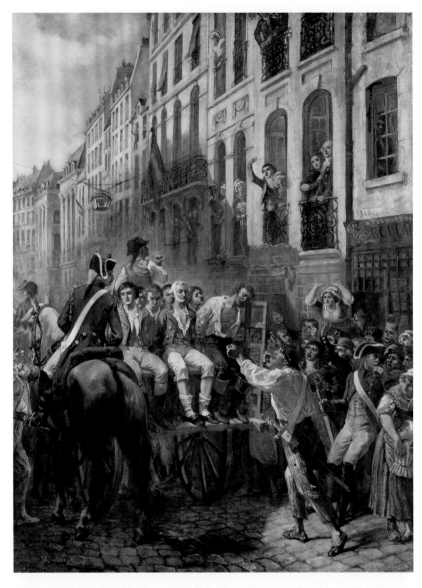

10.12 Alfred Mouillard (1831–1907). *Robespierre (1758–1794) and Saint-Just (1767–1794) Leaving for the Guillotine, 28th July 1794*, 1884. Galerie Dijol, Paris / Bridgeman Images. The "chief Regent," Robespierre, was "levelled with the dust" on July 28, 1794.

Made manifest. 'Come now ye golden times,'
Said I, forth-breathing on those open Sands
A Hymn of triumph, 'as the morning comes
Out of the bosom of the night, come Ye:
Thus far our trust is verified; behold!
They who with clumsy desperation brought
Rivers of blood, and preached that nothing else
Could cleanse the Augean Stable,* by the might
Of their own Helper* have been swept away;
Their madness is declared and visible,   550
Elsewhere will safety now be sought, and Earth
March firmly towards righteousness and peace.'
Then schemes I framed more calmly, when and how
The madding* Factions might be tranquillised,
And, though through hardships manifold and long,
The mighty renovation would proceed:
Thus interrupted by uneasy bursts
Of exultation, I pursued my way
Along that very Shore which I had skimmed
In former times, when spurring from the Vale   560
Of Nightshade and St. Mary's mouldering Fane
And the Stone Abbot, after circuit made
In wantonness of heart, a joyous Crew
Of School-boys, hastening to their distant home,
Along the margin of the moonlight Sea,
We beat with thundering hoofs the level sand.*

CLEANSE . . . STABLE: a labor of Hercules
HELPER: the guillotine
MADDING: to make crazed or unbalanced
WE . . . SAND: repeated from 2.144

10.13 David Cox (1783–1859). *Crossing Lancaster Sands*, mid-1830s. Yale Center for British Art, Paul Mellon Collection. In August 1794, near Rampside on Morecambe Bay, Wordsworth "crossed the Sands with ebb of morning tide" and amidst "a variegated crowd / Of Coaches, Wains, and Travellers, horse and foot," first heard "That *'Robespierre was dead.'*"

From this time forth, in France, as is well known,
Authority put on a milder face,
Yet every thing was wanting* that might give
Courage to them who looked for good by light   570
Of rational experience, good I mean
At hand, and in the spirit of past aims.

■ The Reign of Terror ends, and W hopes that the first revolutionary goals might be fulfilled and spread, achieving similar results at home.

■ The same belief I nevertheless retained;
The language of the Senate and the acts
And public measures of the Government,
Though both of heartless* omen, had not power
To daunt me; in the People was my trust

■ Natural feeling and intuition had replaced, for young souls, bonds of social convention.

And in the virtues which mine eyes had seen,
And to the ultimate repose of things
I looked with unabated confidence.   580
I knew that wound external could not take
Life from the young Republic, that new Foes
Would only follow in the path of shame
Their brethren, and her triumphs be in the end
Great, universal, irresistible.
This faith, which was an object in my mind
Of passionate intuition, had effect
Not small in dazzling me; for thus, through zeal,
Such victory I confounded in my thoughts

■ Those in France who hoped revolutionary ideals might prevail now seek self-preservation, yet W scorns those English wise heads who believe France is doomed.

With one far higher and more difficult,   590
Triumphs of unambitious peace at home
And noiseless fortitude. Beholding still
Resistance strong as heretofore, I thought

That what was in degree the same, was likewise
The same in quality, that as the worse*
Of the two spirits then at strife remained
Untired, the better* surely would preserve
The heart that first had rouzed him, never dreamt
That transmigration could be undergone,
A fall of being suffered, and of hope   600
By creature* that appeared to have received
Entire conviction what a great ascent
Had been accomplished, what high faculties
■ It had been called to. Youth maintains, I knew,
In all conditions of society,
Communion more direct and intimate
With Nature and the inner strength she has,
And hence, oft-times, no less with Reason too,
Than Age or Manhood even. To Nature then
Power had reverted; habit, custom, law   610
Had left an interregnum's open space
For her to stir about in, uncontroled.
The warmest judgments and the most untaught
Found in events which every day brought forth
Enough to sanction them, and far, far more
To shake the authority of canons drawn
■ From ordinary practice. I could see
How Babel-like the employment was of those
Who, by the recent Deluge stupefied,
With their whole souls went culling from the day   620

WANTING: lacking
HEARTLESS: dispiriting

THE WORSE: those allied against France
THE BETTER: France herself
CREATURE: a thing created, here, the French Republic

Its petty promises to build a tower

For their own safety; laughed at gravest heads,

Who, watching in their hate of France for signs

Of her disasters, if the stream of rumour

Brought with it one green branch, conceited* thence

That not a single tree was left alive

In all her forests. How could I believe

That wisdom could in any shape come near

Men clinging to delusions so insane?

And thus, experience proving that no few   630

Of my opinions had been just, I took

Like credit to myself where less was due,

And thought that other notions were as sound,

Yea could not but be right, because I saw

That foolish men opposed them.

10.14 Karl Anton Hickel (1745–1798). *William Pitt Addressing the House of Commons on the French Declaration of War, 1793*, c. 1794. National Portrait Gallery, London / Bridgeman Images. "Our Shepherds . . . Thirsted to make the guardian Crook of Law / A tool of Murder." By 1793, Wordsworth thought Pitt and his ministers nothing more than "vermin working out of reach" to "make an end of Liberty."

To a strain

British leaders, more subtle in deceit than Robespierre, arouse W's contempt, so much so he will shape no verse on it.

More animated I might here give way,

And tell, since juvenile errors are my theme,

What in those days through Britain was performed

To turn all judgments out of their right course;

But this is passion over near ourselves,   640

Reality too close and too intense,

And mingled up with something in my mind

Of scorn and condemnations personal

That would profane the sanctity of verse.

Our Shepherds* (this say merely) at that time

Thirsted to make the guardian Crook of Law

A tool of Murder; they who ruled the State,

Though with such awful proof before their eyes

That he who would sow death, reaps death, or worse,

And can reap nothing better, child-like, longed   650

To imitate, not wise enough to avoid:

Giants in their impiety alone,

But in their weapons and their warfare base

As vermin working out of reach, they leagued

CONCEITED: in their conceit imagined

SHEPHERDS: national leaders of church and state

Their strength perfidiously, to undermine
Justice, and make an end of Liberty.

But from these bitter truths I must return
To my own History. It hath been told
That I was led to take an eager part
In arguments of civil polity   660
Abruptly, and indeed before my time:

■ *The fable of the shield with two sides, germane to judgment.*

■ I had approached, like other Youth, the Shield
Of human nature from the golden* side
And would have fought even to the death to attest
The quality of the metal which I saw.
What there is best in individual Man,
Of wise in passion, and sublime in power,

■ *W reflects with wonder on the possibilities and promise of that time.*

What there is strong and pure in household love,
Benevolent in small societies,
And great in large ones also, when called forth   670
By great occasions, these were things of which
I something knew, yet even these themselves,
Felt deeply, were not thoroughly understood
By Reason; nay far from it, they were yet,
As cause was given me afterwards to learn,
Not proof against the injuries of the day,
Lodged only at the Sanctuary's door,
Not safe within its bosom.* Thus prepared,
And with such general insight into evil,
And of the bounds which sever it from good,   680

GOLDEN: more valuable or optimistic
WITHIN ITS BOSOM: inside the church as protection from prosecution

As books and common intercourse with life
Must needs have given to the noviciate* mind
(When the world travels in a beaten road,
Guide faithful as is needed), I began
To think with fervour upon management
Of Nations, what it is and ought to be,
And how their worth depended on their Laws
And on the Constitution of the State.

O pleasant exercise of hope and joy!
For great were the auxiliars* which then stood   690
Upon our side, we who were strong in love;
Bliss was it in that dawn to be alive,

■ But to be young was very heaven: O times
In which the meagre, stale, forbidding ways
Of custom, law, and statute took at once
The attraction of a Country in Romance;
When Reason seemed the most to assert her rights
When most intent on making of herself
A prime Enchanter to assist the work
Which then was going forwards in her name.   700
Not favoured spots alone, but the whole earth
The beauty wore of promise, that which sets,
To take an image which was felt, no doubt,
Among the bowers of paradise itself,
The budding rose above the rose full blown.*
What temper* at the prospect did not wake

NOVICIATE: novitiate, novice, inexperienced
AUXILIARS: helpers
FULL BLOWN: in full blossom
TEMPER: character, temperament

To happiness unthought-of? The inert*
Were rouzed, and lively natures rapt away:
They who had fed their childhood upon dreams,
The Play-fellows of Fancy, who had made   710
All powers of swiftness, subtlety, and strength
Their ministers, used to stir in lordly wise
Among the grandest objects of the sense
And deal with whatsoever they found there
As if they had within some lurking right
To wield it; they too, who of gentle mood
Had watched all gentle motions, and to these
Had fitted their own thoughts, schemers more mild,
And in the region of their peaceful selves,
Did now find helpers to their hearts' desire,   720
And stuff at hand, plastic* as they could wish,
Were called upon to exercise their skill,
Not in Utopia, subterraneous fields,
Or some secreted Island, Heaven knows where,
But in the very world which is the world
Of all of us, the place in which, in the end,
We find our happiness, or not at all.

■ *He thinks of future time with hope . . .*

Why should I not confess that earth was then
To me what an inheritance new-fallen
Seems, when the first time visited, to one   730
Who thither comes to find in it his home?
He walks about and looks upon the place

INERT: apathetic, apolitical
PLASTIC: amenable, willing to be shaped

With cordial transport, moulds it, and remoulds,
And is half pleased with things that are amiss,
'Twill be such joy to see them disappear.

An active partisan, I thus convoked*
From every object pleasant circumstance
To suit my ends; I moved among mankind
With genial feelings still predominant;
When erring, erring on the better part,   740
And in the kinder spirit; placable,*
Indulgent oft-times to the worst desires
As on one side not uninformed that men
See as it hath been taught them, and that time
Gives rights to error: on the other hand
That throwing off oppression must be work
As well of license as of liberty;

■ And above all, for this was more than all,
Not caring if the wind did now and then
Blow keen upon an eminence that gave   750
Prospect so large into futurity; happy,
In brief, a child of nature, as at first,
Diffusing only those affections wider
That from the cradle had grown up with me,
And losing, in no other way than light
Is lost in light, the weak in the more strong.

CONVOKED: called together, summoned
PLACABLE: able to be moved, conciliatory

In the main outline, such it might be said

■ *. . . until his England*
is at war with France.

■ Was my condition, till with open war
Britain opposed the Liberties of France:
This threw me first out of the pale of love,   760
Soured and corrupted upwards to the source
My sentiments, was not,* as hitherto,
A swallowing up of lesser things in great,
But change of them into their opposites,
And thus a way was opened for mistakes
And false conclusions of the intellect

■ *Events now seem to*
overtake ideals:
the French set out
to conquer.

As gross in their degree, and in their kind
Far, far more dangerous. What had been a pride
Was now a shame; my likings and my loves
Ran in new channels, leaving old ones dry,   770
And thus a blow, which in maturer age
Would but have touched the judgment, struck more deep
Into sensations near the heart: meantime,
As from the first, wild theories* were afloat,
Unto the subtleties of which, at least,
I had but lent a careless ear, assured
Of this, that time would soon set all things right,
Prove that the multitude had been oppressed,
And would be so no more.

             But when events
Brought less encouragement, and unto these   780
The immediate proof of principles no more

Could be entrusted, while the events themselves,
Worn out in greatness and in novelty,
Less occupied the mind, and sentiments
Could through my understanding's natural growth
No longer justify themselves through faith
Of inward consciousness and hope that laid
Its hand upon its object, evidence
Safer, of universal application such
As could not be impeached, was sought elsewhere.   790

■ And now, become Oppressors in their turn,
Frenchmen had changed a war of self-defence
For one of conquest, losing sight of all
Which they had struggled for; and mounted up*
Openly, in the view of earth and heaven,
The scale of Liberty. I read her doom,
Vexed inly somewhat, it is true, and sore,
But not dismayed, nor taking to* the shame
Of a false Prophet; but, rouzed up I stuck
More firmly to old tenets, and to prove   800
Their temper strained them more, and thus in heat
Of contest did opinions every day
Grow into consequence* till round my mind
They clung, as if they were the life of it.

This was the time when all things tended fast
To depravation; the Philosophy

WAS NOT: though there was not
WILD THEORIES: Godwin's *Enquiry Concerning Political Justice*

MOUNTED UP: took possession of
TAKING TO: assuming, admitting to
GROW INTO CONSEQUENCE: gain credibility

10.15 James Northcote (1746–1831). *Portrait of William Godwin*, 1802. National Portrait Gallery, London / De Agostini Picture Library / Bridgeman Images. In London, "wild theories were afloat" in early 1795. Wordsworth mingled with leaders of radical thought including Godwin (1756–1836). He admired Godwin's *Enquiry Concerning Political Justice* (1793): "the Philosophy / That promised to abstract the hopes of man" with reason alone. His admiration did not last long and led to a crisis: "With sorrow, disappointment, vexing thoughts, / Confusion of the judgment, zeal decayed" (11.4–5).

■ *A plea to abstract reason claims to leave all passions far behind, yet lets them in.*

That promised to abstract the hopes of man
Out of his feelings, to be fixed thenceforth
For ever in a purer element,
Found ready welcome. Tempting region that   810
For Zeal to enter and refresh herself,
Where passions had the privilege to work,
And never hear the sound of their own names:
■ But speaking more in charity, the dream
Was flattering to the young ingenuous mind
Pleased with extremes, and not the least with that
Which makes the human Reason's naked self
The object of its fervour: what delight!
How glorious! in self-knowledge and self-rule,
To look through all the frailties of the world   820
And with a resolute mastery shaking off
The accidents of nature, time, and place
That make up the weak being of the past,
Build social freedom on its only basis,
The freedom of the individual mind,
Which, to the blind restraints of general laws
Superior, magisterially adopts
One guide, the light of circumstances, flashed
Upon an independent intellect.

For howsoe'er unsettled, never once   830
Had I thought ill of human kind, or been

Indifferent to its welfare; but, enflamed
With thirst of a secure intelligence

- *With faith in human liberty, he now believes he had misread the way to make it manifest . . .*

- And sick of other passion, I pursued
A higher nature, wished that man should start
Out of the worm-like state in which he is,
And spread abroad the wings of Liberty,
Lord of himself in undisturbed delight,
A noble aspiration. Yet* I feel
The aspiration, but with other thoughts   840
And happier; for I was perplexed and sought
To accomplish the transition by such means
As did not lie in nature, sacrificed
The exactness of a comprehensive mind
To scrupulous and microscopic views
That furnished out materials for a work
Of false imagination, placed beyond
The limits of experience and of truth.

Enough, no doubt, the advocates themselves
Of ancient institutions had performed   850
To bring disgrace upon their very names,*
Disgrace of which custom and written law
And sundry moral sentiments, as props
And emanations of those institutes,

- *. . . and even as the old foundations fall away, he tests in thought the very basis of what now should be.*

- Too justly bore a part. A veil had been
Uplifted; why deceive ourselves? 'Twas so,
'Twas even so, and sorrow for the Man

YET: still, even now
THEIR VERY NAMES: the names of the institutions

Who either had not eyes wherewith to see,
Or seeing hath forgotten. Let this pass;
Suffice it that a shock had then been given   860
To old opinions and the minds of all men
Had felt it; that my mind was both let loose,
Let loose and goaded. After what hath been
Already said of patriotic love,
And hinted at in other sentiments,
We need not linger long upon this theme.
This only may be said, that from the first
Having two natures in me, joy the one
The other melancholy, and withal
A happy man, and therefore bold to look   870
On painful things, slow somewhat too, and stern
In temperament, I took the knife in hand
And stopping not at parts less sensitive,
Endeavoured with my best of skill to probe
The living body of society
Even to the heart: I pushed without remorse
My speculations forward; yea, set foot
On Nature's holiest places. Time may come
When some dramatic Story may afford
Shapes livelier to convey to thee, my Friend,   880
What then I learned, or think I learned, of truth
And the errors into which I was betrayed
By present objects, and by reasonings false
From the beginning, inasmuch as drawn

Out of a heart which had been turned aside

From Nature by external accidents,

And which was thus confounded more and more,

■ *Though Nature now no longer seems an only guide . . .*

■ Misguiding and misguided. Thus I fared,

Dragging all passions, notions, shapes of faith

Like culprits to the bar, suspiciously   890

Calling the mind to establish in plain day

Her titles* and her honours, now believing,

Now disbelieving, endlessly perplexed

With impulse, motive, right and wrong, the ground

Of moral obligation, what the rule

And what the sanction, till, demanding proof

And seeking it in every thing, I lost

All feeling of conviction, and in fine*

Sick, wearied out with contrarieties,

Yielded up moral questions in despair,   900

And for my future studies, as the sole

Employment of the enquiring faculty,

Turned towards mathematics, and their clear

■ *. . . he has Coleridge, who regulates his soul, and Dorothy, who brings him to his better self.*

■ *The voice of liberty in France becomes an empty, pompous show.*

■ And solid evidence—Ah! then it was

That Thou, most precious Friend! about this time*

First known to me, didst lend a living help

To regulate my Soul, and then it was

That the belovèd Woman* in whose sight

Those days were passed, now speaking in a voice

Of sudden admonition, like a brook   910

That does but cross* a lonely road, and now

TITLES: claims

IN FINE: in the end

ABOUT THIS TIME: late 1795

BELOVÈD WOMAN: Dorothy, W's sister

CROSS: hug, repeatedly near while in the same direction

Seen, heard, and felt, and caught at every turn,

Companion never lost through many a league,

Maintained for me a saving intercourse

With my true self: for though impaired and changed

Much, as it seemed, I was no further changed

Than as a clouded, not a waning moon:

She in the midst of all preserved me still

A Poet, made me seek beneath that name

My office upon earth, and nowhere else,   920

And lastly, Nature's self, by human love

Assisted, through the weary labyrinth

Conducted me again to open day,

Revived the feelings of my earlier life,

Gave me that strength and knowledge full of peace,

Enlarged and never more to be disturbed,

Which through the steps of our degeneracy,

All degradation of this age, hath still

Upheld me, and upholds me at this day

In the catastrophe* (for so they* dream,   930

And nothing less) when finally, to close

And rivet up the gains of France, a Pope*

Is summoned in to crown an Emperor;

■ This last opprobrium, when we see the dog

Returning to his vomit,* when the sun

That rose in splendour, was alive, and moved

In exultation among living clouds,

Hath put his function and his glory off,

CATASTROPHE: dramatic conclusion, here, of this degeneracy

THEY: supporters of Napoleon

POPE: Pope Pius VII

DOG . . . VOMIT: 2 Peter 2:19–22

10.16 Jacques-Louis David (1748–1825). *The Consecration of the Emperor Napoleon (1769–1821) and the Coronation of the Empress Josephine (1763–1814) by Pope Pius VII, 2nd December 1804,* 1806–1807. Louvre, Paris / Bridgeman Images. Now "a Pope / Is summoned in to crown an Emperor; / This last opprobrium, when we see the dog / Returning to his vomit."

And, turned into a gewgaw, a machine,
Sets like an opera phantom.   940

Thus, O Friend!
Through times of honour and through times of shame
Have I descended, tracing faithfully
The workings of a youthful mind, beneath
The breath of great events, its hopes no less
Than universal, and its boundless love;
■ A Story destined for thy ear, who now
Among the basest and the lowest fallen
Of all the race of men, dost make abode
Where Etna* looketh down on Syracuse,
The city of Timoleon.* Living God!   950
How are the Mighty prostrated! they first,
They first of all that breathe should have awaked
When the great voice was heard out of the tombs
Of ancient Heroes. If for France I have grieved,
Who* in the judgment of no few hath been
A trifler only, in her proudest day
Have been distressed to think of what she once
Promised, now is, a far more sober cause
Thine eyes must see of sorrow in a Land
Strewed with the wreck of loftiest years,* a Land   960
Glorious indeed, substantially renowned
Of simple virtue once, and manly praise,
Now without one memorial hope, not even

A hope to be deferred; for that would serve
To chear the heart in such entire decay.

But indignation works where hope is not,
And thou, O Friend! wilt be refreshed. There is
One great Society alone on earth,
The noble Living and the noble Dead:
Thy consolation shall be there, and Time   970
And Nature shall before thee spread in store
Imperishable thoughts, the place itself
Be conscious of thy presence, and the dull
Sirocco* air of its degeneracy
■ Turn as thou mov'st into a healthful breeze
To cherish and invigorate thy frame.

Thine be those motions strong and sanative,*
A ladder for thy Spirit to reascend
To health and joy and pure contentedness:
To me the grief confined that Thou art gone   980
From this last spot of earth where Freedom now
Stands single in her only Sanctuary,*
A lonely Wanderer, art gone, by pain
Compelled and sickness, at this latter day,
This heavy time of change for all mankind;
I feel for Thee, must utter what I feel:
The sympathies, erewhile, in part discharged,
Gather afresh, and will have vent again;

*Though Sicily is poor,
its people miserable, its
government corrupt, yet
it holds a charm . . .*

*. . . and W pictures
Coleridge there, reviving,
gaining health.*

ETNA: Mount Etna, an active volcano
TIMOLEON: general who defeated a tyrant
WHO: W himself
LAND . . . YEARS: Sicily, with its many ancient ruins

SIROCCO: dry, hot wind from North Africa
SANATIVE: giving health, restorative
ONLY SANCTUARY: Great Britain

My own delights do scarcely seem to me
My own delights; the lordly Alps themselves,   990
Those rosy Peaks from which the Morning looks
Abroad on many Nations, are not now,
Since thy migration and departure, Friend,
The gladsome image in my memory
Which they were used to be. To kindred scenes
On errand, at a time how different!
Thou tak'st thy way, carrying a heart more ripe
For all divine enjoyment, with the soul
Which Nature gives to Poets, now by thought
Matured, and in the summer of its strength.   1000
Oh! wrap him in your Shades, ye Giant Woods
On Etna's side, and thou, O flowery Vale
Of Enna!* is there not some nook of thine
From the first play-time of the infant earth
Kept sacred to restorative delight?

■ *W regards his dreams of Sicily, long held . . .*

■ *. . . and thinks of Coleridge's return.*

■ Child of the mountains, among Shepherds reared,
Even from my earliest school-day time, I loved
To dream of Sicily; and now a strong
And vital promise wafted from that Land
Comes o'er my heart: there's not a single name   1010
Of note belonging to that honoured Isle,
Philosopher or Bard, Empedocles
Or Archimedes, deep and tranquil Soul,
That is not like a comfort to my grief.

ENNA: in central Sicily, famed of Persephone and renewal

And O Theocritus, so far have some
Prevailed among the Powers of heaven and earth
By force of graces which were theirs, that they
Have had, as thou reportest, miracles
Wrought for them in old time; yea not unmoved
When thinking on my own belovèd Friend,   1020
I hear thee tell how bees with honey fed
Divine Comates, by his tyrant Lord
Within a chest imprisoned impiously,
How with their honey from the fields they came
And fed him there, alive from month to month
Because the Goatherd, blessèd Man! had lips
Wet with the Muses' Nectar.

Thus I soothe
The pensive moments by this calm fire-side
And find a thousand fancied images
That chear the thoughts of those I love, and mine.   1030
Our prayers have been accepted: Thou wilt stand,
Not as an Exile but a Visitant

■ On Etna's top; by pastoral Arethuse*
(Or if that fountain be indeed no more,
Then near some other Spring, which by the name
Thou gratulatest,* willingly deceived)
Shalt linger as a gladsome Votary,*
And not a Captive, pining for his home.

ARETHUSE: the spring Arethusa, linked with Milton and Virgil
GRATULATEST: greet with pleasure, welcome
VOTARY: someone dedicated, a worshipper

10.17 Achille-Etna Michallon (1796–1822). *Ruins of the Theatre at Taormina*, 1821. Louvre, Paris / Giraudon / Bridgeman Images. "I loved / To dream of Sicily . . . there's not a single name / Of note belonging to that honoured Isle . . . That is not like a comfort to my grief."

Book Eleventh
IMAGINATION, HOW IMPAIRED AND RESTORED

Long time hath Man's unhappiness and guilt
Detained us; with what dismal sights beset
For the outward view, and inwardly oppressed
With sorrow, disappointment, vexing thoughts,
Confusion of the judgment, zeal decayed,
And lastly, utter loss of hope itself,
And things to hope for. Not with these began
Our Song, and not with these our Song must end:
Ye motions of delight that through the fields
Stir gently, breezes and soft airs that breathe   10
The breath of paradise, and find your way
To the recesses of the soul! Ye Brooks
Muttering along the stones, a busy noise
By day, a quiet one in silent night,
And you, ye Groves, whose ministry it is
To interpose the covert of your shades,
Even as a sleep, betwixt the heart of man
And the uneasy world, 'twixt man himself,
Not seldom, and his own unquiet heart,
Oh! that I had a music and a voice,   20

11.1 Francis Danby (1793–1861). *Children by a Brook*, 1822. Yale Center for British Art, Paul Mellon Collection. "Ye Brooks / Muttering along the stones . . . And you, ye Groves . . . Oh! that I had a music and a voice, / Harmonious as your own, that I might tell / What ye have done for me."

Harmonious as your own, that I might tell
What ye have done for me. The morning shines,

■ *Despite the tumult of his mind following terrors in France, he still repairs to Nature's counterpoise.*

■ Nor heedeth Man's perverseness; Spring returns,

I saw the Spring return, when I was dead

To deeper hope; yet had I* joy for her,

And welcomed her benevolence, rejoiced

In common with the Children of her Love,

Plants, insects, beast in field, and bird in bower.

So neither were complacency nor peace

Nor tender yearnings wanting* for my good   30

Through those distracted times; in Nature still

Glorying, I found a counterpoise in her,

Which, when the spirit of evil* was at height

Maintained for me a secret happiness:

Her I resorted to, and loved so much

I seemed to love as much as heretofore;

And yet this passion, fervent as it was,

Had suffered change; how could there fail to be

Some change, if merely hence, that years of life

Were going on, and with them loss or gain   40

Inevitable, sure alternative.

This History, my Friend, hath chiefly told

Of intellectual power, from stage to stage

Advancing, hand in hand with love and joy,

And of imagination teaching truth

Until that natural graciousness of mind

Gave way to over-pressure of the times

And their disastrous issues. What availed,

YET HAD I: still I had

WANTING: lacking, absent

SPIRIT OF EVIL: the terror, killing, and war he witnessed

11.2 Anthony Vandyke Copley Fielding (1787–1855). *A View on the Brathay near Ambleside*, undated. Yale Center for British Art, Paul Mellon Collection. "I saw the Spring return, when I was dead / To deeper hope; yet had I joy for her . . . Plants, insects, beast in field, and bird in bower." Ambleside lies three miles southeast of Grasmere.

When Spells forbade the Voyager to land,

The fragrance which did ever and anon   50

Give notice of the Shore, from arbours breathed

Of blessèd sentiment and fearless love?

What did such sweet remembrances avail,

Perfidious then, as seemed, what served they then?

My business was upon the barren seas,

My errand was to sail to other coasts:

Shall I avow that I had hope to see,

I mean that future times would surely see

The man to come parted as by a gulph
From him who had been, that I could no more   60
Trust the elevation which had made me one
With the great Family that here and there
Is scattered through the abyss of ages past,

■ *Disillusioned with violent acts and schemes of thought, to poets he returns . . .*

■ Sage, Patriot, Lover, Hero; for it seemed
That their best virtues were not free from taint
Of something false and weak which could not stand
The open eye of Reason. Then I said,
Go to the Poets; they will speak to thee
More perfectly of purer creatures, yet
If Reason be nobility in man,   70
Can aught be more ignoble than the man
Whom they* describe, would fasten if they may
Upon our love by sympathies of truth.

Thus strangely did I war against myself;
A Bigot to a new Idolatry
Did like a Monk who hath forsworn the world
Zealously labour to cut off my heart
From all the sources of her former strength;
And, as by simple waving of a wand
The wizard instantaneously dissolves   80
Palace or grove, even so did I unsoul
As readily by syllogistic words
Some charm of Logic, ever within reach,
Those mysteries of passion which have made

THEY: the poets

11.3 Unknown artist. *Prospero, Miranda and Ariel, from "The Tempest,"* 1780. Yale Center for British Art, Paul Mellon Fund. His imagination impaired, Wordsworth, like "The wizard [who] instantaneously dissolves / Palace or grove," now "cut off my heart / From all the sources of her former strength" and did "unsoul . . . Those mysteries of passion which have made / And shall continue evermore to make . . . One brotherhood of all the human race." The lines allude to Prospero in Shakespeare's *Tempest* (4.1.148–58), who declares, "Our revels now are ended." The "gorgeous palaces, / The solemn temples . . . shall dissolve."

And shall continue evermore to make
(In spite of all that Reason hath performed
And shall perform to exalt and to refine)
One brotherhood of all the human race
Through all the habitations of past years
And those to come; and hence an emptiness   90

■ *. . . though even they seem shrunk in power.*

■ Fell on the Historian's Page, and even on that
Of Poets, pregnant with more absolute truth.
The works of both withered in my esteem,
Their sentence was, I thought, pronounced; their rights
Seemed mortal, and their empire passed away.

W hat then remained in such eclipse? what light
To guide or chear? The laws of things which lie
Beyond the reach of human will or power;
The life of nature by the God of love
Inspired, celestial presence ever pure;   100

■ *Something yet remains not of human work, though its natural force eludes a mind impaired.*

■ *Logic and understanding can, too much, entrance a young mind bent on truth, which leans on feeling, too.*

■ These left, the soul of Youth must needs be rich,
Whatever else be lost, and these were mine,
Not a deaf echo, merely, of the thought,
Bewildered recollections solitary,
But living sounds. Yet in despite of this,
This feeling, which howe'er impaired or damped,
Yet having been once born can never die.
'Tis true that Earth with all her appanage*
Of elements and organs, storm and sunshine,
With her pure forms and colours, pomp of clouds,   110
Rivers and mountains, objects among which
It might be thought that no dislike or blame,
No sense of weakness or infirmity
Or aught amiss could possibly have come,
Yea, even the visible universe was scanned
With something of a kindred spirit,* fell

APPANAGE: endowments, phenomena

OF A KINDRED SPIRIT: akin to "syllogistic words" of logic

Beneath the domination of a taste
Less elevated, which did in my mind
With its more noble influence* interfere,
Its animation, and its deeper sway.   120

T here comes (if need be now to speak of this
After such long detail of our mistakes),
There comes a time when Reason, not the grand
And simple Reason, but that humbler power
Which carries on its no inglorious work
By logic and minute analysis
Is of all Idols that which pleases most

■
The growing mind. A Trifler would he be
Who on the obvious benefits should dwell
That rise out of this process; but to speak   130
Of all the narrow estimates of things
Which hence originate were a worthy theme
For philosophic Verse; suffice it here
To hint that danger cannot but attend
Upon a Function rather proud to be
The enemy of falsehood, than the friend
Of truth, to sit in judgment than to feel.

O h! soul of Nature excellent and fair
That didst rejoice with me, with whom I too
Rejoiced, through early youth before the winds   140
And powerful waters, and in lights and shades

ITS MORE NOBLE INFLUENCE: that of a felt, imaginative reason

That marched and countermarched about the hills

In glorious apparition, now all eye

And now all ear, but ever with the heart

Employed, and the majestic intellect;

■ *He turns again to natural forms . . .*

■ Oh! soul of Nature that dost overflow

With passion and with life, what feeble men

Walk on this earth! how feeble have I been

When thou wert in thy strength! Nor this through stroke

Of human suffering, such as justifies   150

Remissness and inaptitude of mind,

But through presumption,* even in pleasure pleased

Unworthily, disliking here, and there

Liking, by rules of mimic art transferred

■ *. . . though rules of mimic art, the picturesque, distract him from a deeper might.*

■ To things above all art. But more, for this,*

Although a strong infection of the age,

Was never much my habit, giving way

To a comparison of scene with scene,

Bent overmuch on superficial things,

Pampering myself with meagre novelties   160

Of colour and proportion; to the moods

Of time or season, to the moral power,

The affections, and the spirit of the place,

■ *The power of sight had grown supreme.*

Less sensible.* Nor only did the love

Of sitting thus in judgment interrupt

My deeper feelings, but another cause

More subtle and less easily explained

That almost seems inherent in the Creature,

PRESUMPTION: pride, arrogance

FOR THIS: for the activity just mentioned

LESS SENSIBLE: less aware or engaged

11.4 Rev. William Gilpin (1724–1804). *View in Barnscliff, near Scarborough, when Overflowed by the Derwent*, undated. Yale Center for British Art, Paul Mellon Collection. Wordsworth appreciated the concept of the picturesque initiated by Gilpin, but reacted —as did Jane Austen—against making it a complicated set of "rules of mimic art transferred / To things above all art . . . a strong infection of the age" pursued by figures such as Uvedale Price (1747–1829) and Richard Payne Knight (1750–1824).

Sensuous* and intellectual as he is,

A twofold Frame of body and of mind;   170

■ The state to which I now allude was one

In which the eye was master of the heart,

When that which is in every stage of life

The most despotic of our senses gained

Such strength in me as often held my mind

SENSUOUS: possessing or of the senses

In absolute dominion. Gladly here,
Entering upon abstruser argument,
Would I endeavour to unfold the means

■ *In Mary he beholds a simpler, innate sense of Nature's strength.*

Which Nature studiously employs to thwart
This tyranny, summons all the senses each   180
To counteract the other and themselves,
And makes them all, and the objects with which all
Are conversant, subservient in their turn
To the great ends of Liberty and Power.
But this is matter for another Song;
Here only let me add that my delights,
Such as they were, were sought insatiably,
Though 'twas a transport of the outward sense,
Not of the mind, vivid but not profound:
Yet was I often greedy in the chace,   190
And roamed from hill to hill, from rock to rock,
Still craving combinations of new forms,
New pleasure, wider empire for the sight,
Proud of its own endowments, and rejoiced
To lay the inner faculties asleep.

Amid the turns and counter-turns, the strife
And various trials of our complex being,
As we grow up, such thraldom of that sense
Seems hard to shun: and yet I knew a Maid,*
Who, young as I was then, conversed with things   200
In higher style, from Appetites like these

MAID: Mary Hutchinson (1770–1859) married W in 1802.

She, gentle Visitant, as well she might
Was wholly free, far less did critic rules
Or barren intermeddling subtleties

■ Perplex her mind; but wise as Women are
When genial circumstance hath favored them,
She welcomed what was given, and craved no more.
Whatever scene was present to her eyes,
That was the best, to that she was attuned
Through her humility and lowliness,*   210
And through a perfect happiness of soul
Whose variegated feelings were in this
Sisters, that they were each some new delight:
For she was Nature's inmate.* Her the birds
And every flower she met with, could they but
Have known her, would have loved. Methought such
Of sweetness did her presence breathe around
That all the trees, and all the silent hills
And every thing she looked on should have had
An intimation how she bore herself   220
Towards them and to all creatures. God delights
In such a being; for her common thoughts
Are piety, her life is blessedness.

Even like this Maid, before I was called forth
From the retirement* of my native hills,
I loved whate'er I saw; nor lightly loved
But fervently, did never dream of aught

LOWLINESS: lack of self-importance
INMATE: dweller, resident
RETIREMENT: relative seclusion and removal

More grand, more fair, more exquisitely framed
Than those few nooks to which my happy feet

The elemental force of first devotions now returns, an antidote to recent strife.

■ Were limited. I had not at that time   230
Lived long enough, nor in the least survived
The first diviner influence of this world
As it appears to unaccustomed eyes;
I worshipped then among the depth of things
As my soul bade me: could I then take part
In aught but admiration, or be pleased

The mind may fashion deepest feeling into strength and virtue's aid: the spots of time.

With any thing but humbleness and love?
I felt, and nothing else; I did not judge,
I never thought of judging, with the gift
Of all this glory* filled and satisfied.   240
And afterwards, when through the gorgeous Alps
Roaming, I carried with me the same heart:
In truth, this degradation,* howsoe'er
Induced, effect in whatsoe'er degree
Of custom, that prepares such wantonness
As makes the greatest things give way to least,
Of* any other cause which hath been named,
Or lastly, aggravated by the times,*
Which with their passionate sounds might often make
The milder minstrelsies of rural scenes   250
Inaudible, was transient; I had felt
Too forcibly, too early in my life,

The first is on the moors, alone, confronting stark mortality.

Visitings of imaginative power
For this* to last: I shook the habit off

THIS GLORY: the glory of his native hills
THIS DEGRADATION: impairment of imagination
OF: or of
THE TIMES: events of 1792–1803
THIS: this degradation or impairment

Entirely and for ever, and again
In Nature's presence stood, as I stand now,
A sensitive, and a creative Soul.

■ There are in our existence spots of time,
Which with distinct preeminence retain
A renovating Virtue, whence, depressed   260
By false opinion and contentious thought,
Or aught of heavier or more deadly weight,
In trivial occupations and the round
Of ordinary intercourse, our minds
Are nourished and invisibly repaired,
A virtue by which pleasure is enhanced
That penetrates, enables us to mount
When high, more high, and lifts us up when fallen.
This efficacious spirit chiefly lurks
Among those passages of life in which   270
We have had deepest feeling that the mind
Is lord and master, and that outward sense
Is but the obedient servant of her will.
Such moments worthy of all gratitude
Are scattered every where, taking their date
From our first childhood; in our childhood even
Perhaps are most conspicuous. Life with me,
As far as memory can look back, is full
■ Of this beneficent influence. At a time
When scarcely (I was then not six years old)   280

11.5 Attributed to Peter DeWint (1784–1849). *Near Penrith*, undated. Yale Center for British Art, Paul Mellon Collection. Visiting his stern and unaffectionate maternal grandparents at Penrith in 1775, Wordsworth, age five, rode out one morning alongside the house servant, "honest James." However, they soon became "disjoined" and Wordsworth rode on alone.

My hand could hold a bridle, with proud hopes
I mounted, and we rode towards the hills:
We were a pair of horsemen; honest James*
Was with me, my encourager and guide.
We had not travelled long ere some mischance
Disjoined me from my Comrade and, through fear
Dismounting, down the rough and stony Moor
I led my Horse, and stumbling on, at length
Came to a bottom,* where in former times

JAMES: a family servant or retainer
BOTTOM: lower, flat area

A Murderer had been hung in iron chains.   290
The Gibbet mast was mouldered down, the bones
And iron case were gone; but on the turf
Hard by, soon after that fell* deed was wrought,
Some unknown hand had carved the Murderer's name.
The monumental* writing was engraven
In times long past, and still, from year to year,
By superstition of the neighbourhood
The grass is cleared away; and to this hour

FELL: lethal; cruel or sinister
MONUMENTAL: memorial, related to a resting place

11.6 Jean-François Millet (1814–1875). *The Gust of Wind*, 1871–73. National Museum Wales / Bridgeman Images. "The Beacon on the summit, and more near / A Girl who bore a Pitcher on her head / And seemed with difficult steps to force her way / Against the blowing wind," was, "in truth, / An ordinary sight," but invested with a "visionary dreariness" beyond the realm of "Colours and words" known to man.

■ *He gathers heart from Mary and Dorothy, who to that scene return with him.*

The letters are all fresh and visible.
Faltering, and ignorant where I was, at length   300
I chanced to espy those characters inscribed
On the green sod: forthwith I left the spot
And, reascending the bare Common,* saw
A naked Pool that lay beneath the hills,
The Beacon* on the summit, and more near
A Girl who bore a Pitcher on her head

COMMON: common land on the moor
BEACON: Penrith Beacon (also 6.242)

And seemed with difficult steps to force her way
Against the blowing wind. It was, in truth,
An ordinary sight; but I should need
Colours and words that are unknown to man   310
To paint the visionary dreariness
Which, while I looked all round for my lost Guide,
Did at that time invest the naked Pool,
The Beacon on the lonely Eminence,
The Woman, and her garments vexed and tossed
■ By the strong wind. When, in a blessèd season
With those two dear Ones,* to my heart so dear,
When in the blessèd time of early love,
Long afterwards, I roamed about
In daily presence of this very scene,   320
Upon the naked pool and dreary crags,
And on the melancholy Beacon, fell
The spirit of pleasure, and youth's golden gleam;
And think ye* not with radiance more divine
From these remembrances, and from the power
They left behind? So feeling comes in aid
Of feeling, and diversity of strength
Attends us, if but once we have been strong.
Oh! mystery of Man, from what a depth
Proceed thy honours! I am lost, but see   330
In simple childhood something of the base
On which thy greatness stands, but this I feel,
That from thyself it is that thou must give,

TWO DEAR ONES: Mary Hutchinson and Dorothy, W's sister
YE: you (readers of this poem)

11.7 Itinerant artist. *Mary Wordsworth*, detail from *Wordsworth and Southey family silhouettes, of William Wordsworth, Mary Wordsworth, Dora Wordsworth, Katherine Southey, Edith May Southey, Bertha Southey and unnamed male*, unknown date. The Wordsworth Trust.

11.8 Unknown artist. *Dorothy Wordsworth, sister of W. W.* The Wordsworth Trust.

■ *Deep spirits come from childhood, yet flee the search to hunt them down.*

■ *Another spot of time, at first of dreariness also . . .*

■ *. . . and linked with his father's death—waiting by the wall and hawthorn tree, the single sheep and mist—has become a wellspring for his spirit.*

■ Else never canst receive. The days gone by
Come back upon me from the dawn almost
Of life: the hiding-places of my power
Seem open; I approach, and then they close;
I see by glimpses now; when age comes on
May scarcely see at all, and I would give
While yet we may, as far as words can give,   340
A substance and a life to what I feel:
I would enshrine the spirit of the past
For future restoration. Yet another
Of these to me affecting incidents
With which we will conclude:

                    One Christmas-time,
The day before the Holidays began,
Feverish, and tired, and restless, I went forth
Into the fields, impatient for the sight
Of those two Horses which should bear us home,
■ My Brothers* and myself. There was a Crag,   350
An Eminence, which from the meeting point
Of two high-ways ascending, overlooked
At least a long half-mile of those two roads,
By each of which the expected Steeds might come,
The choice uncertain. Thither I repaired
Up to the highest summit: 'twas a day
Stormy, and rough and wild, and on the grass
I sate, half-sheltered by a naked wall:
Upon my right hand was a single sheep,
A whistling hawthorn on my left, and there,   360
With those companions at my side, I watched,
Straining my eyes intensely, as the mist
Gave intermitting prospect of the wood
And plain beneath. Ere I to School returned
That dreary time, ere I had been ten days
A Dweller in my Father's House, he died,
And I and my two Brothers, Orphans then,
Followed his Body to the Grave. The event
■ With all the sorrow which it brought appeared
A chastisement; and when I called to mind   370
That day so lately passed, when from the crag

BROTHERS: Richard (1768–1816) and John (1772–1805)

11.9 Albert Goodwin (1845–1932). *Mountain Mist,* 1870. Private Collection. Photo © Peter Nahum at The Leicester Galleries, London / Bridgeman Images. Wordsworth recalls "a day / Stormy, and rough and wild . . . as the mist / Gave intermitting prospect of the wood / And plain beneath." On December 19, 1783, he and his brothers, Richard and John, were heading home for Christmas. Their father died on December 30.

I looked in such anxiety of hope,
With trite reflections of morality,
Yet in the deepest passion, I bowed low
To God, who thus corrected my desires:
And afterwards, the wind and sleety rain
And all the business of the elements,
The single sheep, and the one blasted tree,
And the bleak music of that old stone wall,
The noise of wood and water, and the mist   380
Which on the line of each of those two Roads
Advanced in such indisputable* shapes,
All these were spectacles and sounds to which
I often would repair, and thence would drink
As at a fountain: and I do not doubt

That in this later time, when storm and rain
Beat on my roof at midnight, or by day
When I am in the woods, unknown to me
The workings of my spirit thence are brought.

Thou wilt not languish here, O Friend! for whom   390
I travel in these dim uncertain ways;
Thou wilt assist me as a Pilgrim gone
In quest of highest truth. Behold me then
Once more in Nature's presence, thus restored
Or otherwise,* and strengthened once again
(With memory left of what had been escaped)
To habits of devoutest sympathy.

INDISPUTABLE: palpable, undeniable

THUS . . . OTHERWISE: restored by this or other means

Book Twelfth

SAME SUBJECT, CONTINUED

From Nature doth emotion come, and moods
Of calmness equally are Nature's gift,
This is her glory; these two attributes
Are sister horns that constitute her strength;
This twofold influence is the sun and shower
Of all her bounties, both in origin
And end alike benignant. Hence it is,
That Genius, which exists by interchange
Of peace and excitation, finds in her
His best and purest Friend, from her receives   10
That energy by which he seeks the truth,
Is rouzed, aspires, grasps, struggles, wishes, craves
From her that happy stillness of the mind
Which fits him to receive it when unsought.

■ *He recognizes Nature once again as guide and friend . . .*

■ *. . . moral anchor of worth and love, holding fast in humble things.*

■ Such benefit may souls of humblest frame
Partake of, each in their degree: 'tis mine
To speak of what myself have known and felt,
Sweet task! for words find easy way, inspired
By gratitude and confidence in truth.

Long time in search of knowledge desperate,   20
I was benighted, heart and mind; but now*
On all sides day began to reappear,
And it was proved indeed that not in vain
I had been taught to reverence a Power
That is the very quality and shape
And image of right reason, that matures
Her processes by steady laws, gives birth
To no impatient or fallacious hopes,
No heat of passion or excessive zeal,
No vain conceits, provokes to no quick turns   30
Of self-applauding intellect, but lifts
The Being into magnanimity,*
Holds up before the mind, intoxicate
With present objects and the busy dance
Of things that pass away, a temperate shew
Of objects that endure, and by this course
Disposes her, when over-fondly set
On leaving her incumbrances behind,
To seek in Man, and in the frame of life
Social and individual, what there is   40
Desirable, affecting, good or fair
Of kindred permanence, the gifts divine
And universal, the pervading grace
■ That hath been, is, and shall be. Above all
Did Nature bring again that wiser mood
More deeply reestablished in my soul,

NOW: about 1796, after events of Book Eleventh
MAGNANIMITY: elevation or greatness of soul

12.1 Sir Edwin Henry Landseer (1802–1873). *A Highland Landscape*, 1830. Yale Center for British Art, Paul Mellon Collection. "From Nature doth emotion come, and moods / Of calmness equally are Nature's gift . . . This twofold influence is the sun and shower / Of all her bounties."

Which, seeing little worthy or sublime
In what we blazon* with the pompous names
Of power and action, early tutored me
To look with feelings of fraternal love   50
Upon those unassuming things that hold
A silent station in this beauteous world.

Thus moderated, thus composed, I found
Once more in Man an object of delight,
Of pure imagination, and of love;
And, as the horizon of my mind enlarged,
Again I took the intellectual eye
For my instructor, studious more to see
Great Truths than touch and handle little ones.
Knowledge was given accordingly: my trust   60
Was firmer in the feelings which had stood
The test of such a trial; clearer far
My sense of what was excellent and right;
The promise of the present time retired
Into its true proportion; sanguine* schemes,
Ambitious virtues pleased me less; I sought
For good in the familiar face of life
And built thereon my hopes of good to come.

■ With settling judgments now of what would last
And what would disappear, prepared to find   70
Ambition, folly, madness in the men

■ *Some famous views present a narrowed sense of common life.*

BLAZON: highlight, adorn
SANGUINE: optimistic, (overly) confident

Who thrust themselves upon this passive world
As rulers of the world, to see in these,
Even when the public welfare is their aim,
Plans without thought, or bottomed on* false thought
And false philosophy: having brought to test
Of solid life and true result the Books
Of modern Statists,* and thereby perceived
The utter hollowness of what we name
The wealth of Nations,* where alone that wealth   80
Is lodged, and how encreased, and having gained
A more judicious knowledge of what makes
The dignity of individual Man,
Of Man no composition of the thought,
Abstraction, shadow, image, but the man
Of whom we read, the man whom we behold
With our own eyes, I could not but* inquire,
Not with less interest than heretofore,
But greater, though in a spirit more subdued,
Why is this glorious Creature to be found   90
One only in ten thousand? What one is,
Why may not many be? What bars are thrown
By nature in the way of such a hope?
Our animal wants and the necessities
Which they impose, are these the obstacles?
If not, then others vanish into air.
Such meditations bred an anxious wish
To ascertain how much of real worth

BOTTOMED ON: built or based on
STATISTS: philosophers of political economy
WEALTH OF NATIONS: alluding to Adam Smith, *Wealth of Nations* (1776)
I COULD NOT BUT: "having brought to test . . . I could not but"

And genuine knowledge, and true power of mind
Did at this day exist in those who lived   100
By bodily labour, labour far exceeding
Their due proportion, under all the weight
Of that injustice which upon ourselves
By composition of society

■ *He seeks that life in fields and roads . . .*

■ Ourselves entail.* To frame such estimate
I chiefly looked (what need to look beyond?)
Among the natural abodes of men,
Fields with their rural works, recalled to mind
My earliest notices, with these compared
The observations of my later youth   110
Continued downwards to that very day.

For time had never been in which the throes
And mighty hopes of Nations, and the stir
And tumult of the world to me could yield,
How far soe'er transported and possessed,
Full measure of content; but still I craved
An intermixture of distinct regards*
And truths of individual sympathy
Nearer ourselves. Such often might be gleaned
From that great City,* else it must have been   120
A heart-depressing wilderness indeed,
Full soon to me a wearisome abode;
But much was wanting;* therefore did I turn
To you, ye Pathways, and ye lonely Roads

ENTAIL: burden

REGARDS: observations

CITY: London

WANTING: lacking

Sought you enriched with everything I prized,
With human kindness, and with Nature's joy.

Oh! next to one dear state of bliss vouchsafed
Alas! to few in this untoward* world,
The bliss of walking daily in Life's prime
Through field or forest with the Maid we love   130
While yet our hearts are young, while yet we breathe
Nothing but happiness, living in some place,
Deep Vale, or any where, the home of both,
From which it would be misery to stir;
Oh! next to such enjoyment of our youth,
In my esteem, next to such dear delight
Was that of wandering on from day to day
Where I could meditate in peace, and find
The knowledge which I loved, and teach the sound
Of Poet's music to strange fields and groves,   140
Converse with Men, where if we meet a face
We almost meet a friend, on naked Moors
With long, long ways before, by Cottage Bench
Or Well-spring, where the weary Traveller rests.

I love a public road: few sights there are
That please me more; such object hath had power
O'er my imagination since the dawn
Of childhood, when its disappearing line,
Seen daily afar off, on one bare steep

UNTOWARD: difficult, not kind

12.2 John Warwick Smith (1749–1831). *Village of Stonethwaite and Eagle Cragg, Borrowdale*, 1792. Yale Center for British Art, Paul Mellon Collection. So "therefore did I turn / To you, ye Pathways, and ye lonely Roads / Sought you enriched with everything I prized, / With human kindness, and with Nature's joy."

Beyond the limits which my feet had trod,   150
Was like a guide into eternity,
At least to things unknown and without bound.*
Even something of the grandeur which invests
The Mariner who sails the roaring sea
Through storm and darkness early in my mind
Surrounded, too, the Wanderers of the Earth,
Grandeur as much, and loveliness far more:
Awed have I been by strolling Bedlamites,*
From many other uncouth Vagrants, passed
In fear, have walked with quicker step; but why   160

■ *. . . and on his walks descries a depth in humankind.*

■ Take note of this? When I began to inquire,
To watch and question those I met, and held
Familiar talk with them, the lonely roads
Were schools to me in which I daily read
With most delight the passions of mankind,
There saw into the depth of human souls,
Souls that appear to have no depth at all

■ *An inclination to love is our inheritance, though poverty and exploitation may beat it down.*

To vulgar* eyes. And now convinced at heart
How little that to which alone we give
The name of education hath to do   170
With real feeling and just sense, how vain
A correspondence with the talking world
Proves to the most, and called to make good search
If man's estate, by doom of Nature yoked
With toil, is therefore yoked with ignorance,
If virtue be indeed so hard to rear,

SINCE . . . BOUND: a memory from childhood in Cockermouth
BEDLAMITES: severely mentally disabled; insane (7.132)
VULGAR: common, average

And intellectual strength so rare a boon,
I prized such walks still more; for there I found
Hope to my hope, and to my pleasure peace,
And steadiness, and healing, and repose   180
To every angry passion. There I heard
From mouths of lowly men, and of obscure,
A tale of honour, sounds in unison
With loftiest promises of good and fair.

There are who think that strong affections, love
Known by whatever name, is falsely deemed
A gift, to use a term which they would use,
Of vulgar* Nature, that its growth requires
Retirement, leisure, language purified
By manners thoughtful and elaborate,   190
That whoso feels such passion in excess
Must live within the very light and air
Of elegances that are made by man.

■ True is it, where oppression worse than death
Salutes the Being at his birth, where grace
Of culture hath been utterly unknown,
And labour in excess and poverty
From day to day preoccupy the ground
Of the affections, and to Nature's self
Oppose a deeper nature, there indeed,   200
Love cannot be; nor does it easily thrive
In cities, where the human heart is sick,

VULGAR: common, ubiquitous

12.3 John Watkins Chapman (1832–1903). *In the Library*, 19th century. Private Collection / Photo © Bonhams, London / Bridgeman Images. "How Books mislead us, looking for their fame / To judgments of the wealthy Few who see / By artificial lights."

And the eye feeds it not, and cannot feed:
Thus far, no further, is that inference* good.

Yes, in those wanderings deeply did I feel
How we mislead each other, above all
How Books mislead us, looking for their fame
To judgments of the wealthy Few who see
By artificial lights, how they debase
The Many for the pleasure of those Few,   210

INFERENCE: that love is not the gift of common nature

Effeminately level down the truth
To certain general notions for the sake
Of being understood at once, or else
Through want of better knowledge in the men
Who frame them, flattering thus our self-conceit
With pictures that ambitiously set forth
The differences, the outside marks by which
Society has parted man from man,
Neglectful of the universal heart.

Here calling up to mind what then I saw   220
A youthful Traveller, and see daily now
Before me in my rural neighbourhood,
Here might I pause and bend in reverence
To Nature, and the power of human minds,
To Men as they are Men within themselves.
How oft high service is performed within
When all the external man is rude in shew,
Not like a temple rich with pomp and gold
But a mere mountain Chapel such as shields
Its simple worshippers from sun and shower.   230
Of these, said I, shall be my Song; of these,
If future years mature me for the task,
Will I record the praises, making Verse
Deal boldly with substantial things, in truth
And sanctity of passion, speak of these
That justice may be done, obeisance paid

12.4 George Delamotte (active 1809–1821). *A Country Lane with a Farm Labourer Climbing a Five-bar Gate*, 1808. Yale Center for British Art, Paul Mellon Collection. "Before me in my rural neighbourhood, / Here might I pause and bend in reverence . . . To Men as they are Men within themselves."

12.5 Samuel Davis (1757–1819). *Church with a Wooden Belfry*, undated. Yale Center for British Art, Paul Mellon Collection. Wordsworth admires the "high service" of someone "rude in shew" to be "Not like a temple rich with pomp and gold / But a mere mountain Chapel such as shields / Its simple worshippers from sun and shower."

As might befit a prophet new inspired, he vows to tell the feeling tales of common life.

■ Where it is due: thus haply shall I teach,
Inspire, through unadulterated ears

Pour rapture, tenderness, and hope, my theme
No other than the very heart of man   240
As found among the best of those who live
Not unexalted by religious hope,
Nor uninformed by books, good books though few,
In Nature's presence: thence may I select
Sorrow that is not sorrow but delight,
And miserable love that is not pain

To hear of, for the glory that redounds
Therefrom to human kind and what we are.
Be mine to follow with no timid step
Where knowledge leads me; it shall be my pride   250
That I have dared to tread this holy ground,
Speaking no dream but things oracular,
Matter not lightly to be heard by those
Who to the letter of the outward promise

■ *Such glances of existence seem more true than high language and eloquence alone.*

■ Do read the invisible soul, by men adroit
In speech and for communion with the world
Accomplished, minds whose faculties are then
Most active when they are most eloquent,
And elevated most when most admired.

■ *No theme of artifice can steal the prize from Nature or the "works of man," which W now perceives afresh, his mind allied with Nature's strength.*

Men may be found of other mold than these   260
Who are their own upholders, to themselves
Encouragement, and energy and will,
Expressing liveliest thoughts in lively words
As native passion dictates. Others, too,
There are among the walks of homely life
Still higher, men for contemplation framed,
Shy, and unpractised in the strife of phrase,
Meek men, whose very souls perhaps would sink
Beneath them, summoned to such intercourse:
Theirs is the language of the heavens, the power,   270
The thought, the image, and the silent joy;
Words are but under-agents in their souls;
When they are grasping with their greatest strength

They do not breathe among them:* this I speak
In gratitude to God, who feeds our hearts
For his own service, knoweth, loveth us
When we are unregarded by the world.

Also about this time did I receive
Convictions still more strong than heretofore
Not only that the inner frame* is good,   280
And graciously composed, but that no less
Nature through all conditions hath a power
To consecrate, if we have eyes to see,
The outside of her creatures, and to breathe
Grandeur upon the very humblest face

■ Of human life. I felt that the array
Of outward circumstance and visible form
Is to the pleasure of the human mind
What passion makes it, that meanwhile the forms
Of Nature have a passion in themselves   290
That intermingles with those works of man
To which she summons him, although the works
Be mean,* have nothing lofty of their own;
And that the genius of the Poet hence
May boldly take his way among mankind
Wherever Nature leads, that he hath stood
By Nature's side among the Men of old,
And so shall stand for ever. Dearest Friend,*
Forgive me if I say that I, who long

THEM: words
INNER FRAME: versus "letter of the outward promise" (l. 254)
MEAN: ordinary
FRIEND: Coleridge

Had harboured reverentially a thought   300

That Poets, even as Prophets, each with each

Connected in a mighty scheme of truth,

Have, each for his peculiar dower,* a sense

By which he is enabled to perceive

Something unseen before; forgive me, Friend,

If I, the meanest of this Band, had hope

That unto me had also been vouchsafed

An influx,* that in some sort I possessed

A privilege, and that a work of mine,

Proceeding from the depth of untaught things,   310

Enduring and creative, might become

■ *He recalls a long walk on Salisbury Plain, a dozen years before his writing now.*

■ A power like one of Nature's. To such mood,

Once above all, a Traveller at that time*

Upon the Plain of Sarum* was I raised;

There on the pastoral Downs without a track

To guide me, or along the bare white roads

Lengthening in solitude their dreary line,

While through those vestiges of ancient times

I ranged, and by the solitude o'ercome,

I had a reverie and saw the past,   320

Saw multitudes of men, and here and there

A single Briton in his wolf-skin vest

With shield and stone axe, stride across the Wold;*

The voice of spears was heard, the rattling spear

Shaken by arms of mighty bone, in strength

Long mouldered of barbaric majesty.

DOWER: gift, ability

INFLUX: inspiration, special influence

AT THAT TIME: summer 1793

PLAIN OF SARUM: Salisbury Plain in southern England

WOLD: rolling plain

I called upon the darkness; and it took,

A midnight darkness seemed to come and take

All objects from my sight; and lo! again

The desart visible by dismal flames!   330

It is the sacrificial Altar, fed

With living men, how deep the groans, the voice

Of those in the gigantic wicker* thrills

Throughout the region far and near, pervades

The monumental hillocks;* and the pomp

Is for both worlds, the living and the dead.

At other moments, for through that wide waste

Three summer days I roamed, when 'twas my chance

To have before me on the downy Plain*

Lines, circles, mounts, a mystery of shapes   340

Such as in many quarters yet survive,

With intricate profusion figuring o'er

The untilled ground, the work, as some divine,

Of infant science, imitative forms

By which the Druids covertly expressed

Their knowledge of the heavens, and imaged forth

The constellations, I was gently charmed,

Albeit with an antiquarian's dream,

I saw the bearded Teachers, with white wands

Uplifted, pointing to the starry Sky   350

Alternately, and Plain below, while breath

Of music seemed to guide them, and the Waste

Was cheared with stillness and a pleasant sound.

WICKER: wicker case believed used in sacrificial burning

MONUMENTAL HILLOCKS: burial mounds

DOWNY PLAIN: a rolling plain, one with downs

12.6 John Constable (1776–1837). *Stonehenge*, 1835. Victoria & Albert Museum, London / Bridgeman Images. Neolithic and Bronze Age peoples built Stonehenge as a cremation and burial site, astronomical calendar, and place for rites. Reports of "gigantic wicker" cases and sacrificial burning by Druids were mistaken. Wordsworth walked alone on Salisbury Plain and came upon these stones, a place for "both worlds, the living and the dead," in early August 1793. These impressions stayed with him the rest of his life.

This for the past, and things that may be viewed
Or fancied in the obscurities of time.

■ *A new world revealed now promises its own revolution.*

■ Nor is it, Friend, unknown to thee, at least
Thyself delighted, Thou for my delight
Hast said, perusing some imperfect verse
Which in that lonesome journey was composed,
That also I must then have exercised   360
Upon the vulgar forms of present things
And actual world of our familiar days
A higher power, have caught from them a tone,
An image, and a character, by books
Not hitherto reflected. Call we this
But a persuasion taken up by Thee

In friendship: yet the mind is to herself
Witness and judge, and I remember well
That in life's every-day appearances
I seemed about this period to have sight   370
Of a new world, a world, too, that was fit
To be transmitted and made visible
To other eyes, as having for its base
That whence our dignity originates,
That which both gives it being and maintains
A balance, an ennobling interchange
Of action from within and from without,
The excellence, pure spirit, and best power
Both of the object seen, and eye that sees.

13.1 Philippe-Jacques de Loutherbourg (1740–1812). *Snowdon from Capel Curig*, 1787. Yale Center for British Art, Paul Mellon Collection. Wordsworth took his trek up Snowdon in the summer of 1791, probably between mid-June and early August. Capel Curig (Curig's Chapel, lower right) lies east of Snowdon about seven miles. Snowdon, 3,560 feet, is the highest peak in Wales and England.

Book Thirteenth
CONCLUSION

In one of these excursions,* travelling then
Through Wales on foot, and with a youthful Friend,*
I left Bethkelet's* huts at couching-time,*
And westward took my way to see the sun
Rise from the top of Snowdon. Having reached
The Cottage at the Mountain's foot, we there
Rouzed up the Shepherd, who by ancient right
Of office is the Stranger's usual Guide,
And after short refreshment sallied forth.

■ *The ascent of*
Snowdon . . .

■ It was a Summer's night, a close warm night,   10
Wan, dull and glaring,* with a dripping mist
Low-hung and thick that covered all the sky,
Half threatening storm and rain; but on we went
Unchecked, being full of heart and having faith
In our tried Pilot. Little could we see,
Hemmed round on every side with fog and damp,
And, after ordinary travellers' chat
With our Conductor, silently we sank
Each into commerce with his private thoughts:

THESE EXCURSIONS: walks or "wanderings" mentioned in Book Twelfth
YOUTHFUL FRIEND: Robert Jones (1769–1835; 6.339–40)
BETHKELET: Beddgelert, village about four miles south of Snowdon
COUCHING-TIME: bedtime, which would be late in summer
GLARING: clammy, humid

13.2 Anthony Vandyke Copley Fielding (1787–1855). *A View of Snowdon from the Sands of Traeth Mawr, taken at the Ford Between Pont Aberglaslyn and Tremadoc,* 1834. Yale Center for British Art, Paul Mellon Collection. "It was a Summer's night, a close warm night, / Wan, dull and glaring, with a dripping mist / Low-hung and thick that covered all the sky, / Half threatening storm and rain." Snowdonia is among the wettest areas of the United Kingdom with over 170 inches of rain each year. Traeth Mawr, estuary of Afon Glaslyn, is several miles south of Beddgelert. The village of Tremadog (Tremadoc) was not built until about 1805.

Thus did we breast the ascent, and by myself   20
Was nothing either seen or heard the while
Which took me from my musings, save that once
The Shepherd's Cur did to his own great joy
Unearth a hedgehog in the mountain crags
Round which he made a barking turbulent.
This small adventure, for even such it seemed
In that wild place and at the dead of night,

Being over and forgotten, on we wound
In silence as before. With forehead bent
Earthward, as if in opposition set   30
Against an enemy, I panted up
With eager pace, and no less eager thoughts.
Thus might we wear perhaps an hour away,
Ascending at loose distance each from each,
And I, as chanced, the foremost of the Band,
When at my feet the ground appeared to brighten,
And with a step or two seemed brighter still,
Nor had I time to ask the cause of this,
For instantly a Light upon the turf
Fell like a flash. I looked about, and lo!   40
The Moon stood naked in the Heavens, at height
Immense above my head, and on the shore
I found myself of a huge sea of mist,

■ . . . and when its great   Which meek and silent rested at my feet:
scene passes, an image   A hundred hills their dusky backs upheaved
appears.   All over this still Ocean, and beyond,
Far, far beyond the vapours shot themselves
In headlands, tongues, and promontory shapes
Into the Sea, the real Sea, that seemed
To dwindle, and give up its majesty,   50
Usurped upon as far as sight could reach.
Meanwhile the Moon looked down upon this shew
In single glory, and we stood, the mist
Touching our very feet: and from the shore

At distance not the third part of a mile
Was a blue chasm, a fracture in the vapour,
A deep and gloomy breathing-place through which
Mounted the roar of waters, torrents, streams
Innumerable, roaring with one voice.
The universal spectacle throughout   60
Was shaped for admiration and delight,
Grand in itself alone, but in that breach
Through which the homeless voice of waters rose,
That dark deep thorough-fare, had Nature lodged
The Soul, the Imagination of the whole.

A meditation rose in me that night
Upon the lonely Mountain when the scene
Had passed away, and it appeared to me
The perfect image of a mighty Mind,
■ Of one that feeds upon infinity,   70
That is exalted by an under-presence,
The sense of God, or whatsoe'er is dim
Or vast in its own being, above all
One function of such mind had Nature there
Exhibited by putting forth, in midst
Of circumstance most awful and sublime,
That domination which she oftentimes
Exerts upon the outward face of things,
So moulds them, and endues, abstracts, combines,
Or by abrupt and unhabitual influence   80

13.3 Joseph Wright of Derby (1734–1797). *Snowdown by Moonlight*, 1792. University of Liverpool Art Gallery & Collections / Bridgeman Images. "The Moon stood naked in the Heavens, at height / Immense above my head, and on the shore / I found myself of a huge sea of mist." "A meditation rose in me that night . . . The perfect image of a mighty Mind . . . The sense of God, or whatsoe'er is dim / Or vast in its own being."

Doth make one object so impress itself
Upon all others and pervade them so
That even the grossest minds must see and hear

A transformative power shapes the world, and human minds commune with it.

And cannot chuse but feel. The Power which these*
Acknowledge when thus moved, which Nature thus
Thrusts forth upon the senses, is the express
Resemblance, in the fullness of its strength
Made visible, a genuine Counterpart
And Brother of the glorious faculty
Which higher minds bear with them as their own;   90
This is the very spirit in which they deal
With all the objects of the universe.
They from their native selves can send abroad

Liberty and love accompany it.

Like transformation, for themselves create
A like existence, and whene'er it is
Created for them, catch it by an instinct;
Them the enduring and the transient both
Serve to exalt; they build up greatest things
From least suggestions, ever on the watch,
Willing to work and to be wrought upon,   100
They need not extraordinary calls*
To rouze them, in a world of life they live,
By sensible impressions not enthralled,
But quickened, rouzed, and made thereby more fit
To hold communion with the invisible world.
Such minds are truly from the Deity,
For they are Powers; and hence the highest bliss

That can be known is theirs, the consciousness
Of whom they are habitually infused
Through every image, and through every thought,   110
And all impressions: hence religion, faith,
And endless occupation for the soul
Whether discursive or intuitive,
Hence sovereignty within and peace at will,
Emotion which best foresight need not fear,
Most worthy then of trust when most intense,
Hence chearfulness in every act of life,
Hence truth in moral judgements and delight
That fails not in the external universe.

Oh! who is he that hath his whole life long   120
Preserved, enlarged, this freedom in himself!
For this alone is genuine Liberty.
Witness, ye Solitudes! where I received
My earliest visitations, careless* then
Of what was given me, and where now I roam,
A meditative, oft a suffering Man,
And yet, I trust, with undiminished powers,
Witness, whatever falls* my better mind,
Revolving with the accidents of life,
May have sustained, that, howsoe'er misled,   130
I never in the quest of right and wrong
Did tamper with myself* from private aims;
Nor was in any of my hopes the dupe

THESE: these, "even the grossest," minds
EXTRAORDINARY CALLS: strong or violent sensations

CARELESS: not realizing the import
FALLS: hardships, difficulties
MYSELF: i.e., my conscience

Of selfish passions; nor did wilfully

Yield ever to mean cares and low* pursuits;

But rather did with jealousy* shrink back

From every combination that might aid

The tendency, too potent in itself,

Of habit to enslave the mind, I mean

Oppress it by the laws of vulgar sense,　　　　140

And substitute a universe of death,*

The falsest of all worlds, in place of that

Which is divine and true. To fear and love,

To love as first and chief, for there fear ends,

Be this ascribed; to early intercourse,

In presence of sublime and lovely Forms,

With the adverse principles of pain and joy,

Evil, as one* is rashly named by those

Who know not what they say. From love, for here

Do we begin and end, all grandeur comes,　　　　150

All truth and beauty, from pervading love,

That gone, we are as dust. Behold the fields

In balmy spring-time, full of rising flowers

And blissful Creatures: see that Pair, the Lamb

And the Lamb's Mother, and their tender ways

Shall touch thee to the heart; in some green bower

Rest, and be not alone, but have thou there

The One who is thy choice of all the world,

There linger, lulled and lost, and rapt away,

Be happy to thy fill; thou call'st this love　　　　160

13.4 Jessica Landseer (1807–1880). *Village Scene (possibly Colickey Green, Essex)*, early 19th century. Yale Center for British Art, Paul Mellon Fund. All fear ends "From love, for here / Do we begin and end, all grandeur comes, / All truth and beauty, from pervading love . . . see that Pair, the Lamb / And the Lamb's Mother, and their tender ways / Shall touch thee to the heart."

And so it is, but there is higher love

Than this, a love that comes into the heart

With awe and a diffusive* sentiment;

Thy love is human merely; this proceeds

More from the brooding Soul, and is divine.

This love more intellectual cannot be

Without Imagination, which in truth

Is but another name for absolute strength

And clearest insight, amplitude of mind,

Such love and imagination are linked.

And reason in her most exalted mood.

This faculty hath been the moving Soul

They carry joy and sympathy.

Of our long labour: we have traced the stream

From darkness, and the very place of birth

In its blind cavern, whence is faintly heard

The sound of waters, followed it to light

And open day, accompanied its course

Among the ways of Nature; afterwards

Lost sight of it bewildered and engulphed,

Then given it greeting, as it rose once more

With strength, reflecting in its solemn breast   180

The works of man and face of human life;

And lastly, from its progress have we drawn

The feeling of life endless, the one thought

By which we live, Infinity and God.

W addresses Dorothy . . .

Imagination having been our theme,

So also hath that intellectual* love,

For they are each in each, and cannot stand

Dividually.*—Here must thou be, O Man!

Strength to thyself; no Helper hast thou here;

Here keepest thou thy individual state,   190

No other can divide with thee this work,

No secondary hand can intervene

To fashion this ability;* 'tis thine,

The prime and vital principle is thine

INTELLECTUAL: also carrying a spiritual sense
DIVIDUALLY: apart, separately
THIS ABILITY: for imagination and intellectual love

In the recesses of thy nature, far

From any reach of outward fellowship,

Else 'tis not thine at all.—But joy to him   170

Oh! joy to him who here hath sown, hath laid

Here the foundations of his future years!

For all that friendship, all that love can do,   200

All that a darling countenance can look

Or dear voice utter to complete the man,

Perfect him, made imperfect in himself,

All shall be his: and he whose soul hath risen

Up to the height of feeling intellect

Shall want no humbler tenderness, his heart

Be* tender as a nursing Mother's heart,

Of female softness shall his life be full,

Of little loves and delicate desires,

Mild interests and gentlest sympathies.   210

Child of my Parents! Sister of my Soul!*

Elsewhere* have strains of gratitude been breathed

To thee for all the early tenderness

Which I from thee imbibed.* And true it is

That later seasons owed to thee no less;

For spite of thy sweet influence and the touch

Of other kindred hands that opened out

The springs of tender thought in infancy,

And spite of all which singly I had watched

Of elegance, and each minuter charm   220

BE: shall be
CHILD . . . SOUL: Dorothy, his sister
ELSEWHERE: 6.213–18, 10.908–20, and some other poems
IMBIBED: drank in

In nature or in life, still to the last,

■ . . . then Coleridge.

Even to the very going out* of youth,

The period* which our Story now hath reached,

I too exclusively esteemed that love,

And sought that beauty, which, as Milton sings,*

Hath terror in it. Thou didst soften down

This over-sternness: but for thee, sweet Friend,

My soul, too reckless of mild grace, had been

Far longer what by Nature it was framed,

Longer retained its countenance severe,   230

A rock with torrents roaring, with the clouds

Familiar, and a favourite of the Stars:

But thou didst plant its crevices with flowers,

Hang it with shrubs that twinkle* in the breeze,

And teach the little birds to build their nests

And warble in its chambers. At a time*

When Nature, destined to remain so long

Foremost in my affections, had fallen back

Into a second place, well pleased to be

A Hand-maid to a nobler than herself,   240

When every day brought with it some new sense

Of exquisite regard for common things,

And all the earth was budding with these gifts

Of more refined humanity, thy breath,

■ He hopes his own devel-
opment now means that
he may write a work of
greater scale.

Dear Sister, was a kind of gentler spring

That went before my steps.

GOING OUT: final days

PERIOD: about 1796

AS MILTON SINGS: in *Paradise Lost* (9.490–92)

TWINKLE: move their leaves in air, as if winking

AT A TIME: about 1796–98

With such a theme,

■ Coleridge! with this my argument, of thee

Shall I be silent? O most loving Soul!

Placed on this earth to love and understand,

And from thy presence shed the light of love,   250

Shall I be mute ere thou be spoken of?

Thy gentle Spirit to my heart of hearts

Did also find its way; and thus the life

Of all things and the mighty unity

In all which we behold, and feel, and are,

Admitted more habitually a mild

Interposition, and closelier gathering thoughts

Of man and his concerns, such as become

A human Creature, be he who he may,

Poet, or destined to an humbler name;   260

And so the deep enthusiastic joy,

The rapture of the Hallelujah sent

From all that breathes and is, was chastened, stemmed,

And balanced by a Reason which indeed

Is Reason, duty and pathetic* truth;

And God and Man divided, as they ought,

Between them the great system of the world

Where Man is sphered, and which God animates.

■ And now, O Friend!* this History is brought

To its appointed close: the discipline   270

And consummation* of the Poet's mind

PATHETIC: feeling, passionate

FRIEND: Coleridge

CONSUMMATION: full creation

In every thing that stood most prominent
Have faithfully been pictured; we have reached
The time (which was our object from the first)
When we may, not presumptuously, I hope,
Suppose my powers so far confirmed, and such
My knowledge, as to make me capable
Of building up a work that should endure,
Yet much hath been omitted, as need was,
Of Books how much! and even of the other wealth   280
Which is collected among woods and fields,
Far more: for Nature's secondary grace,
That outward illustration* which is hers,
Hath hitherto been barely touched upon,
The charm more superficial, and yet sweet,
Which from her works finds way, contemplated*
As they hold forth a genuine counterpart
And softening mirror of the moral world.

Yes, having tracked the main essential Power,
Imagination, up her way sublime,   290
In turn might Fancy also be pursued
Through all her transmigrations, till she too
Was purified, had learned to ply her craft
By judgment steadied. Then might we return
And in the Rivers and the Groves behold
Another face; might hear them from all sides
Calling upon the more instructed mind

OUTWARD ILLUSTRATION: of "the moral world" (l. 288)

CONTEMPLATED: then stressed on the second syllable

13.5 Unknown artist, after Robert Hancock (1730–1817) and Peter Vandyke (1729–1799). *William Wordsworth, Samuel Taylor Coleridge and a woman, possibly Dorothy Wordsworth*, 1803. The Wordsworth Trust. "Child of my Parents! Sister of my Soul!" and "Coleridge! . . . O most loving Soul!" The drawing of Wordsworth, lower right, is based on Hancock's 1798 profile (see illustration 9.12), that of Coleridge on Vandyke's 1795 portrait.

To link their images with subtle skill
Sometimes, and by elaborate research

13.6 George Vincent (1796–1832). *A View of Cheddar Gorge*, c. 1820. Yale Center for British Art, Paul Mellon Collection. On May 16, 1798, two days after the birth of Coleridge's second son Berkeley, William, Dorothy, and Coleridge walked twenty-five miles to see Cheddar Gorge, one of England's greatest natural wonders. This event is the last one recorded in Dorothy's *Alfoxden Journal*.

With forms and definite appearances   300
Of human life, presenting them sometimes
To the involuntary sympathy
Of our internal being, satisfied
And soothed with a conception of delight
Where meditation cannot come, which thought
Could never heighten. Above all how much
Still nearer to ourselves is overlooked
In human nature and that marvellous world
As studied first in my own heart, and then
In life among the passions of mankind   310
And qualities commixed and modified
By the infinite varieties and shades
Of individual character. Herein

■ *His capacities owe something to early circumstance at school . . .*

■ It was for me (this justice bids me say)
No useless preparation to have been
The pupil of a public School,* and forced
In hardy independence to stand up
Amid conflicting passions and the shock
Of various tempers, to endure and note
What was not understood though known to be: 320
Among the mysteries of love and hate,

■ *. . . to his sister . . .*

Honour and shame, looking to right and left,
Unchecked by innocence too delicate
And moral notions too intolerant,
Sympathies too contracted. Hence, when called
To take a station among Men, the step

■ *. . . and to a young man for whom he cared in illness. His generosity released W to devote himself to poetry.*

A PUBLIC SCHOOL: Hawkshead Grammar School, for any boy of merit

Was easier, the transition more secure,
More profitable also; for the mind
Learns from such timely exercise to keep
In wholesome separation the two natures,   330
The one that feels, the other that observes.

Let one word more of personal circumstance,
Not needless, as it seems, be added here.
Since I withdrew unwillingly from France*
The Story hath demanded less regard
To time and place; and where I lived, and how,
Hath been no longer scrupulously marked.
■ Three years, until a permanent abode
Received me with that Sister of my heart
Who ought by rights the dearest to have been   340
Conspicuous through this biographic Verse,
Star seldom utterly concealed from view,
I led an undomestic Wanderer's life.
In London chiefly was my home, and thence
Excursively,* as personal friendships, chance
Or inclination led, or slender means
Gave leave, I roamed about from place to place
Tarrying in pleasant nooks, wherever found
Through England or through Wales. A Youth (he bore
■ The name of Calvert;* it shall live if words   350
Of mine can give it life) without respect
To prejudice or custom, having hope

SINCE . . . FRANCE: for lack of funds (10.188–201)
EXCURSIVELY: on excursions, but returning to London
CALVERT: Raisley Calvert (1773–1795) bequeathed W £900.

That I had some endowments by which good
Might be promoted, in his last decay
From his own Family withdrawing part
Of no redundant Patrimony, did
By a Bequest sufficient for my needs
Enable me to pause for choice, and walk
At large and unrestrained, nor damped too soon
By mortal cares. Himself no Poet, yet   360
Far less a common Spirit of the world,
He deemed that my pursuits and labours lay
Apart from all that leads to wealth, or even
Perhaps to necessary maintenance,
Without some hazard to the finer sense;
He cleared a passage for me, and the stream
Flowed in the bent of Nature.

                    Having now
Told what best merits mention, further pains
Our present labour seems not to require,

■ *He thinks of when he first began this poem . . .*

■ And I have other tasks. Call back to mind   370
The mood in which this Poem was begun,
O Friend! the termination of my course
Is nearer now, much nearer; yet even then
In that distraction and intense desire
I said unto the life which I had lived,
Where art thou?* Hear I not a voice from thee
Which 'tis reproach to hear? Anon* I rose

WHERE ART THOU?: After the Fall, God asks this of Adam, Genesis 3:9.
ANON: soon, immediately

13.7 Unknown artist. *Valley of Rocks, Devon*, 1851. Yale Center for British Art, Paul Mellon Collection. In November 1797 (Wordsworth later recalled it as spring 1798), he, Dorothy, and Coleridge walked from Nether Stowey and Alfoxden to Lynton and the Valley of Rocks. During their walk Coleridge and Wordsworth discussed the plan of *The Rime of the Ancient Mariner*, which the following summer became part of their collaborative, ground-breaking effort, *The Lyrical Ballads* (1798): "That summer when on Quantock's grassy Hills . . . Thou . . . Didst speak the Vision of that Ancient Man, / The bright-eyed Mariner."

As if on wings, and saw beneath me stretched
Vast prospect of the world* which I had been
And was; and hence this Song, which like a lark   380
I have protracted in the unwearied Heavens
Singing, and often with more plaintive voice
Attempered to the sorrows of the Earth,
Yet centring all in love, and in the end
All gratulant* if rightly understood.

THE WORLD: the life and state of being
GRATULANT: expressing joy and pleasure

Than any sweetest sight of yesterday

■ That summer when on Quantock's grassy Hills*

Far ranging, and among her sylvan Coombs,*

Thou in delicious words, with happy heart,

Didst speak the Vision of that Ancient Man,

The bright-eyed Mariner, and rueful woes

Didst utter of the Lady Christabel;

And I, associate with such labour, walked

Murmuring of him who, joyous hap! was found,   400

After the perils of his moonlight ride

Near the loud Waterfall; or her who sate

In misery near the miserable Thorn;

When thou dost to that summer turn thy thoughts,

And hast before thee all which then we were,

To thee, in memory of that happiness

It will be known, by thee at least, my Friend,

Felt, that the history of a Poet's mind

Is labour not unworthy of regard.

To thee the work shall justify itself.   410

The last and later portions of this Gift*

Which I for Thee design have been prepared

In times which have from those wherein we first

■ Together wantoned in wild Poesy

Differed thus far, that they* have been, my Friend,

Times of much sorrow, of a private grief*

Keen and enduring, which the frame of mind

13.8 John Constable (1776–1837). *Weymouth Bay*, 1816. Private Collection / The Stapleton Collection / Bridgeman Images. "Times of much sorrow, of a private grief / Keen and enduring": on February 5, 1805, three months before Wordsworth completed the final three books of *The Prelude*, his beloved brother John, captain of one of the largest East Indiamen, the *Earl of Abergavenny*, drowned in a violent storm two miles off this dangerous coast of Weymouth near Portland Bill. More than 250 souls perished. John's sudden death was devastating to Wordsworth.

■ *... and then of that miraculous year, 1798, when Coleridge wrote* The Rime of the Ancient Mariner *and first part of* Christabel, *W* The Idiot Boy *and* The Thorn: *chief characters in them are remembered.*

■ *In times of personal sorrow he completes this gift to Coleridge, conceived as prelude to more ambitious work.*

Whether to me shall be allotted life,

And with life power to accomplish aught of worth

Sufficient to excuse me in men's sight

For having given this Record of myself,

Is all uncertain: but, belovèd Friend!   390

When looking back thou seest in clearer view

QUANTOCK'S GRASSY HILLS: Quantock Hills, north and northwest of Taunton
SYLVAN COOMBS: wooded hollows or valleys on flanks of hills
THIS GIFT: this poem, "Addressed to S. T. Coleridge"
THAT THEY: in that the times of writing later parts of it
A PRIVATE GRIEF: See illustration caption 13.8.

That in this meditative History
Hath been described more deeply makes me feel,
Yet likewise hath enabled me to bear   420
More firmly; and a comfort now, a hope,
One of the dearest which this life can give,
Is mine; that Thou art near, and wilt be soon
Restored to us in renovated health:
When after the first mingling of our tears,
'Mong other consolations we may find
Some pleasure from this Offering of my love.

Oh! yet a few short years of useful life,
And all will be complete, thy race be run,
Thy monument of glory will be raised.   430
Then, though, too weak to tread the ways of truth,
This Age fall back to old idolatry,
Though men return to servitude as fast
As the tide ebbs, to ignominy and shame

By Nations sink together, we shall still
Find solace in the knowledge which we have,
Blessed with true happiness if we may be
United helpers forward of a day
Of firmer trust, joint-labourers in the work
(Should Providence such grace to us vouchsafe)   440
Of their redemption, surely yet to come.
Prophets of Nature, we to them will speak
A lasting inspiration, sanctified
By reason and by truth: what we have loved
Others will love; and we may teach them how,
Instruct them how the mind of Man becomes
A thousand times more beautiful than the earth
On which he dwells, above this Frame of things
(Which 'mid all revolution in the hopes
And fears of Men doth still remain unchanged)   450
In beauty exalted, as it is itself
Of substance and of fabric more divine.

TO WILLIAM WORDSWORTH

S. T. Coleridge

On successive evenings after Christmas 1806, probably in early January 1807, Wordsworth read aloud to Coleridge the thirteen-book poem he had completed in spring of 1805, the "poem to Coleridge." Also present were Dorothy, Mary Wordsworth, and Mary's sister Sara Hutchinson. Coleridge until then had known only earlier versions, most recently the first five books completed in spring 1804 before he left for Malta. In January 1807, after hearing what he called Wordsworth's "recitation," Coleridge wrote what later become known as *To William Wordsworth*. He soon wrote a second manuscript version with variations, eventually printed in his own *Poetical Works* (1893), Appendix H, though that manuscript is now apparently lost. The poem was first published in *Sibylline Leaves* (1817), but without Wordsworth's name mentioned.

Instead, Coleridge entitled the published poem "*To A Gentleman.* Composed on the night after his recitation of a Poem on the Growth of an Individual Mind." In the surviving manuscript now held by the Wordsworth Trust at the Jerwood Centre in Grasmere, he had written: "To W. Wordsworth Lines composed for the greater part on the Night, on which he finished the recitation of his Poem (in thirteen Books) concerning the growth and history of his own mind." Only in the 1834 edition of Coleridge's *Poetical Works*, one authorized by him, does Wordsworth's name finally appear. Wordsworth had earlier wished the poem to remain unpublished, in part because he felt uneasy about what he considered advance praise, in part because Coleridge had for years urged him to write a different, greater, and more philosophical poem, one that Wordsworth envisioned as *The Recluse*, but on which he had made limited progress. Part of it he published as *The Excursion* (1814), along with a Prospectus to *The Recluse*, but Wordsworth, at least in his own mind, never fulfilled its ambition.

In his Preface to *The Excursion*, Wordsworth turns Coleridge's own somewhat self-castigating line, "And Genius given, and knowledge won in vain" (l. 70) into a compliment. He mentions his own unpublished poem that eventually became known as *The Prelude:* "That Work, addressed to a dear friend, most distinguished for his knowledge and genius, and to whom the Author's Intellect is deeply indebted, has long been finished."

Coleridge's poem is complex. It expresses too much nuance and conflict to summarize in a headnote. It seems that hearing his friend's long poem, no matter how much he admired it, did not raise in him the joy and health that Wordsworth had hoped it would. There are elements of self-pity, even estrangement. Yet, there is high praise, too, and we might recall that Coleridge, more than anyone, championed Wordsworth as standing among the greatest of poets, a claim Coleridge made when Wordsworth was still young. Coleridge in his poem recognizes the importance of the tumultuous time in France that Wordsworth depicts in detail, a time prior to their friendship. Lines 11–47 constitute a rough outline of the progress of Wordsworth's entire thirteen books.

The poem is deeply personal and self-consciously literary to a high degree. It is saturated with allusions and references, some impossible to trace to one source. For example, "patient toil" (l. 72) appears in a 1719 translation of Le Bossu on epic poetry, soon after in *Oppian's Halieuticks*, a translation by John Jones of an ancient Greek poetic treatise on fishing (1722), in an anti-Lucretius poem in the *Gentleman's Magazine* (November 1753), and, most popularly, in John Dyer's *The Fleece* (1757). Perhaps prompted by Coleridge's use of the phrase, Wordsworth employed it in his own *Ode 1814*, composed in January 1816, where it becomes "Sculpture's patient toil." The phrase "vernal Hours" (l. 90) Coleridge apparently drew from Erasmus Darwin's *The Botanic Garden* (1789), though it occurs in earlier eighteenth-century poems by John Dalton, Richard Savage, Edward Lovibund, and John Scott. Coleridge records this phrase in an early Notebook, probably in early 1795 when he was, in fact, reading Darwin. The phrase may also elicit in his mind, as in Wordsworth's, happier times—spring awakenings—associated with his first personal acquaintance with Wordsworth later in 1795, suggested by "the memory of that hour / Of thy communion with my nobler mind" (ll. 83–84). "The howl of more than wintry storms" (l. 89) evokes an image Coleridge elsewhere in his writing connects with personal distress and trauma originating in early childhood. That howl is now to be calmed by the Halcyon bird. The literary allusions and plucked phrases do not detract from—they are blended with and in many ways strengthen—Coleridge's felt sense of the occasion, its personal associations, and his immediate recognition of the remarkable nature of Wordsworth's achievement.

The lines "Eve following eve, / Dear tranquil time, when the sweet sense of Home / Is sweetest!" refer to the successive evenings on which Wordsworth read the long poem aloud. (Coleridge would not enjoy a stable home between 1804 and 1816. On December 21, 1806, recently separated from his wife, he had arrived with his young son Hartley to stay with the Wordsworths at Coleorton. He remained there until April 17, 1807). The succeeding lines, "Driven as in surges . . . yet swelling to the Moon," contain a memory that Coleridge associated with the sea voyage that he took with William and Dorothy to Germany in 1798, just as the first edition of *Lyrical Ballads* appeared.

The text is from Coleridge's 1829 *Poetical Works*. Accent marks are added to the final syllables of preterit forms where they are to be voiced.

Friend of the Wise! and Teacher of the Good!
Into my heart have I received that Lay
More than historic, that prophetic Lay
Wherein (high theme by thee first sung aright)
Of the foundations and the building up
Of a Human Spirit thou has dared to tell
What may be told, to the understanding mind
Revealable; and what within the mind
By vital Breathings secret as the soul
Of vernal growth, oft quickens in the Heart   10
Thoughts all too deep for words!*—

THOUGHTS . . . WORDS: an echo of W's *Ode: Intimations of Immortality*

Theme hard as high!*
Of smiles spontaneous, and mysterious fears
(The first-born they of Reason and twin-birth)
Of tides obedient to external force,
And currents self-determined, as might seem,
Or by some inner Power; of moments awful,
Now in thy inner life, and now abroad,
When Power streamed from thee, and thy soul received
The light reflected, as a light bestowed—
Of Fancies fair, and milder hours of youth,   20
Hyblean* murmurs of Poetic Thought
Industrious in its Joy, in Vales and Glens
Native or outland, Lakes and famous Hills!
Or on the lonely High-road, when the Stars
Were rising;* or by secret Mountain-streams,
The Guides and the Companions of thy way!

Of more than Fancy, of the Social Sense
Distending wide, and man beloved as Man,
Where France in all her Towns lay vibrating
Like some becalmèd Bark beneath the burst   30
Of Heaven's immediate Thunder, when no cloud
Is visible, or shadow on the Main.*
For thou wert there, thine own brows garlanded,
Amid the tremor of a realm aglow,
Amid a mighty nation jubilant,
When from the general Heart of Human kind

THEME HARD AS HIGH: Milton speaks of epic ambitions similarly.
HYBLEAN: Hybla, city and mountain in Sicily known for honey; *Prelude* 10.1019–27
OR . . . RISING: brings to mind *Prelude* 4.363–91
OF . . . MAIN: alludes to Horace, *Odes* I, 34; varies *Prelude* 9.48–49

Hope sprang forth like a full-born Deity!
—Of that dear Hope afflicted and struck down,
So summoned homeward, thenceforth calm and sure
From the dread Watch-Tower of man's absolute Self,   40
With light unwaning on her eyes, to look
Far on—herself a glory to behold,
The Angel of the vision!* Then (last strain)
Of Duty, chosen Laws controlling choice,
Action and Joy!—An orphic song* indeed,
A song divine of high and passionate thoughts,
To their own Music chaunted!

O great Bard!
Ere yet that last strain dying awed the air,
With stedfast eye I viewed thee in the choir
Of ever-enduring men. The truly Great   50
Have all one age, and from one visible space
Shed influence! They, both in power and act,
Are permanent, and Time is not with *them*,
Save as it worketh *for* them, they *in* it.*
Nor less a sacred Roll, than those of old,
And to be placed, as they, with gradual fame
Among the Archives of Mankind, thy work
Makes audible a linkèd lay of Truth,
Of Truth profound a sweet continuous lay,
Not learnt, but native, her own natural notes!*   60
Ah! as I listened with a heart forlorn

The pulses of my Being beat anew:
And even as Life returns upon the Drowned,
Life's joy rekindling roused a throng of Pains—
Keen pangs of Love, awakening as a babe
Turbulent, with an outcry in the heart;
And Fears self-willed, that shunned the eye of Hope;
And Hope that scarce would know itself from Fear;
Sense of past Youth, and Manhood come in vain,
And Genius given, and knowledge won in vain;*   70
And all which I had culled in Wood-walks wild,
And all which patient toil* had reared, and all,
Commune with *thee* had opened out—but Flowers
Strewed on my corse, and borne upon by Bier,*
In the same Coffin, for the self-same Grave!

That way no more! and ill beseems it me,
Who came a welcomer in Herald's Guise,
Singing of Glory, and Futurity,
To wander back on such unhealthful road,
Plucking the poisons of self-harm! And ill   80
Such intertwine beseems triumphal wreaths
Strewed before *thy* advancing!

Nor do thou,
Sage Bard! impair the memory of that hour
Of thy communion with my nobler mind
By Pity or Grief, already felt too long!

ANGEL OF THE VISION: perhaps alludes to "the great vision" of the angel Michael in Milton's *Lycidas*
ORPHIC SONG: Orpheus, ancient Greek oracular poet and musician; *Prelude* 1.234
THE TRULY . . . IN IT: parallel to *Prelude* 10.968–72
NATIVE . . . NATURAL NOTES: echoes Milton's praise of Shakespeare in *L'Allegro*

AND GENIUS . . . IN VAIN: See headnote.
PATIENT TOIL: See headnote.
BORNE . . . BIER: echoing Shakespeare, sonnet 12

Nor let my words import more blame than needs.
The tumult rose and ceased: for Peace is nigh
Where wisdom's voice has found a listening heart.
Amid the howl of more than wintry storms,
The Halcyon* hears the voice of vernal Hours*   90
Already on the wing.

                        Eve following eve,
Dear tranquil time, when the sweet sense of Home
Is sweetest! moments for their own sake hailed
And more desired, more precious for thy song,
In silence listening, like a devout child,
My soul lay passive, by thy various strain
Driven as in surges now beneath the stars,
With momentary Stars of my own birth,

Fair constellated Foam, still darting off
Into the darkness; now a tranquil sea,   100
Outspread and bright, yet swelling to the Moon.

    And when—O Friend! my comforter and guide!*
Strong in thyself, and powerful to give strength!—
Thy long sustainèd Song finally closed,
And thy deep voice had ceased—yet thou thyself
Wert still before my eyes, and round us both
That happy vision of beloved Faces—
Scarce conscious, and yet conscious of its close
I sate, my being blended in one thought
(Thought was it? or Aspiration? or Resolve?)   110
Absorbed, yet hanging still upon the sound—
And when I rose, I found myself in prayer.

HALCYON: legendary bird believed to calm waters and winds
VERNAL HOURS: See headnote.

MY . . . GUIDE: W's final *River Duddon* sonnet, XXXIII (1820), "my partner and my guide"

A Note on the Text and Editorial Practice

The poem has been edited from original manuscripts, most importantly Dove Cottage MS 52 and MS 53, also referred to, respectively, as MS A and MS B. While this is not a definitive scholarly edition but rather one for common pleasure and student use, every attempt has been made to produce an accurate text that reflects the manuscript record of the poem. A list of detailed scholarly editions appears at the end of the Selected Bibliography.

The first publication of the 1805 *Prelude* was Ernest de Selincourt's edition of 1926. He and later scholars edited the poem from DC MS 52 (MS A), and only the recent Norton Critical edition edited by Nicholas Halmi (2014) prints a text of the 1805 *Prelude* based primarily on DC MS 53 (MS B). The text in the present volume results from consulting equally both of these two fair copy manuscripts completed in 1805-06, MS A and MS B. Dorothy, William's sister, made the fair copy now known as MS A, and Mary, his wife, made the duplicate (but not perfectly identical) fair copy now known as MS B.

There is no reason to believe that Wordsworth himself directly authorized the punctuation, spelling, or capitalization in either MS A or MS B. (While he used both manuscripts as the basis for some later revisions, he did so more with MS A, and hence editors have favored it. On the other hand, Coleridge himself read and annotated MS B.) In certain instances, therefore, punctuation in this edition is occasionally supplied or deleted in a manner that seems more appropriate to the sense and meter of the poem as they are aligned with modern practices of reading and punctuation. Thus, in some instances, if it seems better to aid the reader in obtaining sense and preserving meter, punctuation that appears in neither MS A nor MS B is supplied. In some other cases, punctuation that appears in one or both of the manuscripts is deleted. Every editor

has to some degree altered the punctuation found in the manuscripts. As Nicholas Halmi notes, "All 'reading texts' of the poem . . . supplement the original punctuation." In some cases this means deleting punctuation, in other cases adding to or altering it slightly, though in every case attempting to retain and make clear the sense and meter of the passages involved. Punctuation and capitalization in one manuscript not infrequently differ from punctuation and capitalization in the other, and within each manuscript the punctuation and capitalization are not internally consistent. Wordsworth sometimes capitalized common nouns to emphasize the importance of a particular instance of that noun, but this practice is not reflected consistently in the two fair copy manuscripts. Thus, "that belovèd Vale" refers to the Vale of Grasmere, but the word can be capitalized in other contexts: "In what Vale / Shall be my harbour?" The same word can also appear without capitalization: "the sun in heaven / Beheld not vales more beautiful than ours."

Spelling had not in the early nineteenth century become fully standardized. In the two fair copy manuscripts, or even in the same one, we find, for example, both *honorable* and *honourable*, both *show* and *shew*. When different spellings of what is clearly the same word do not dictate different pronunciations, this edition generally strives for consistency. It does not Americanize spelling. If something unusual occurs in spelling, a clarifying note may be given in favor of modernizing the word, though generally the reader will recognize these relatively rare, older spellings easily enough, for example, *atchieved* for *achieved*, *huxter* for *huckster*, and *Desart* for *desert*. The spelling of place names often changed over the years. Spelling of place names in the original manuscripts has generally been retained, with modern spelling noted if clarification seems needed.

When preterit verb forms that end with *'d* in the manuscripts do not represent a separate, voiced syllable in pronunciation, a very common occurrence, then they are consistently given with the modern spelling that ends with *ed*. For example, *pursued* is read as two syllables, *loved* as one. When the *ed* ending of words is pronounced as a separate, distinct syllable, somewhat unusual but not rare, an accent is added, for example, "belovèd Vale," where the adjective is pronounced as three syllables.

Certain words are usually elided in pronunciation as one syllable, such as *tower*, *heaven*, and *given*. Some polysyllabic words might be pronounced in one instance with elision and in another instance without it. The best guide is to follow the meter of the poem, iambic pentameter. Sometimes, elision in pronunciation occurs between two words as well as within one word. Thus, the line "So sweetly 'mid the gloom the invisible Bird" is pronounced "So sweetly mid the gloom th'invis'ble Bird." It is unadvisable and would be distracting to change spelling to indicate all such elisions. The best practice is to pay attention to the meter so that the rhythm, flow, and music of blank verse are obtained, generally ten syllables in each line, five stressed syllables alternating with five unstressed ones. For example, a line such as "Internal echo of the imperfect sound" is read by eliding *the* with *imperfect*: "Internal echo of th'imperfect sound" achieves the ˘ / ˘ / ˘ / ˘ / ˘ / meter (where ˘ = an unstressed syllable; / = a stressed syllable). Of course, iambic pentameter exhibits some variation, and at times two stressed or two unstressed syllables occur in succession.

If a word might be pronounced more than one way and guidance seems advisable, a note indicates what is appropriate. Ampersands (&), common in MS A, are rendered as *and*. When Wordsworth employs an unusual word or a word in a sense no longer common, a brief note clarifies the meaning. For example, he uses *redundant* to mean overflowing or exuberant, not repetitive or uselessly excessive. The decision to create verse paragraphs (they are not called stanzas) with a line of space generally follows the two manuscript fair copies, which agree quite consistently on this point, though the sense of the verse and decisions of previous modern editors have been considered, too.

Marginal glosses are provided simply to aid the reader in following the flow and design of the poem. They are not intended as adequate summary or interpretation. Occasionally, a gloss will contain pertinent information too long for the short form of the notes. Many long poems in English provide a prefatory prose "argument" for each book or part of the poem. *Paradise Lost* was first printed without such prose arguments but Milton soon provided them, and together they run to many hundreds of words. Seamus Heaney provided marginal glosses with his translation of *Beowulf*. Coleridge wrote marginal glosses for *The Rime of the Ancient Mariner* when it was published in 1817, almost two decades after the first and second versions of the poem appeared in the first and second editions of *Lyrical Ballads* (1798 and 1800).

CHRONOLOGY

While useful for quickly checking particular events and dates, a chronology read through also has power as the outline of a larger narrative. Parenthetical references refer to book and line numbers of *The Prelude*. While multiple sources, primary and secondary, have been consulted, even primary sources occasionally give or suggest slightly different dates for the same event.

November 27, 1741
John Wordsworth, William's father, is born at Appleby, Westmorland, near Penrith, 23 miles northeast of Grasmere.

January 20, 1748
Ann Cookson, William's mother, is born at Penrith.

October 25, 1760
George William Frederick (1738–1820), George III, is crowned King of Great Britain and Ireland.

December 1764
John Wordsworth, an attorney and law-agent for "Wicked Jimmy," Sir James Lowther (1736–1802), Collector of Customs at Whitehaven, later Earl of Lonsdale, and the richest man in Cumberland, moves into the finest house in Cockermouth, owned by Lowther, 20 miles northwest of Grasmere (1.286–304).

February 5, 1766
John Wordsworth marries Ann Cookson.

June 22, 1766
Annette Vallon, future lover of William, is born at Blois.

August 31, 1767
Thomas Nicholson is hung near Penrith on a "Gibbet mast" for murdering Thomas Parker (11.279–316).

August 19, 1768
Richard Wordsworth, older brother of William, is born at Cockermouth.

April 7, 1770
William Wordsworth is born at ten in the evening at Cockermouth.

August 16, 1770
Mary Hutchinson, William's future wife, is born at Penrith.

December 25, 1771
Dorothy Wordsworth, William's sister, is born at Cockermouth.

October 21, 1772
Samuel Taylor Coleridge is born at Ottery St. Mary, Devon.

December 4, 1772
John Wordsworth, William's younger brother, is born at Cockermouth.

May 10, 1774
Louis XVI is crowned King of France at age nineteen.

June 9, 1774
Christopher Wordsworth, the youngest brother, is born at Cockermouth.

May 15, 1775
William lives in Penrith with his mother at his grandparents' home for almost one year. He probably attends Dame Ann Birkett's infant school and meets schoolmate Mary Hutchinson. He visits the Penrith Beacon (11.279–316).

March 8, 1778
Ann Wordsworth, William's mother, dies at age thirty, probably from pneumonia (5.256–60).

June 13, 1778
Dorothy Wordsworth is sent to live with relatives William and Elizabeth Threlkeld in Halifax, Yorkshire.

July 2, 1778
Jean-Jacques Rousseau (1712–1778) dies in Paris.

May 15, 1779
William and Richard attend Hawkshead Grammar School, 5 miles south of Grasmere. They live with Ann Tyson and her husband Hugh. William's younger brothers will follow later.

June 18, 1779
William discovers on the shore of Esthwaite Water the clothes of a drowned man, schoolmaster James Jackson from Sawrey (5.450–81).

January 1781
Rev. William Taylor (1754–1786), a Cambridge man of learning who loves poetry (Gray, Chatterton, Collins, Beattie, Young, and Thomson) becomes headmaster at Hawkshead Grammar School. He soon has profound influence on young William.

January 1781
William Pitt the Younger is given a seat in the House of Commons in the pocket borough of Appleby-in-Westmorland (near Penrith) with the help of Sir James Lowther, John Wordsworth's employer, on condition that Pitt resign should his views and those of his patron diverge.

1782
Rousseau's *Confessions* is published posthumously.

Spring 1782
Wordsworth and friends hunt for ravens' eggs near Yewdale Crag (1.333–50).

1783
The Tysons move to the hamlet of Colthouse, a quarter mile east of Hawkshead.

April 1783
Wordsworth discovers "the charm / Of words in tuneful order" (5.575–607).

December 1783
William Pitt the Younger becomes Prime Minister at twenty-four.

December 19, 1783
William, Richard, and John wait in stormy weather for horses to take them back to Cockermouth for Christmas holidays (11.345–64; 12.287–305).

December 30, 1783
William's father dies suddenly at age forty-two (5.364–89). Sir James Lowther's refusal to reimburse the Wordsworth family for debts owed to the estate (£4,625) impoverishes the Wordsworth children for years.

February 28, 1784
Hugh Tyson dies at Colthouse.

September 1784
William composes his first poem assigned by his teacher William Taylor on the subject of *The Summer Vacation.*

June 12, 1786
Taylor, William's headmaster since 1781, dies at thirty-two. He is buried in the churchyard of Cartmel Priory at Grange-over-Sands, southern Cumbria (10.486–514).

May 22, 1787
Society for Effecting the Abolition of the Slave Trade is formed and led by Granville Sharp and Thomas Clarkson. Clarkson later becomes Wordsworth's close friend.

Summer 1787
Wordsworth and Dorothy meet again at Penrith (6.208–45; 11.316–26).

October 30, 1787
Wordsworth begins studies at St. John's College, Cambridge (Book Third; 8.641–77; 9.226–36).

December 19, 1787
William's grandfather, William Cookson, dies at Penrith.

Summer 1788
Wordsworth spends summer vacation in Hawkshead visiting Ann Tyson (Book Fourth). He spots the discharged soldier in Far Sawrey, three miles from Hawkshead above the Windermere ferry (4.369–504).

November 1788
George III, suffering perhaps from porphyria, sparks the regency crisis.

May 5, 1789
In Paris the Estates-General meets for the first time since 1614.

May 28, 1789
The Third Estate begins to meet on its own, calling themselves *"communes"* (commons).

June 20, 1789
The Third Estate/National Assembly are locked out of meeting houses; the Third Estate issues the *Serment du Jeu de Paume* (The Tennis Court Oath), not to dissolve itself until a constitution is established.

June 27, 1789
Louis recognizes the validity of the National Assembly and orders the First and Second Estates to join the Third.

Summer 1789
Wordsworth "roved / Dovedale, or Yorkshire Dales" with Dorothy and perhaps Mary Hutchinson (6.208–10). The three visit Brougham Castle and the border beacon at Penrith.

July 12, 1789
Camille Desmoulins announces the dismissal of Necker to the Paris crowd (Book Ninth).

July 14, 1789
Crowds storm the Bastille. Only seven prisoners were held there. The governor of the Bastille and three officers are beheaded. Almost 100 citizens and eight prison guards are murdered.

August 26, 1789
French National Assembly issues the "Declaration of the Rights of Man and of the Citizen."

July–October 1790
Wordsworth and college friend Robert Jones undertake a walking tour through France, the Alps, Chamonix, the Simplon Pass, Lake Maggiore, and Lake Como (6.332–705). See map, page xvii.

November 1790
Edmund Burke publishes *Reflections on the Revolution in France.* Mary Wollstonecraft publishes *Vindication of the Rights of Men.*

January 21, 1791
Wordsworth graduates from Cambridge (BA without distinction) and moves to London (Book Seventh).

February 22, 1791
Thomas Paine publishes Part I of *Rights of Man.*

April 19, 1791
Parliament rejects William Wilberforce's bill to abolish the slave trade.

May–September 1791
Wordsworth and Robert Jones take a walking tour of Wales and ascend Mount Snowdon to see the sunrise from its summit (13.1–65).

June 20, 1791
Louis XVI and his family, attempting to flee and reach the frontier, are captured.

July 11, 1791
Voltaire is reinterred at Sainte-Geneviève Church, later the Panthéon.

July 14, 1791
Riots drive Joseph Priestley, supporter of the French Revolution, from Birmingham.

July 17, 1791
Members of the French National Guard under command of General Lafayette open fire on radical Jacobins at the Champ de Mars, Paris, killing as many as 50.

September 3, 1791
French Constitution is passed by the French National Assembly.

September 13, 1791
Louis XVI accepts the new Constitution.

October 1, 1791
The National Constituent Assembly in Paris is dissolved; Parisians hail Maximilien Robespierre and Jérôme Pétion as patriots.

November 21, 1791
Colonel Napoleon Bonaparte is promoted to full general and appointed Commander-in-Chief of the Armies of the French Republic.

November 26, 1791
Wordsworth returns to France via Dieppe. He soon reaches Paris and visits the National Assembly.

December 5, 1791
Wordsworth departs Paris for Orléans (9.80–125). He meets Annette Vallon (the story of Vaudracour and Julia, 9.550–936, is associated with her) and follows her to Blois. There he meets Michel Beaupuy and absorbs his republican ideals (9.113–554).

January 25, 1792
John Frost and Thomas Hardy found The London Corresponding Society, a moderate-radical group.

March 20, 1792
The guillotine is adopted as the official means of execution in France.

May 21, 1792
Due to radical political thought inspired by the French Revolution and Paine's *Rights of Man*, George III issues a proclamation against seditious publications.

June 13, 1792
Louis XVI dismisses the French government.

June 20, 1792
Louis XVI refuses to abandon his decision to veto the wishes of the Legislative Assembly and the Girondin ministers. The last chance to obtain a peaceful ending and constitutional monarchy fails. Crowds storm the Tuileries.

July 27, 1792
Michel Beaupuy's regiment leaves Blois for the Rhine frontier.

August 10, 1792
Parisian mobs attack the palace of Louis XVI. The king is deposed (10.39–54).

August 13, 1792
Louis XVI is arrested and sent to the Temple, an ancient Paris fortress used as a prison (10.41–44).

August 19, 1792
Coalition troops led by the Duke of Brunswick invade France.

September 2–6, 1792
Austria invades France, provoking a massacre of royalist and other prisoners in Paris. The September Massacres take place (10.31–69).

September 3, 1792
Wordsworth returns to Orléans from Blois.

September 22, 1792
The National Assembly declares France a republic and abolishes the monarchy.

October 29, 1792
Wordsworth leaves Orléans and arrives in Paris (10.1–136).

October 31, 1792
French revolutionary leader Jacques Pierre Brissot and twenty-seven of Brissot's Girondin colleagues are guillotined in Paris.

November 18, 1792
Wordsworth possibly attends a banquet of English radicals at White's Hotel in Paris, which would call attention to himself.

November 1792
Wordsworth returns to London (10.188–226; 13.334–48).

December 11, 1792
Accused of high treason and crimes against the state, Louis XVI is tried before the Convention. Robespierre argues, "Louis must die, so that the country may live."

December 15, 1792
Wordsworth's daughter Anne-Caroline is born in Orléans (d. July 8, 1862).

January 15, 1793
The Convention finds Louis XVI guilty. A day later, deputies vote to execute him.

January 21, 1793
Louis XVI is guillotined in Paris (Book Tenth).

January 29, 1793
Richard Watson, Bishop of Llandaff, in an appendix to an older sermon, condemns republican tyranny in France and praises the British constitution. This angers Wordsworth.

January 29, 1793
Wordsworth's *An Evening Walk* and *Descriptive Sketches* are published to critical neglect.

February 1, 1793
France declares war on England (10.233).

February 11, 1793
England declares war on France (10.228–90, 758–74).

February 16, 1793
William Godwin publishes *An Enquiry Concerning Political Justice* (10.805–29; illustration 10.5).

June 2, 1793
Jacobins arrest Girondin deputies to the National Convention.

June 1793
Wordsworth writes *A Letter to the Bishop of L[l]andaff on the extraordinary avowal of his Political Principles contained in the Appendix to his late Sermon*. In this attack on the Bishop for sympathies with "the personal sufferings of the late royal martyr," Wordsworth looks forward to a day when England will be a republic. The letter was not printed by his publisher, Joseph Johnson, perhaps avoiding charges of seditious libel and likely imprisonment.

Late June 1793
Wordsworth and friend William Calvert spend a month on the Isle of Wight in view of the gathering English fleet (10.291–307).

July 13, 1793
Charlotte Corday assassinates Jean-Paul Marat.

July 27, 1793
Robespierre is elected to the Committee of Public Safety.

July 28, 1793
Convention proscribes twenty-one Girondin deputies as enemies of France.

Late July 1793
Wordsworth and Calvert depart the Isle of Wight and, after a carriage accident, part near Salisbury. Walking alone, Wordsworth reaches Stonehenge and experiences a near visionary episode (12.312–53). Later, he passes Tintern Abbey and Goodrich Castle.

Late July 1793
Coleridge reads Wordsworth's *Descriptive Sketches* and later recalls it as "the emergence of an original poetic genius above the literary horizon."

August–October 1793
Wordsworth told Thomas Carlyle in 1840 that during these months he returned to France and witnessed the execution of Gorsas in Paris on October 7, 1793. As an Englishman and friend of the defeated Girondins, he would have been at risk.

September 5, 1793
The Reign of Terror begins (10.307–60).

September 6–8, 1793
The Duke of York's English army are routed near Dunkirk by green but larger French forces. Wordsworth welcomes the loss (10.259–64, 283–99).

October 7, 1793
Gorsas is executed by guillotine.

October 16, 1793
Marie Antoinette is executed by guillotine.

October 27, 1793
General Beaupuy, leading a Republican army in a losing battle against a Loyalist group at Entrammes, is seriously wounded but recovers.

October 31, 1793
Execution of Girondins at Paris during the Reign of Terror (Book Tenth).

November 8, 1793
Madame Roland is guillotined, part of the purge of the Girondins (Book Tenth; illustration 10.11).

April 5, 1794
Danton and Desmoulins are guillotined.

April 1794
Wordsworth and Dorothy leave Kendal, walk along Windermere, and spend the night at Grasmere. They walk past *The Dove and Olive Branch* inn, where they will settle five years later.

May 17, 1794
Parliament suspends Habeas Corpus until July 1795 and again from April 1798 to March 1801. In London elements considered radical, led by John Horne Tooke, Thomas Hardy, and especially John Thelwall, a man Wordsworth would know personally later, are brought to trial and charged with high treason.

May 1794
Terminally ill friend and political radical Raisley Calvert leaves Wordsworth a legacy of £900.

June 1794
Wordsworth expresses criticism of the English government to William Matthews: "I disapprove of monarchical and aristocratical governments, however modified."

June–July 1794
Robespierre and the Committee of Public Safety execute more than 1300 people by guillotine (10.329–45).

July 28, 1794
Robespierre is executed (10.530–657).

August 20, 1794
Wordsworth visits the grave of his schoolmaster William Taylor at Cartmel Priory (10.486–538). On this trip he learns of Robespierre's execution.

October 9, 1794
French troops occupy 's-Hertogenbosch.

October 1794
Wordsworth begins to doubt his enthusiasm for France—now "oppressors in their turn"—but sticks "firmly to old tenets" and revolutionary ideals (10.791–804).

January 9, 1795
Raisley Calvert dies at Penrith from tuberculosis (13.349–67). Wordsworth likely attends the funeral at Greystoke, Cumberland.

February 1795
Wordsworth travels to London and meets Basil Montagu and his young son. The boy will live with William and Dorothy at £50 per year.

February 27, 1795
Wordsworth meets William Godwin for the first time (Book Tenth). From March to August the two often converse. Godwin claims that at their first meeting he converted Wordsworth "from the doctrine of self-love to that of benevolence." Wordsworth tells a student to "throw aside your books of chemistry and read Godwin on Necessity."

July 27, 1795
Spain and France sign peace treaty.

August 15, 1795
Wordsworth departs London for Bristol and waits for Dorothy to join him. A friend of Basil Montagu, John Pinney, will allow William and Dorothy to rent free a large, unoccupied house, Racedown Lodge, in West Dorset.

August–September 1795
In Bristol, Wordsworth meets Coleridge and Robert Southey for the first time.

September 26, 1795
William, Dorothy, and young Basil Montagu arrive at Racedown Lodge.

October 4, 1795
Coleridge marries Sara Fricker in Bristol at St. Mary Redcliffe Church, where Chatterton had grown up and later claimed to have found the Rowley manuscripts.

March 1796
Wordsworth experiences a deepening moral crisis, in part due to his disappointments in reading the second edition of Godwin's *Political Justice* (10.878–907). Wordsworth and Coleridge begin regular correspondence.

May 13, 1796
Coleridge proclaims his "very dear friend" Wordsworth is "the best poet of the age."

August 19, 1796
Spain and France sign an anti-British alliance.

September 19, 1796
Hartley Coleridge is born.

October 5, 1796
Spain declares war on England.

October 19, 1796
General Beaupuy dies at the battle of Emmendingen in what is now southern Germany.

December 31, 1796
Coleridge and his wife Sara move into a small, damp cottage in Nether Stowey, 27 miles north of Racedown Lodge.

February 22, 1797
A French Revolutionary force of over 1,000 lands at Fishguard in northwestern Wales (the last invasion of England). They surrender but cause great concern. Wordsworth and Coleridge face the possibility of being pressed into military duty to protect the coast.

March 30, 1797
Wordsworth visits Coleridge at Nether Stowey.

April 18, 1797
France and Austria sign ceasefire.

May 12, 1797
Napoleon conquers Venice.

June 4, 1797
Coleridge arrives at Racedown to stay almost four weeks. He soon tells Robert Southey that "Wordsworth is a very great man—the only man, to whom *at all times* & in *all modes of excellence* I feel myself inferior."

July 2–4, 1797
William and Dorothy visit Coleridge at Nether Stowey. They discover that a large, unoccupied house, Alfoxden Park, three miles from Nether Stowey, is available.

July 16, 1797
William and Dorothy move to Alfoxden Park in the Quantock Hills (13.386–410).

July 18, 1797
Coleridge, his wife Sara, Dorothy, William, and John Thelwall have "a most philosophical party" at Alfoxden. Thelwall's reputation makes neighbors and the landlord suspicious. A government spy determines they are "a nest of a gang of disaffected Englishmen." The Wordsworths lose their lease. About this time, or perhaps the next summer, Coleridge writes *Kubla Khan*.

November 1797
Coleridge and Wordsworth plan a poem that becomes Coleridge's *Rime of the Ancient Mariner*. The two soon project a book of poems that becomes *Lyrical Ballads* (13.390–410).

January 20, 1798
Dorothy begins her *Alfoxden Journal:* "The young wheat is streaked by silver lines of water running between the ridges, the sheep are gathered together on the slopes."

February 1798
15,000 French troops occupy Mulhouse and Biel/Bienne in Switzerland and establish a puppet government. Wordsworth and Coleridge perhaps lose final sympathy with revolutionary France.

March 1798
Coleridge believes that poetry can become "the living image rather than the abstract explanation of higher truths." He sees in Wordsworth a poet to achieve this and tells Joseph Cottle, "The Giant Wordsworth—God love him!" Encouraged by Coleridge to write a philosophical poem, Wordsworth begins writing verse for *The Recluse*. What becomes *The Prelude* he later describes as an ante-chapel or portico, the "least important" aspect of this poem.

May 14, 1798
Berkeley Coleridge is born at Nether Stowey.

June 25, 1798
Wordsworth and Dorothy leave Alfoxden.

July 1, 1798
Napoleon invades Egypt with 400 ships and 54,000 men.

July 3, 1798
Wordsworth and Dorothy arrive in Bristol then walk in Wales for four days and see Tintern Abbey, Goodrich Castle, and the Wye valley.

August 2, 1798
Admiral Nelson defeats the French at the Battle of the Nile.

August 13, 1798
Wordsworth and Dorothy reach London. They leave five-year-old Basil Montagu under the care of Basil's aunt.

August 22, 1798
French troops land in County Mayo to aid Wolfe Tone's United Irishmen's Rebellion.

September 16, 1798
Lyrical Ballads is published anonymously in Bristol. Wordsworth, Dorothy, and Coleridge sail for Hamburg, Germany.

October 4, 1798
Lyrical Ballads is reissued, again anonymously, by J. & A. Arch in London.

October 6, 1798
Wordsworth and Dorothy part with Coleridge and head for Goslar. Wordsworth soon writes lines that will become part of the "poem to Coleridge," which he composes at various times until May 1805. After later revisions, it is published posthumously in 1850 as *The Prelude*.

February 10, 1799
Berkeley Coleridge dies.

February 23, 1799
After a brutal winter, one of the coldest in a century, William and Dorothy leave Goslar (1.1–54; 7.1–9).

April 20, 1799
Wordsworth and Dorothy meet Coleridge in Göttingen. They discuss being near each other in England. Wordsworth says he wishes to live in the Lake District.

April 26, 1799

After sailing to England with Coleridge, William and Dorothy live for a time near family at Sockburn-on-Tees.

July 29, 1799

Coleridge returns to Nether Stowey.

October 26, 1799

Visiting Wordsworth at Sockburn-on-Tees, Coleridge meets Mary Hutchinson's younger sister Sara.

October 27, 1799

Wordsworth and Coleridge embark on a walking tour of the Lake District. They meet by chance William's favorite brother John, at twenty-six an officer on the East Indiaman, the *Earl of Abergavenny*, recently back from India and China.

November 3, 1799

Wordsworth, John, and Coleridge arrive in Grasmere. William finds a "small house" (Dove Cottage) for rent.

November 9, 1799

A coup d'état overthrows the Directory in France. Napoleon gains power as First Consul.

November 11, 1799

Wordsworth and Coleridge spend the night at Buttermere and meet "the Maid of Buttermere," Mary Robinson (7.311–64).

November 20, 1799

John Wordsworth and Coleridge leave William, who returns to Grasmere and signs a lease for Dove Cottage, then returns to Sockburn on November 29.

December 20, 1799

William and Dorothy move to Dove Cottage at Town End, Grasmere. They remain there until May 1, 1808.

January 1800

John visits William and Dorothy until September 29, 1800.

Late February 1800

Mary Hutchinson arrives at Dove Cottage for six weeks. She meets John Wordsworth and develops a "tender love" or fondness for him. John falls in love with Mary but seems too shy to tell her.

April 6, 1800

Coleridge visits Wordsworth and Dorothy at Dove Cottage for the first time and stays a month.

May 14, 1800

Wordsworth and his brother John visit Yordas Cave (8.711–41). Dorothy writes the first entry in her *Grasmere Journals*.

May 21, 1800

Coleridge and his family move to Greta Hall in Keswick, 13 miles north of Grasmere. He and Wordsworth meet often, forming, as Coleridge puts it, "a gang" that includes Dorothy and Mary and Sara Hutchinson.

September 5, 1800

French forces at Malta surrender to the British after a long blockade.

September 17, 1800

Struggling with the composition of *Christabel*, Coleridge writes James Tobin, "I abandon Poetry altogether—I leave the higher and deeper kinds to Wordsworth."

September 29, 1800

John Wordsworth departs from Grasmere. He makes a covenant with William to seek a fortune at sea and return to aid William achieve greatness as a poet. John begins writing affectionate letters to Mary Hutchinson.

October 4, 1800

Coleridge visits Dove Cottage and reads to William and Dorothy the unfinished second part of *Christabel* on the day after they encountered a leech gatherer. According to Dorothy's *Journal*, after initial delight, her brother within two days decides not to include *Christabel* in *Lyrical Ballads*, primarily, he will say, for reasons of style and continuity.

December 9, 1800

Wordsworth completes *Michael*, which will replace Coleridge's *Christabel* in the 1800 edition of *Lyrical Ballads*.

December 19, 1800

Coleridge, twenty-eight, writes to Francis Wrangham of Wordsworth: "He is a great, a true Poet—I am only a kind of a Metaphysician."

January 7, 1801

John Wordsworth is sworn in as captain of the *Earl of Abergavenny*.

January 25, 1801

Second edition of *Lyrical Ballads* (date given as 1800), published in London by Longman and including a Preface, prints "W. Wordsworth" as author.

April 19, 1801

Wordsworth and Dorothy visit Coleridge at Greta Hall and find him "very, very unwell," perhaps due in part to his use of opium, which had deepened that winter.

November 12, 1801

William asks Mary to marry him and she accepts.

March 27, 1802

England signs the Peace of Amiens with France. Lasting until May 16, 1803, it allows Wordsworth to visit Annette and their daughter.

June 1802

Third edition of *Lyrical Ballads* is published with an enlarged Preface.

August 1, 1802

William and Dorothy arrive at Calais and spend one month with Annette and William's daughter Anne-Caroline. Napoleon declares himself First Consul for Life.

September 7, 1802

William and Dorothy visit Bartholomew Fair with Charles Lamb and his sister Mary (7.649–707).

September 11, 1802

In London Wordsworth tells his brother John of his impending marriage with Mary. Although John and Mary never see each other again, John writes a last letter to her, finishing: "But whatever fate Befall me I shall love [thee] to the last and bear thy memory with me to the grave."

October 4, 1802

William and Mary are married in the Church of All Saints in Brompton-by-Sawdon, a North Yorkshire village. Few members of her family attend. Dorothy stays home due to "nervous uneasiness." The newlyweds receive but one present: John Wordsworth sends a dress obtained on a recent voyage to the Far East.

October 4, 1802
Coleridge chooses the day of Wordsworth's marriage, the seventh anniversary of his own, the date he read the second part of *Christabel* to William and Dorothy, and the date on which he recalls that his own father died, to publish *Dejection: An Ode*. It is also the date on which his play with Southey, *The Fall of Robespierre*, was first sold in Cambridge in 1794, and the date of the second issue of the first edition of *Lyrical Ballads* in 1798.

October 11, 1802
Coleridge publishes in *The Morning Post* a poem, "Spots in the Sun." It seems to allude unkindly and privately to Wordsworth's affair with Annette Vallon.

October 16, 1802
Mary and Dorothy return to Dove Cottage, William the next day.

May 1803
Britain's war with France resumes. Coleridge reconsiders his earlier radicalism: "My *opinions* were the drivel of a Babe."

June 18, 1803
William and Mary's first child, John (d. 1875), is born at Grasmere.

August 15, 1803
William, Dorothy, and Coleridge set off on a tour of Scotland. They stop in Carlisle and Coleridge visits in jail the bigamist Hatfield, the forger who violated the innocence of Mary of Buttermere (7.317–60).

September 25, 1803
William and Dorothy return to Grasmere.

October 3, 1803
Due to a possible French invasion, Wordsworth and others enlist with the Grasmere Volunteers.

January 4, 1804
Coleridge records that Wordsworth read to him the "second Part of his divine Self-biography," probably Book Second.

January 14, 1804
"Sorely ill," Coleridge begins travel preparations for Malta to take a diplomatic post and to restore his health.

March 6, 1804
Wordsworth writes to William Matthews concerning the poem "on my own earlier life": "This Poem will not be published these many years, and never during my lifetime, till I have finished a larger and more important work . . . a moral and Philosophical poem . . . the chief force of my mind."

March 1804
Still lacking from Coleridge notes that might assist him with *The Recluse*, Wordsworth completes a five-book version of what will become *The Prelude* and sends it to Coleridge.

April 3, 1804
William Pitt returns to govern as Prime Minister.

April 9, 1804
Before sailing for Malta on *Speedwell* (6.256), Coleridge receives a discouraging letter from Sara Hutchinson that puts "despair into [his] Heart." He does not return to England until August 17, 1806.

August 16, 1804
Wordsworth's daughter Dora (d. 1847) is born at Grasmere.

August 1804
Coleridge climbs Etna twice, the mountain Wordsworth mentions in Book Tenth (10.1006–38).

December 2, 1804
Pope Pius VII crowns Napoleon Emperor of France (10.918–40).

February 5, 1805
In a severe storm off Portland Bill, Wordsworth's brother John drowns aboard the *Earl of Abergavenny* (13.415–21).

February 11, 1805
Wordsworth learns of John's drowning. He writes to his brother Richard, "The set is now broken" and, devastated, stops composing his autobiographical poem until

April. The brotherly covenant is shattered: "I will work for you [at sea] and you shall attempt to do something for the world."

March 20, 1805
John Wordsworth's body is recovered near Weymouth and buried the next day in the churchyard at Wyke Regis.

March 26, 1805
Wordsworth receives a letter from Coleridge, dated January 19, that indicates that Coleridge's notes to assist Wordsworth's composition of *The Recluse* have been burnt as plague papers while in the possession of someone else.

April 24, 1805
Wordsworth resumes writing what will become *The Prelude*. He appears to pay tribute to John (12.260–77).

May 20, 1805
Wordsworth completes thirteen books of his "biographic verse." Over the years, he revises the poem but never publishes it. He considers it as preparatory or tributary for the "task of his life": *The Recluse*, never completed.

June 3, 1805
Wordsworth writes to his friend and benefactor, Sir George Beaumont, to inform him that he has finished the poem about his own development: "I had looked forward to the day as a most happy one, and I was indeed grateful to God for giving me life to complete the work, such as it is; but it was not a happy day for me I was dejected on many accounts; when I look back upon the performance it seemed to have a dead weight about it, the reality so far short of the expectation . . . and the doubt whether I should ever live to write the Recluse. . . . This work may be considered as a sort of portico to the Recluse, part of the same building, which I hope to be able erelong to begin with in earnest; and if I am permitted to bring it to conclusion, and to write, further, a narrative Poem of the Epic kind, I shall consider the *task* of my life as over."

October–November 1805
In a Notebook Coleridge writes of Wordsworth, "O that my spirit purged by Death of its Weaknesses, which are alas! my *identity* might flow into *thine*, & live and act in

thee, & be Thou." This also alludes to the fate of the poet philosopher Empedocles.

October 20, 1805
Nelson's ships destroy the French fleet near Cape Trafalgar off Spain. Nelson is killed in the action.

December 2, 1805
Napoleon defeats the Russians and Austrians at Austerlitz.

Early 1806
Wordsworth and Mary begin attending Anglican Church services.

January 9, 1806
Nelson receives a state funeral and is laid to rest in St. Paul's Cathedral.

January 23, 1806
William Pitt the Younger dies at age forty-six.

Summer 1806
Now thirty-six, Wordsworth completes the first book of *The Recluse (Home at Grasmere)* and begins to compose *Elegiac Stanzas Suggested by a Picture of Peele Castle*, a response to his brother John's death.

August 17, 1806
Coleridge returns to England in poor condition, his opium use unabated. He does not return to his family in the Lake District until late October.

September 1806
Wordsworth meets the painter John Constable at Brathay.

October 26, 1806
Wordsworth and Dorothy reunite with Coleridge in Kendal. They are shaken by his appearance and manner.

November 7, 1806
Sir George Beaumont offers the Wordsworths use of a large farmhouse in Coleorton, Leicestershire, for the winter. Wordsworth invites Coleridge to live there for a time.

November 24, 1806
Coleridge separates from his wife.

December 21, 1806
Coleridge and his son Hartley live with the Wordsworths for four months at Coleorton Hall. Wordsworth begins some revisions of the 1805 "poem to Coleridge."

January 7, 1807
Wordsworth completes reading aloud to Coleridge the thirteen books of what will become *The Prelude*. In response, Coleridge writes *To William Wordsworth* (see pp. 261–64).

March 25, 1807
Parliament votes to abolish the slave trade throughout the British Empire.

April 17, 1807
Coleridge departs from the Wordsworth family.

May 8, 1807
Wordsworth's *Poems, in Two Volumes* is published. Reviews are unfavorable.

July 7, 9, 1807
France, Russia, and Prussia sign Treaties of Tilsit.

July 1807
The Wordsworths return to Dove Cottage.

February 1808
William and Dorothy visit Coleridge and are alarmed at his condition, dependent on opium, and offer to have him live in their home to be at Allan Bank, Grasmere.

Late May 1808
The Wordsworth family, including Sara Hutchinson, move to Allan Bank, regarded by them as a "temple of abomination" when built in 1805.

September 1, 1808
Coleridge arrives at Allan Bank. By "a very painful Effort of moral Courage," he reduces use of opium and begins a periodical, *The Friend*, parts dictated to Sara Hutchinson. It engages principles, philosophy, morality, and law.

May 27, 1809
Wordsworth's *The Convention of Cintra* is published.

March 1810
Last number of *The Friend* is published. Sara Hutchinson leaves Allan Bank for Wales.

April 12, 1810
Dorothy writes to a friend that she and William no longer "have hope of him" (Coleridge). Without their help, he is "the slave of stimulants as ever . . . employed in deceiving himself, and seeking to deceive others."

May 2, 1810
Coleridge departs Allan Bank and returns to Greta Hall.

October 28, 1810
Basil Montagu imprudently informs Coleridge that Wordsworth said Coleridge was "a rotten drunkard . . . rotting out his entrails by intemperance" and "an absolute nuisance in the family." Wordsworth and Coleridge become estranged. Coleridge tells Mary Lamb, "Wordsworth, Wordsworth has given me up."

March 25, 1811
Percy Bysshe Shelley is expelled from Oxford for publication of his pamphlet *The Necessity of Atheism*.

May 1811
Wordsworth family moves to the Rectory, Grasmere.

February 7, 1812
Byron gives maiden speech in the House of Lords.

May 1812
Wordsworth and Coleridge achieve some reconciliation through letter writing encouraged by mutual friends. They meet several times in London. Coleridge writes, "I never ceased to have faith in you, to love & revere you." Yet, he writes to Thomas Poole, "O no! no! that I fear, never can return . . . there remains an immedicable *But*." To indicate his hurt he uses the image of a storm out of the blue (from Horace), an image he used in *To William Wordsworth* (see p. 262). On May 11, Spencer Perceval, England's Prime Minister, is assassinated.

June 4, 1812
Catharine, William and Mary's daughter, dies suddenly.

September 15, 1812
A French army of nearly 500,000 reaches Moscow.

October 30, 1812
Sara Hutchinson writes to Thomas Poole of Wordsworth and Coleridge: "there will never more be *that* between them which was in days of yore."

November 29, 1812
Napoleon's army begins retreat from Russia. Most men perish in the harsh winter.

December 1, 1812
Wordsworth's son Thomas dies of pneumonia.

April 26, 1813
Wordsworth is appointed Distributor of Stamps for Westmoreland.

May 1813
Wordsworth family moves to Rydal Mount, Wordsworth's home until his death in 1850.

February 1, 1814
Byron's *Corsair* sells 10,000 copies on its first day of publication.

March 31, 1814
Forces allied against Napoleon capture Paris.

April 11, 1814
Napoleon abdicates, is exiled to Elba, but allowed to keep the title of Emperor.

May 3, 1814
Cheering crowds meet Louis XVIII in Paris.

May 30, 1814
The Treaty of Paris returns French borders to their 1792 extent.

August 1814
The Excursion, a narrative poem in nine books, planned as part of *The Recluse*, is published to mixed reviews. Wordsworth alludes in the Preface to an introductory portico, biographical and already "long finished," that "conducts the history of the Author's mind to the point when he was emboldened to hope that his faculties were sufficiently matured for entering upon the arduous labour which he had proposed to himself" (*The Recluse* as a whole).

March 20, 1815
Escaped from Elba, Napoleon enters Paris to begin his *Cent Jours* (100-day rule).

April 3, 1815
Coleridge tells Lady Beaumont that *The Excursion* was not as good as Book First of the unpublished *Prelude*. Wordsworth writes Coleridge for an explanation.

April 11, 1815
Wordsworth publishes *Poems* in two volumes. Three poems are by Dorothy.

May 30, 1815
Coleridge writes Wordsworth and outlines what *The Recluse* might contain.

June 2, 1815
Wordsworth publishes *The White Doe of Rylstone*.

June 18, 1815
At Waterloo British forces of 67,000 under Wellington, with 45,000 Prussian troops under Blücher, defeat Napoleon and his 69,000. Dead and wounded exceed 43,000.

August 9, 1815
Napoleon is banished for life and exiled to the South Atlantic island of St. Helena, where he dies six years later.

November 20, 1815
The Quadruple Alliance of Russia, Prussia, Austria, and England is signed in Paris "for the maintenance of peace in Europe."

February 28, 1816
Wordsworth and Annette Vallon's daughter, Anne-Caroline, marries Jean Baptiste Martin Baudouin in Paris. Her unmarried last name is officially corrected from Wordswodsth to Wordsworth.

May 1816
Coleridge, now living with the Gillmans at Highgate, publishes *Christabel* (never finished) and *Kubla Khan*.

1816–19
Wordsworth makes extensive revisions to the 1805 manuscript of what will become *The Prelude*.

July 1817
Coleridge publishes *Biographia Literaria*, originally intended as a preface to a volume of his own poems and an answer to the 1800/1802 Preface that Wordsworth wrote for *Lyrical Ballads*. Coleridge also publishes *Sibylline Leaves*.

December 28, 1817
Wordsworth meets John Keats at the "Immortal Dinner" in Haydon's studio. At two other dinner parties in late December he has tense exchanges with Coleridge.

April 1819
Wordsworth's *Peter Bell* is published.

May 1819
Wordsworth's *The Waggoner* is published.

January 29, 1820
George III dies and is succeeded by George IV.

May 1820
Wordsworth's *River Duddon* sonnets are published. He uses passages from Book Ninth of the unpublished thirteen-book *Prelude* for *Vaudracour and Julia*.

July 1820
Retracing his route through the Alps in 1790, Wordsworth takes a tour with Mary and Dorothy.

October 1820
In Paris the Wordsworth party visits Annette Vallon, Caroline Baudouin, and her husband for several weeks.

February 23, 1821
Keats dies in Rome from tuberculosis at age twenty-five.

February 1822
Wordsworth's *Ecclesiastical Sketches* (sonnets) and *Memorials of a Tour of the Continent* are published.

July 8, 1822
Percy Shelley drowns at age twenty-nine during a storm in the Gulf of Spezia while sailing a small boat.

April 19, 1824
Byron dies at Missolonghi, age thirty-six.

December 1824
Dorothy writes that her "brother has not yet looked at *The Recluse*; he seems to feel the task so weighty that he shrinks from beginning with it."

February 7, 1827
Wordsworth's friend and patron Sir George Beaumont dies.

June 21, 1828
Wordsworth, Dora, and Coleridge embark on a six-week Netherlands and Rhineland tour. In his Notebook in July, Coleridge writes in German, presumably to keep it from companions, that Wordsworth's "grand flowerings of philosophic and poetic genius have withered and dried."

April 13, 1829
Parliament grants British and Irish Catholics emancipation. Wordsworth opposes the bill, asking, "Are not the same Arguments that induced our Forefathers to withdraw from the Roman faith 300 years ago still applicable?"

June 26, 1830
George IV dies and is succeeded by his brother William IV.

December 25, 1830
Wordsworth and Coleridge meet for the last recorded time for dinner in London. Coleridge writes, "a happy Christmas Day throughout." They perhaps meet again in 1831.

1831–32
Wordsworth makes further revisions to what will become *The Prelude*. He tells the artist Benjamin Robert Haydon, "The Muse has forsaken me."

June 4, 1832
The Great Reform Act is passed. It changes parliamentary representation to "take effectual Measures for correcting divers Abuses that have long prevailed in the Choice of Members to serve in the Commons House of Parliament." Wordsworth thinks the authors of the Act "have already gone so far towards committing a greater political crime than any recorded in History."

June 5, 1832
French Republicans revolt when Jean-Maximilien Lamarque's funeral procession reaches the Place de la Bastille. King Louis-Philippe reclaims the streets. Many who shout "Liberty or Death" die in vain. The monarchy is secured.

1833
Dorothy Wordsworth's health begins to fail and her mental capacities to diminish.

July 31, 1833
Parliament passes a bill to abolish slavery throughout the British Empire, to take effect one year later.

July 25, 1834
Age sixty-one, Coleridge dies at Highgate. Wordsworth writes four days later that, "his mind has been habitually present with me, with an accompanying feeling that he was still in the flesh." He calls Coleridge the "most *wonderful* man" he had ever known.

January 1835
Wordsworth's *Yarrow Revisited, and Other Poems* is published.

June 24, 1835
Sara Hutchinson dies of rheumatic fever. Dorothy is ill.

1836
The Excursion is republished without reference to its original plan as part of *The Recluse*.

June 20, 1837
Upon the death of her uncle William IV, Victoria becomes queen at age eighteen.

1838–39
Apparently for the last time, Wordsworth makes revisions to what will become *The Prelude*.

1840
Wordsworth tells a friend that he regrets not completing *The Recluse*: the poet Gray "had undertaken something beyond his powers to accomplish. And that is my case."

January 10, 1841
Annette Vallon dies and is buried in Père Lachaise in Paris.

April 1842
Wordsworth's *Poems, Chiefly of Early and Late Years; including The Borderers, A Tragedy* is published.

April 1843
Wordsworth is named Poet Laureate succeeding Robert Southey.

April 25, 1845
Wordsworth meets Queen Victoria at the Queen's Ball.

July 9, 1847
Wordsworth's beloved daughter Dora dies at forty-two from tuberculosis.

January 6, 1849
Coleridge's son Hartley, "child of all the Vale," dies at fifty-two.

1849–1850
The Poetical Works of William Wordsworth, DCL, Poet Laureate: A New Edition appears in six volumes.

April 23, 1850
Wordsworth dies at age eighty from pneumonia and is buried in the churchyard of St. Oswald's in Grasmere.

July 1850
Originally the "poem to Coleridge," now *The Prelude, or Growth of a Poet's Mind: An Autobiographical Poem*, its title given by Mary, is published in fourteen books by Wordsworth's executors. Few are aware that an earlier, thirteen-book version exists.

January 25, 1855
Dorothy Wordsworth dies at eighty-four and is buried near her brother.

January 17, 1859
Mary Wordsworth, "the Solitary Lingerer," dies and is laid to rest next to William.

1926
Ernest de Selincourt (1870–1943) publishes Wordsworth's long unknown thirteen-book *Prelude*.

2016
The Prelude (1805) is fully illustrated for the first time.

Selected Bibliography and Scholarly Editions of *The Prelude*

This list, not intended to be comprehensive, offers material especially regarding the themes of nature and the environment, place, and illustration. Following it appear some scholarly editions of *The Prelude* that readers may wish to consult.

Bate, Jonathan. *Romantic Ecology: Wordsworth and the Environmental Tradition* (London and New York: Routledge, 1991). Bate also discusses Wordsworth and *The Prelude* in *The Song of the Earth* (Cambridge MA: Harvard University Press, 2000).

Bushell, Sally. *Wordsworth's Sense of Place*: "Home at Grasmere" (The Wordsworth Centre of Lancaster University and The Wordsworth Trust, 2007), DVD.

Clark, Kenneth. *Moments of Vision*, with wood engravings by Reynolds Stone, an expanded version of the Romanes Lecture delivered May 11, 1954 (London: John Murray, 1973). Clark discusses Wordsworth's "Moments of Vision" and "visual obsession." The Clarendon Press published the original lecture in 1954. In 1981 J. Murray published a longer work with the same title.

Hess, Scott. *William Wordsworth and the Ecology of Authorship* (Charlottesville: University of Virginia Press, 2012), chapter 1, "Picturesque Vision, Photographic Subjectivity, and the (Un)framing of Nature," and chapter 2, "Wordsworth Country: The Lake District and the Landscape of Genius."

Huson, Thomas. *Round About Helvellyn*, twenty-four plates with notes by the artist and descriptive passages from Wordsworth's poems (London: Seeley and Co., 1895). Modern reprints may be available.

Iddon, Henry E. *Spots of Time: The Lake District Photographed by Night* (Grasmere: The Wordsworth Trust, 2008). Wordsworth frequently walked Lake District roads and paths at night.

Jarvis, Simon. *Wordsworth's Philosophic Song* (Cambridge UK: Cambridge University Press, 2007). Wordsworth's thinking as a poet, with parts devoted to *The Prelude*.

Knight, William. *The English Lake District as Interpreted in the Poems of Wordsworth* (Edinburgh: David Douglas, 1878, 1891; Folcroft Library Editions, 1977).

Lindop, Grevel. *A Literary Guide to the Lake District* (London: Chatto & Windus, 1993).

McCracken, David. *Wordsworth and the Lake District: A Guide to the Poems and Their Places* (Oxford: Oxford University Press, 1984), illustrated and with maps. A superb treatment.

Milnes, Tim. *The Prelude* (London: Palgrave Macmillan, 2009). A guide to the poem, the history of its reception, and changing critical views of it.

Newlyn, Lucy. "'The noble living and the noble dead': community in *The Prelude*," chapter 4 in *The Cambridge Companion to William Wordsworth*, ed. Stephen Gill (Cambridge UK: Cambridge University Press, 2003).

Powell, Cecilia. *Savage Grandeur and Noblest Thoughts: Discovering the Lake District 1750–1820* (Grasmere: The Wordsworth Trust, 2010). A splendid illustrated exhibition catalogue.

Robertson, Eric S. *Wordsworthshire: Wordsworth and the English Lake Country: An Introduction to a Poet's Country* (New York: D. Appleton, 1911), illustrated with forty-seven drawings by Arthur Tucker and with maps.

Stafford, Fiona. "Wordsworth's Poetry of Place," chapter 17 in *The Oxford Handbook of William Wordsworth*, ed. Richard Gravil and Daniel Robinson (Oxford: Oxford University Press, 2015); also Stafford's *Local Attachments: The Province of Poetry* (Oxford: Oxford University Press, 2010), especially chapter 3, "Local Attachments and Adequate Poetry," though Wordsworth appears throughout the volume.

Tejblum, Julia. "Wordsworth and the *Relief of Central Switzerland*," *The Wordsworth Circle* 46:2 (Spring 2015): 116–20. Wordsworth had a decades-long fascination with a large, three-dimensional landscape model of central Switzerland. This model can still be viewed today in Lucerne, the city where he saw it in 1790 and 1820.

Trott, Nicola. "Wordsworth and the Picturesque: A Strong Infection of the Age," *The Wordsworth Circle* 18:3 (Summer 1987): 114–21. Wordsworth's involvement with a theory and practice of art and landscape.

Wordsworth, Dorothy. *The Grasmere Journals*, ed. Pamela Woof (Oxford: The Clarendon Press, 1991).

Wordsworth, William. *Guide to the Lakes*, ed. Ernest de Selincourt, with a new preface by Stephen Gill (London: Frances Lincoln, 2004).

Our English Lakes, Mountains and Waterfalls as seen by William Wordsworth, photographically illustrated (London: A.W. Bennett, 1864). Photographs by Thomas Ogle, printed by William Russell Sedgfield and J. Eliot. Some prints vary among copies.

The Poems of William Wordsworth, selected, edited, and introduced by Jonathan Wordsworth, illustrated by John O'Connor (Cambridge UK: Cambridge University Press for the Limited Editions Club, 1973).

Poems from Wordsworth, edited by T. Sturge Moore, illustrated by wood-cuts designed and engraved by T. S. Moore (London: Vale Press, Ballantyne Press, 1902).

The Deserted Cottage [Wordsworth's *Ruined Cottage*], illustrated with twenty-one designs by Birket Foster, J. Wolf, and John Gilbert, engraved by the Brothers Dalziel [Edward and George] (London: George Routledge and Co., 1859).

The Prelude, illustrated by David Esslemont, edited with an essay by Robert Woof and Introduction by Stephen Gill (Grasmere: The Wordsworth Trust, 2007). A rare, special edition illustrated with abstract watercolors.

The Illustrated Wordsworth's Guide to the Lakes, ed. Peter Bickell, Foreword by Alan G. Hill (Exeter: Webb & Bower, 1984).

Wordsworth at Cambridge: A Record of the Commemoration Held at St. John's College, Cambridge, in April 1950 (Cambridge UK: Cambridge University Press, 1950?), with illustrations. Originally appearing in the annual record of St. John's, *The Eagle*, 54:237 (1950–51): 73–143.

The Wordsworth Centre, Lancaster University, www.wordsworthcentre.co.uk

The Wordsworth Trust, Grasmere, www.wordsworth.org.uk

Scholarly Editions of *The Prelude*

The Prelude (text of 1805), ed. Ernest de Selincourt (Oxford: The Clarendon Press, 1926). The first publication of the 1805 text of thirteen books. In 1970 Oxford issued a second edition with corrections by Stephen Gill.

The Thirteen-Book Prelude, ed. Mark L. Reed, The Cornell Wordsworth, 2 vols. (Ithaca: Cornell University Press, 1991). The authoritative, scholarly edition of the poem as Wordsworth originally completed it in thirteen books.

The Fourteen-Book Prelude, ed. W. J. B. Owen, The Cornell Wordsworth (Ithaca: Cornell University Press, 1985). The authoritative, scholarly edition of the poem as Wordsworth revised it after 1805. *The Prelude* in fourteen books was first published in 1850 after his death.

The Prelude, 1798–1799, ed. Stephen Parrish, The Cornell Wordsworth (Ithaca: Cornell University Press, 1977). Contains the earliest version of the two-part *Prelude* of 1798–1799 with transcriptions of its manuscripts.

The Five-Book Prelude, ed. Duncan Wu (Oxford and Cambridge MA: Blackwell, 1997). An edition of the poem in its state of early 1804.

Wordsworth's Poetry and Prose, ed. Nicholas Halmi (New York and London: W. W. Norton, 2014). This anthology prints the 1805 *Prelude* with substantial annotation and pertinent criticism.

William Wordsworth, ed. Stephen Gill, 21st-Century Oxford Authors (Oxford: Oxford University Press, 2010). This anthology contains the 1805 *Prelude* with concise, helpful notes.

The Prelude, 1799, 1805, 1850, ed. Jonathan Wordsworth, M. H. Abrams, and Stephen Gill (New York and London: W. W. Norton, 1979). Spelling is modernized and punctuation at times significantly altered.

The Prelude, 1798, 1799, 1805, 1850, ed. Jonathan Wordsworth (Harmondsworth and New York: Penguin, 1995).

www.digitalwordsworth.org

Acknowledgments

This book is not the labor of two or three people but the product of work and cooperation by many. The volume would not enjoy its aesthetic and visual merit were it not for the superb eye and judgment of the designer Howard I. Gralla. Editing *The Prelude* (1805), even when consulting manuscripts directly, leans on previous editors, and they are thanked deeply: Ernest de Selincourt, Mark L. Reed, Stephen Gill, Nicholas Halmi, Jonathan Wordsworth, Duncan Wu, and M. H. Abrams. Without the previous labor of these editors there would be more errors than whatever the present edition might contain, and the effort of writing notes and making decisions concerning editorial matters would have been more vexing. All good editorial practice and scholarship stand on earlier good practice. The work of these editors is acknowledged as instrumental to the production of this volume.

We are deeply grateful to The Wordsworth Trust for access to the manuscripts of *The Prelude* and for permission to reproduce the entire text of this major poem. Without this permission, publication of the current edition would not have been possible. We also express gratitude to the Trust for providing many superb illustrations from its collection. At the Trust we thank especially Jeff Cowton, Michael McGregor, Melissa Mitchell, and Linda Nordgreen, as well as Seamus Perry for his kind offices. The Yale Center for British Art has been wonderfully generous with its resources. Gillian Forrester, Maria Singer, Kurt Heumiller, and Matthew Hargraves at the Center have been equally generous with their time. Richard Hyde of Cumbrian Discoveries, a Blue Guide, showed us places in the Lake District that we otherwise would have missed or misidentified. His help was invaluable. At Bridgeman Images we thank Leslie Wong; at Art Resource we are grateful to Diana Reeve and Ann Miniutti; at Tate Images we benefitted from the aid of Clive Coward. Maps in this book are from the hand of Mick and Jennifer Ashworth of Ashworth Maps, Glasgow. Work of Fiona Stafford and Sally Bushell on the idea of place in Wordsworth's poetry has been extremely helpful. Samantha Harvey and Michael McCue provided astute suggestions and important information. The incomparable Library of Harvard University was indispensable for research. The Fred Robinson and Hyder E. Rollins Funds of the Department of English, the Anne and Jim Rothenberg Fund for Humanities Research, and the Tenured Faculty Publication Fund, all of Harvard University, supported this publication. We extend profound thanks to these funds and to the generosity of their donors. Early on, Elizabeth Wilson helped forward this project, and Alison MacKeen at Yale University Press gave sound advice. We are indebted to the books listed in the Selected Bibliography and Scholarly Editions of *The Prelude*.

The original conception of an edition of Wordsworth's great poem fully illustrated with works of art, themselves created generally at or near the time of the composition of the poem, came from Michael Raymond, who completed his doctoral work on the 1805 version. David R. Godine, our publisher, believed in this project. Our gratitude to him personally, and for his vision of this book, cannot be overstated. We extend thanks to Sue Ramin and Chelsea Bingham. Finally, we express warm thanks to our families, who not only tolerated our absences in travel and in study, but who encouraged and loved us in this endeavor as in all things.

About the Editors

JAMES ENGELL is Gurney Professor of English and Professor of Comparative Literature at Harvard University, where he chaired the Department of English for six years. He is author of four books and more than forty articles and book chapters treating eighteenth-century and romantic literature, as well as the present state of higher education in America. He has contributed to and edited eight additional volumes, including Samuel Taylor Coleridge's *Biographia Literaria* (with W. Jackson Bate) and *Environment: An Interdisciplinary Anthology* (with three co-editors). A recipient of national academic awards and university teaching prizes, he was named a Senior Fellow at the National Humanities Center and elected a member of the American Academy of Arts and Sciences.

MICHAEL D. RAYMOND has studied the poetry of William Wordsworth for decades—a catalyst for his own life-long search for deeply rooted, private places of remembrance. After earning a B.A. in English from Yale, he received his M.A. from Harvard with a thesis entitled *Wordsworth on Salisbury Plain: Noetic Insights, Natural Mysticism, and the Absence of Ideology*. Fordham conferred his doctoral degree. His dissertation is *John Wordsworth on Snowdon: The Elegiac Sublime and the Spectacle of Woe*. He has travelled with a particular passion to walk the paths and routes described in *The Prelude*, from Cockermouth and Grasmere to London, Paris, the Alps, and the northern Italian lakes, including Como and Maggiore. For four decades president of his own financial services firm, Raymond Wealth Advisors, he lives with his wife in North Haven, Connecticut, near their three children and four grandchildren.

THE PRELUDE

This illustrated edition is composed in the Bell types,
an elegant transitional typeface that was originally engraved by
Richard Austin in 1788 for John Bell's British Letter Foundry.
The distinguished typographic historian, Stanley Morison, wrote that Austin
"imparted a note of brilliance, rare at the time, to the British punches he cut for Bell."
The Bell types are known to have been used as early as 1792 in America.
Henry O. Houghton, the Boston publisher, imported the type for use at
the Riverside Press in 1864 where it was later discovered and used
under different names by Daniel Berkeley Updike and Bruce Rogers.
The digitized version of Bell used here is based upon the revival of
the type recut in 1930 by The Monotype Corporation Limited.

Printed & bound by C & C Offset Printing Co., Ltd., China

Design & typography by Howard I. Gralla